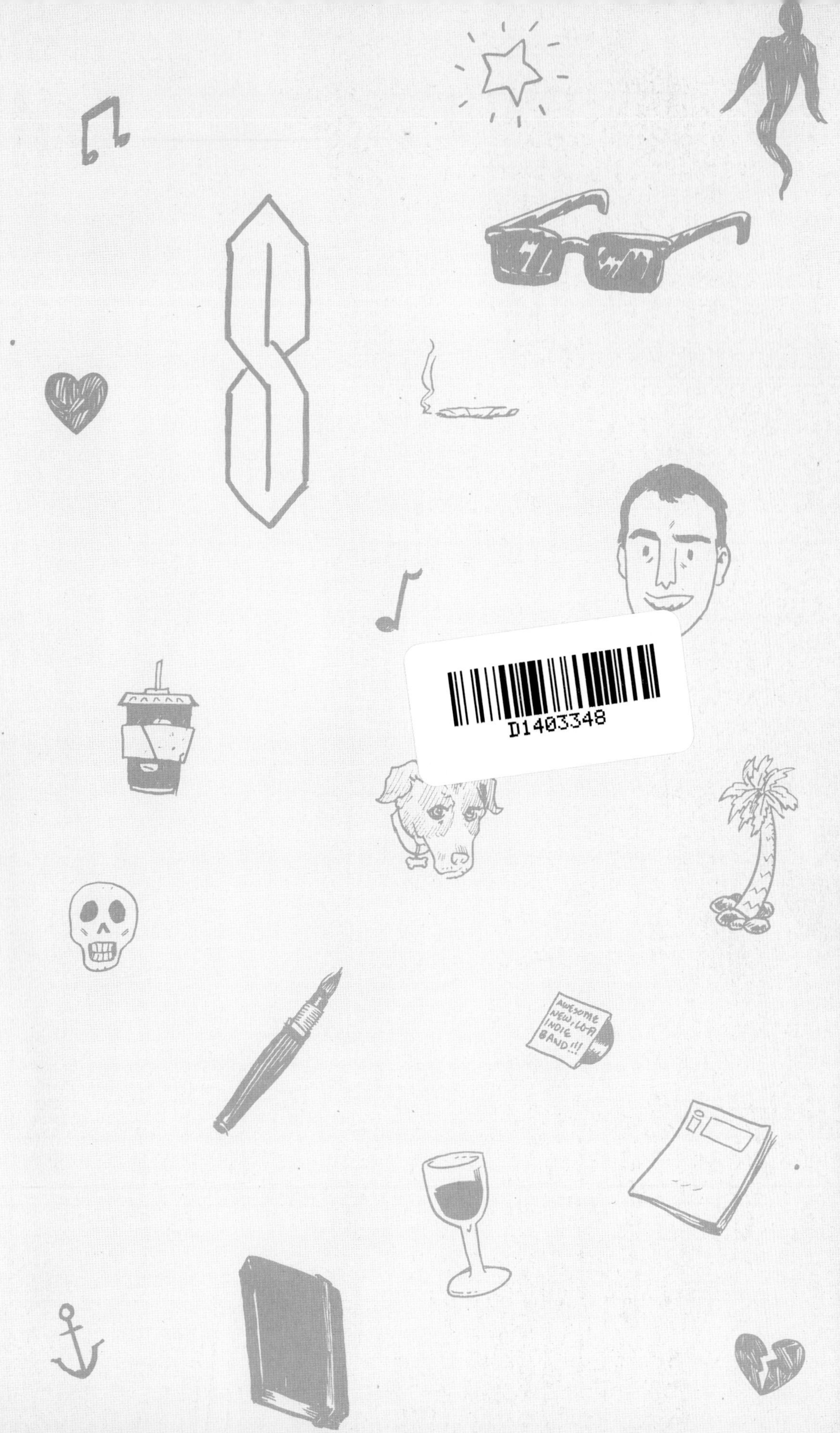
S
AWESOME NEW, LO-FI INDIE BAND!!!

IMAGE COMICS PRESENTS

SELF-OBSESSED

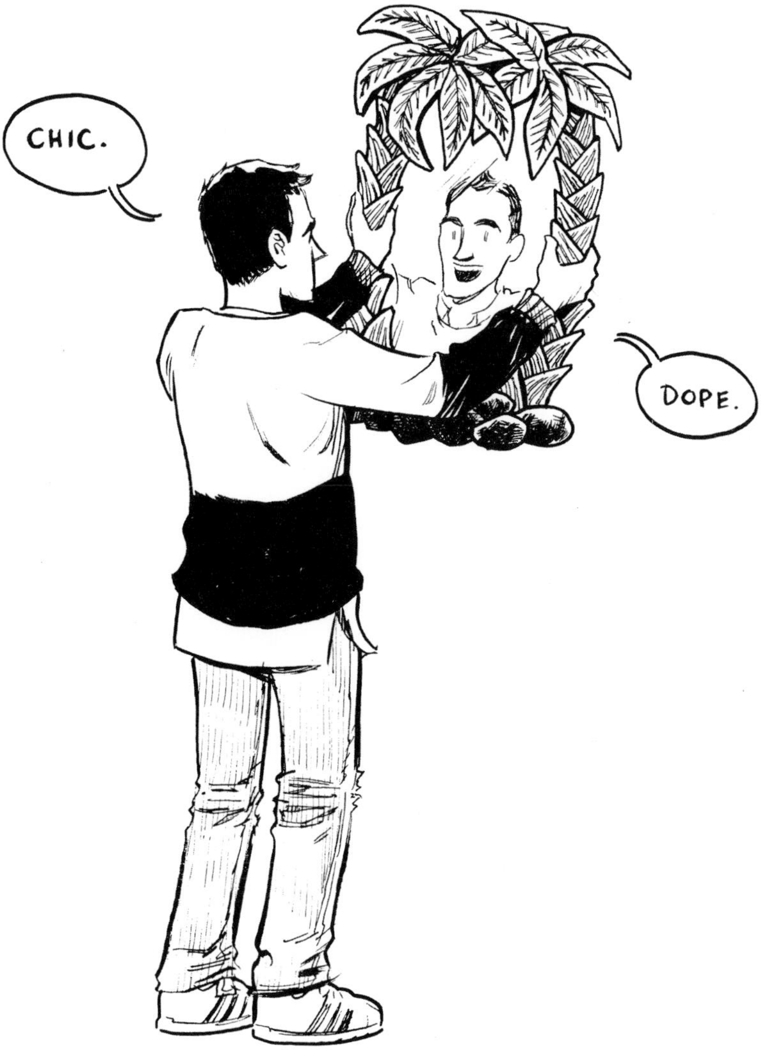
CHIC.
DOPE.

WRITTEN & ILLUSTRATED BY SINA GRACE

VISIT SOUNDCLOUD.COM/SELFOBSESSEDSINA FOR YOUR AUDIOBOOK DOWNLOAD
(AVAILABLE AFTER 10/10/2015)

BACK COVER COVER BY BRAD PRESENTATI

DESIGN BY SINA GRACE, TIM DANIEL, & SYDNEY NICHOLS

SHOPPING PHOTO BY INDIA BROOKOVER-COLEMAN

MIRROR PHOTO BY MEGAN MACK

ALL ADDITIONAL PHOTOGRAPHY BY NICHOLAS FREEMAN

THE ESSAYS "THE LIZZIE MCGUIRE MOVIE IS ACTUALLY REALLY GOOD," "I LIKE BIG GAY BEARS," AND "ADVICE FOR PEOPLE WHO WANT TO QUIT THEIR JOBS" ORIGINALLY APPEARED ON THOUGHTCATALOG.COM

THE ESSAY "THAT TIME I ALMOST BOUGHT SJPS" ORIGINALLY APPEARED ON THETANGENTIAL.COM

THE STRIP "BABA AB DAD" (THE ONE ABOUT MY DAD) ORIGINALLY APPEARED IN DADDY ISSUES, ISSUE ONE

THE STRIP "THAT TIME I ALMOST WENT DOWN ON A GIRL" ORIGINALLY APPEARED IN THE CBLDF 2015 LIBERTY ANNUAL

FOR MORE INFORMATION, VISIT WWW.SINAGRACE.COM

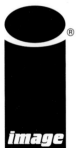

IMAGE COMICS, INC.
Robert Kirkman – Chief Operating Officer
Erik Larsen – Chief Financial Officer
Todd McFarlane – President
Marc Silvestri – Chief Executive Officer
Jim Valentino – Vice-President

Eric Stephenson – Publisher
Corey Murphy – Director of Sales
Jeremy Sullivan – Director of Digital Sales
Kat Salazar – Director of PR & Marketing
Emily Miller – Director of Operations
Branwyn Bigglestone – Senior Accounts Manager
Drew Gill – Art Director
Jonathan Chan – Production Manager
Meredith Wallace – Print Manager
Randy Okamura – Marketing Production Designer
David Brothers – Branding Manager
Ally Power – Content Manager
Addison Duke – Production Artist
Vincent Kukua – Production Artist
Sasha Head – Production Artist
Tricia Ramos – Production Artist
Emilio Bautista – Digital Sales Associate
Chloe Ramos-Peterson – Administrative Assistant
IMAGECOMICS.COM

SELF-OBSESSED. First Printing. September 2015. Published by Image Comics, Inc. Office of publication: 2001 Center Street, 6th Floor, Berkeley, CA 94704. Parts of this book were previously printed in single-magazine form as SELF-OBSESSED ONE-SHOT. Copyright © 2015 Sina Grace. All rights reserved. "Self-Obsessed," the Self-Obsessed logo, and all character likenesses herein are trademarks of Sina Grace unless expressly noted. "Image" and the Image Comics logos are registered trademarks of Image Comics, Inc. No part of this publication may be reproduced or transmitted, in any form or by any means (except short excerpts for journalistic or review purposes) without the express written permission of Sina Grace or Image Comics, Inc. All names, characters, events, and locales in this publication are entirely fictional. Any resemblance to actual persons (living or dead) or events or places, without satiric intent, is coincidental. PRINTED IN THE U.S.A. For information regarding the CPSIA on this printed material call: 203-595-3636 and provide reference # RICH – 646815.
Representation: Law Offices of Harris M. Miller II, P.C. (rightsinquiries@gmail.com).
ISBN: 978-1-63215-449-1

WHEN I WAS AROUND EIGHT YEARS OLD, MY BEST FRIEND MOVED TO COSTA RICA.

I SPENT THE FIRST FEW MONTHS HE WAS GONE HIDING UNDER MY BED, WEARING MY MOM'S SHAWL BACKWARDS AS IF I WAS LYDIA DEETZ AND SUMMONING GHOSTS TO KEEP ME COMPANY.

I WOULD SPEND HOURS UNDER THERE, MAINTAINING LONG CONVERSATIONS WITH A BEST FRIEND WHO WAS THOUSANDS OF MILES AWAY.

FROM THE OUTSIDE LOOKING IN, I WAS SAD AND ALONE.

THE TRUTH IS THAT I DON'T THINK THERE WAS A HAPPIER TIME THAN WHEN I WAS ALONE, TELLING STORIES TO MYSELF.

THIS BOOK IS DEDICATED TO THAT LITTLE KID AND ALL OF HIS IMAGINARY FRIENDS.

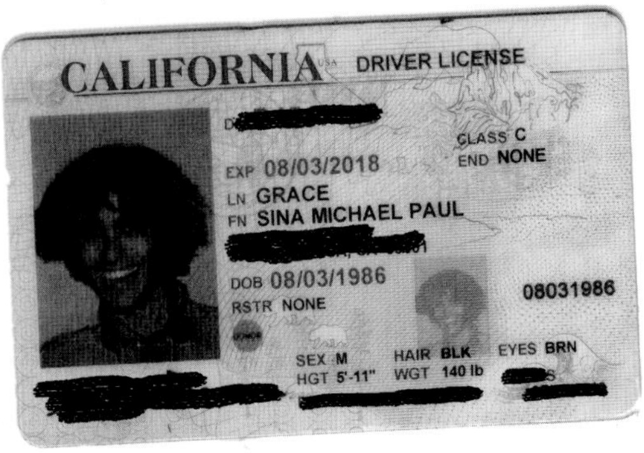

CALIFORNIA DRIVER LICENSE

D [redacted]

CLASS C
END NONE

EXP 08/03/2018
LN GRACE
FN SINA MICHAEL PAUL
[redacted]

DOB 08/03/1986
RSTR NONE

08031986

SEX M
HGT 5'-11"
HAIR BLK
WGT 140 lb
EYES BRN

[redacted]

INTRODUCTION

Sometimes it's okay to be self-obsessed. It's what you do with it that counts.

Self-indulgence is a part of being a cartoonist. Drawing even one page of comics is tedious and time consuming work, often done alone, hunched over a desk. It's hard not to get lost in your own head. Even if it's a work of fiction, a cartoonist's personality works their way into every pen line or brush stroke. The drawings become like handwriting or their fingerprints, every artist's style totally unique to them. This is why I love comics. It's the most intimate storytelling medium in existence. Not even the greatest prose writer nor the most auteur filmmaker can create a work that bears as much of their personality in the finished product. They have type and the screen between them and their audience. With comics it's all there, every line and every drawing right from the artist's hand.

If I'm to be proven right about comics being the most intimate modern storytelling medium, then Sina Grace's *Self-Obsessed* may be one of the best arguments I've ever read that helps prove my case.

Sina has created something wonderful here. Something only he could make. *Self-Obsessed* is him. He has turned his brush on himself and created a one hundred and forty-page self-portrait that is as funny and charming as it is painful and revealing. What makes this book so special is that it not only captures Sina's personality, it's that his personality actually becomes comics. It's like his inner self is spilled out and flows from page to page, every sequence using the language of comics in a totally singular way.

But it's not all pretty. My favorite parts of *Self-Obsessed* are the inclusion of Sina's older, early comics. These formative efforts are worked into the narrative of *Self-Obsessed* in a really clever and natural way, they stand out as a bit crude and awkward in comparison to the more elegant and polished brushwork Sina uses today. But I love them. I love the crudeness. I love the awkwardness. I love how much they reveal about who he was and who he is.

Sina certainly isn't afraid to share everything here. He doesn't hold back. The good the bad and the ugly are all here. But it doesn't feel self-indulgent in any negative sense. It feels like we're on a journey with him. And he's used comics as the vehicle that will take us, and him, somewhere new, somewhere better.

Sometimes it's okay to be self-obsessed. It's what you do with it that counts. Sina Grace has done something wonderful with it. He's made art. And now we get to share it with him.

JEFF LEMIRE
Toronto, Canada

Jeff Lemire is the award-winning creator of
Essex County, *Sweet Tooth* and *Descender*.
He also writes *The Extraordinary X-Men* for Marvel.

The Ways One Can Read This Book...

1- The Post-Modern Approach

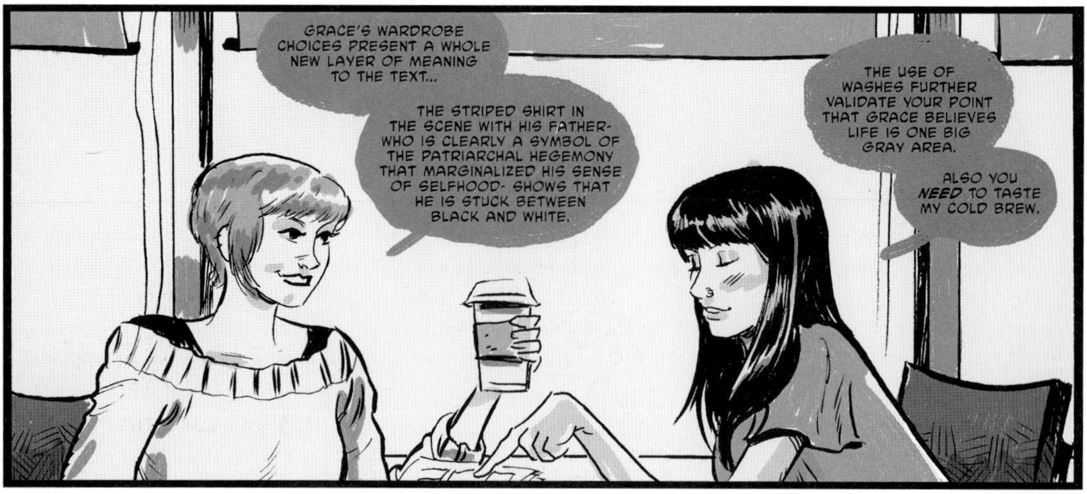
GRACE'S WARDROBE CHOICES PRESENT A WHOLE NEW LAYER OF MEANING TO THE TEXT...
THE STRIPED SHIRT IN THE SCENE WITH HIS FATHER- WHO IS CLEARLY A SYMBOL OF THE PATRIARCHAL HEGEMONY THAT MARGINALIZED HIS SENSE OF SELFHOOD- SHOWS THAT HE IS STUCK BETWEEN BLACK AND WHITE.
THE USE OF WASHES FURTHER VALIDATE YOUR POINT THAT GRACE BELIEVES LIFE IS ONE BIG GRAY AREA.
ALSO YOU *NEED* TO TASTE MY COLD BREW.

2- The "Just Like Me" Approach

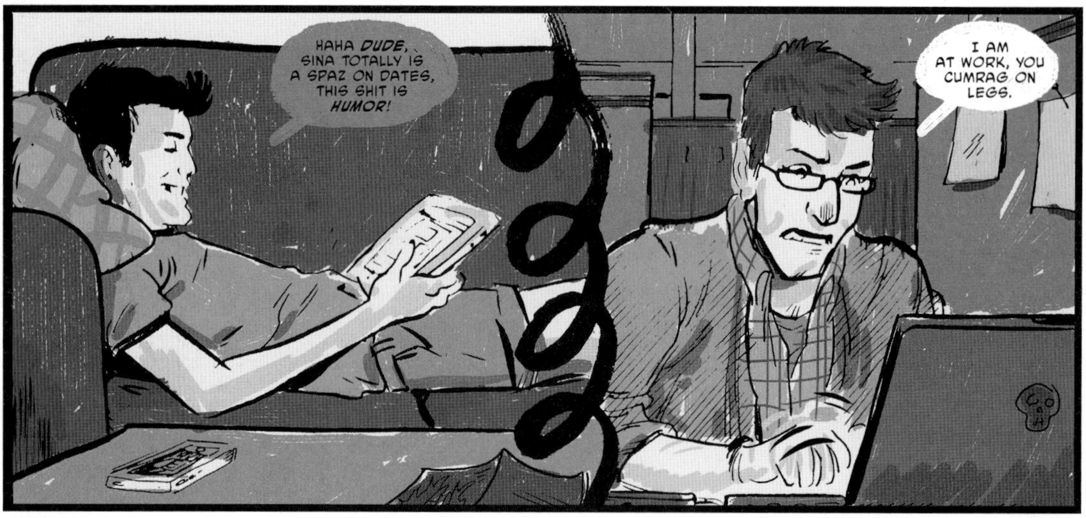
HAHA *DUDE*, SINA TOTALLY IS A SPAZ ON DATES, THIS SHIT IS *HUMOR*!
I AM AT WORK, YOU CUMRAG ON LEGS.

3- The Path of Most Resistance Approach

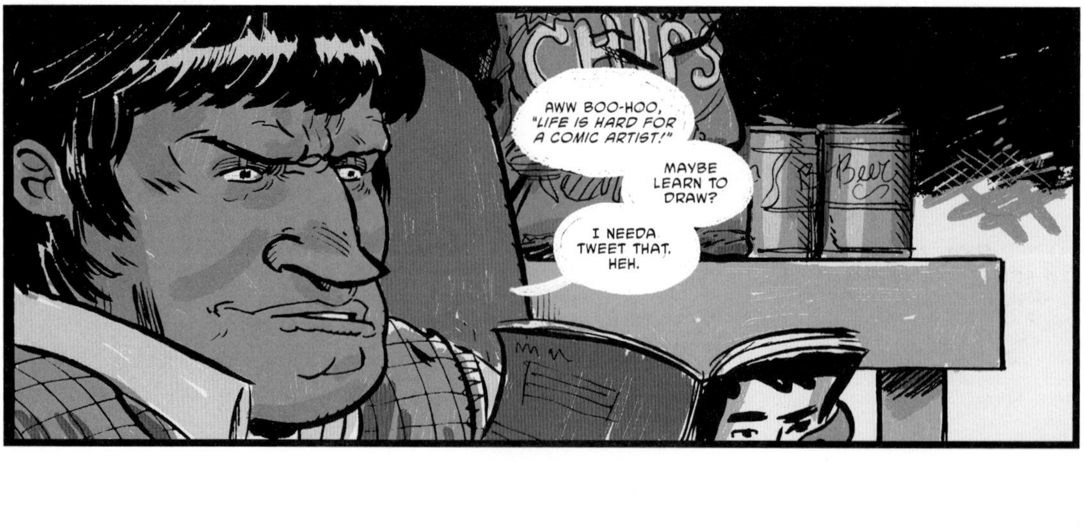
AWW BOO-HOO, *"LIFE IS HARD FOR A COMIC ARTIST!"*
MAYBE LEARN TO DRAW?
I NEEDA TWEET THAT. HEH.

The Cast

SINA (ME!)

JUST A REGULAR DUDE
LIVING THE DREAM OF MAKING
COMICS FULL-TIME.

AND SO MUCH MORE.

MY MOM
SHE RAISED ME
AND PULLED OFF A
FULL-TIME JOB.
SINGLE PARENT FTW

MY SISTER
SIX YEARS OLDER
THAN ME, & HAS ALWAYS
HAD MY BACK.

MY DAD
WASN'T AROUND WHEN
I WAS A KID. HE LOVES
ME MAYBE?

SCHMORGASBOARD
A SUPER ANNOYING
AMALGAM OF EVERYTHING
I HATE ABOUT OTHER
PEOPLE, OR REALLY
MYSELF??

GHOSTS
USUALLY SPECTERS
REPRESENTING FOLKS
FROM RELATIONSHIPS
PAST & OTHER
DARK FEELS.

DANIEL
A FRIEND SINCE GRADE
SCHOOL, WE CREATED
A COMIC TOGETHER
AND LIVED SUPER
CLOSE TO EACH
OTHER.

AMBER
A FRIEND AND COLLEAGUE.
WE MADE A KIDS BOOK
TOGETHER, AND SHE
ALWAYS GIVES ME GREAT
ADVICE ABOUT LIFE
AND ART.

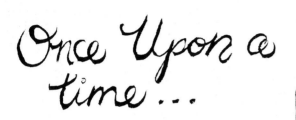
Once Upon a time...

I'M GONNA LOVE YOU SO MUCH!

A REALLY BEAUTIFUL AND SMART PERSIAN WOMAN GAVE BIRTH TO A YOUNG BOY IN THE EARLY DAYS OF AUGUST, 1986. SHE CHOSE TO RAISE THE CHILD WITHOUT HIS FATHER, KNOWING THE BOY WOULD BE IN SAFE ARMS IF SHE WAS ALWAYS HOLDING HIM.

GROWING UP, THE BOY WAS HAPPY. HIS FATHER DIDN'T COME AROUND MUCH, BUT HE HAD OTHER MEN IN HIS LIFE: HEROES. ADVENTURERS. POWER RANGERS. THEY TAUGHT HIM HOW TO BE BRAVE, AND GAVE LESSONS ON BEING DIFFERENT.

THE BOY WANTED NOTHING ELSE BUT TO LIVE WITH HIS HEROES, AND SPENT HIS DAYS DRAWING THEIR STORIES.

WHEN ASKED WHAT HE WANTED TO BE WHEN HE GREW UP, THE BOY HAD ONE ANSWER.

Sina Grace
Comic Book Illustrator
My favorite memory was the last day of school.

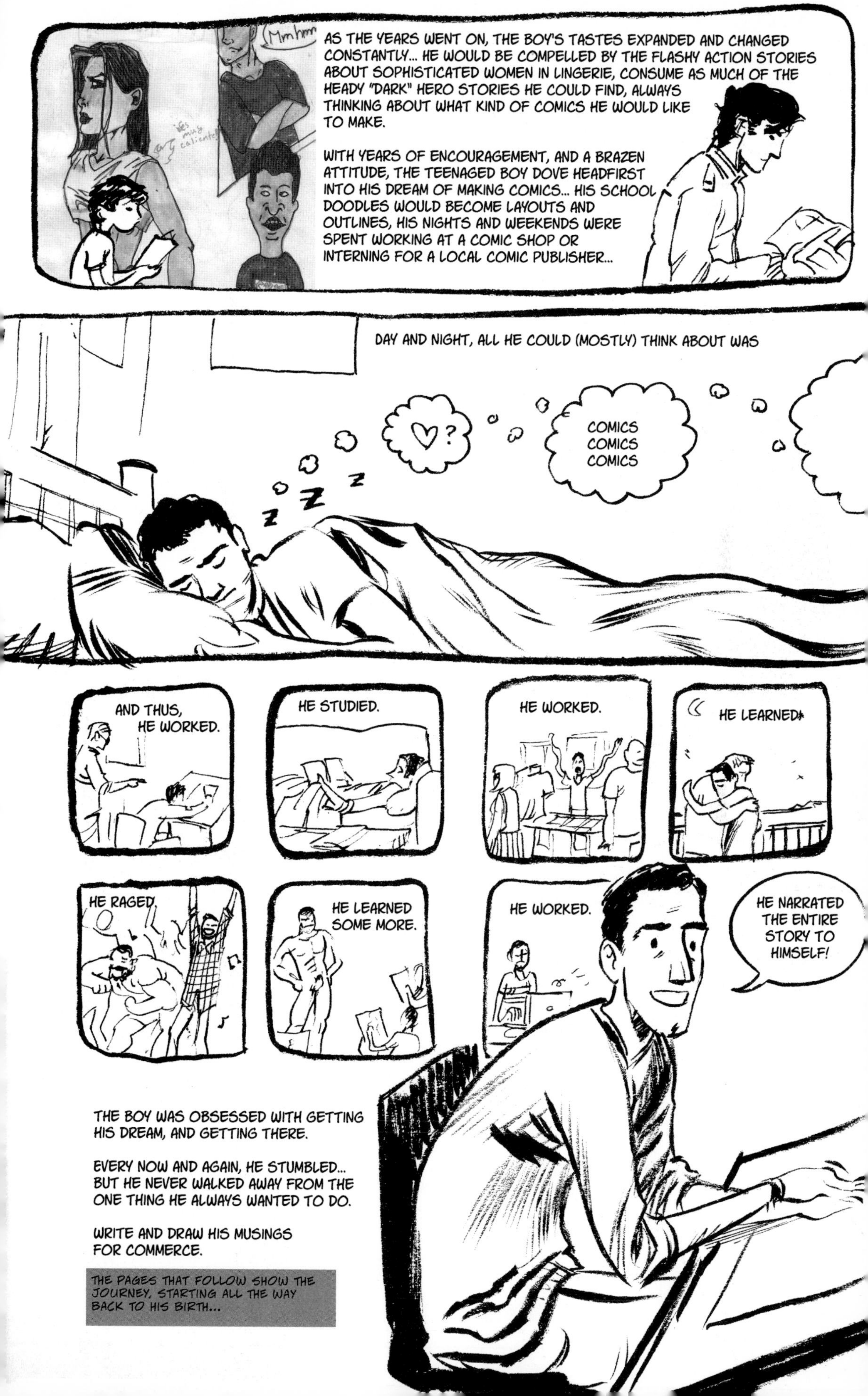
Mrmhmm
¡Es muy caliente!
AS THE YEARS WENT ON, THE BOY'S TASTES EXPANDED AND CHANGED CONSTANTLY... HE WOULD BE COMPELLED BY THE FLASHY ACTION STORIES ABOUT SOPHISTICATED WOMEN IN LINGERIE, CONSUME AS MUCH OF THE HEADY "DARK" HERO STORIES HE COULD FIND, ALWAYS THINKING ABOUT WHAT KIND OF COMICS HE WOULD LIKE TO MAKE.
WITH YEARS OF ENCOURAGEMENT, AND A BRAZEN ATTITUDE, THE TEENAGED BOY DOVE HEADFIRST INTO HIS DREAM OF MAKING COMICS... HIS SCHOOL DOODLES WOULD BECOME LAYOUTS AND OUTLINES, HIS NIGHTS AND WEEKENDS WERE SPENT WORKING AT A COMIC SHOP OR INTERNING FOR A LOCAL COMIC PUBLISHER...
DAY AND NIGHT, ALL HE COULD (MOSTLY) THINK ABOUT WAS
♡ ?
COMICS COMICS COMICS
Z Z Z
AND THUS, HE WORKED.
HE STUDIED.
HE WORKED.
HE LEARNED.
HE RAGED.
HE LEARNED SOME MORE.
HE WORKED.
HE NARRATED THE ENTIRE STORY TO HIMSELF!
THE BOY WAS OBSESSED WITH GETTING HIS DREAM, AND GETTING THERE.
EVERY NOW AND AGAIN, HE STUMBLED... BUT HE NEVER WALKED AWAY FROM THE ONE THING HE ALWAYS WANTED TO DO.
WRITE AND DRAW HIS MUSINGS FOR COMMERCE.
THE PAGES THAT FOLLOW SHOW THE JOURNEY, STARTING ALL THE WAY BACK TO HIS BIRTH...

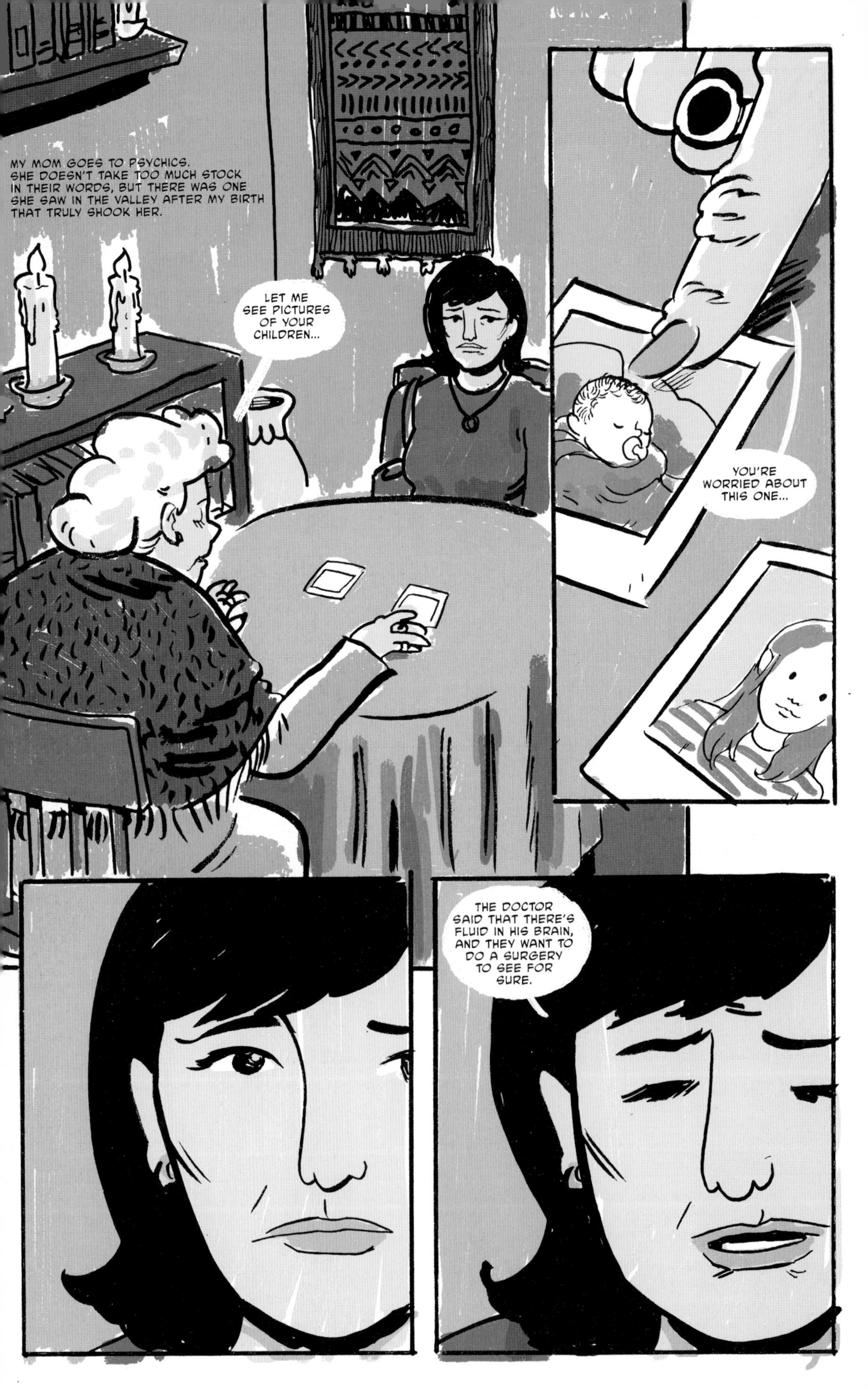
MY MOM GOES TO PSYCHICS. SHE DOESN'T TAKE TOO MUCH STOCK IN THEIR WORDS, BUT THERE WAS ONE SHE SAW IN THE VALLEY AFTER MY BIRTH THAT TRULY SHOOK HER.
LET ME SEE PICTURES OF YOUR CHILDREN...
YOU'RE WORRIED ABOUT THIS ONE...
THE DOCTOR SAID THAT THERE'S FLUID IN HIS BRAIN, AND THEY WANT TO DO A SURGERY TO SEE FOR SURE.

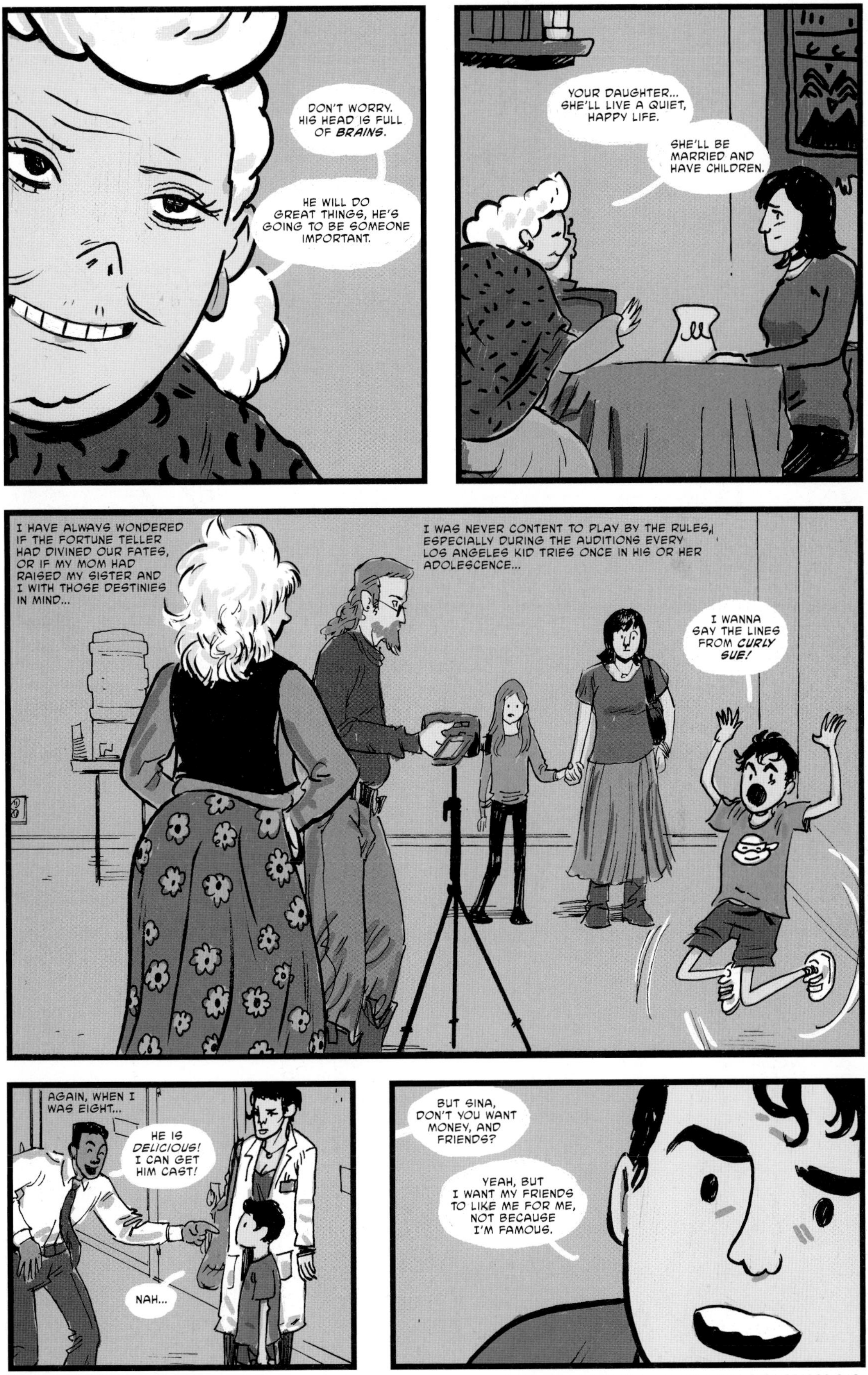
DON'T WORRY. HIS HEAD IS FULL OF BRAINS.
HE WILL DO GREAT THINGS, HE'S GOING TO BE SOMEONE IMPORTANT.
YOUR DAUGHTER... SHE'LL LIVE A QUIET, HAPPY LIFE.
SHE'LL BE MARRIED AND HAVE CHILDREN.
I HAVE ALWAYS WONDERED IF THE FORTUNE TELLER HAD DIVINED OUR FATES, OR IF MY MOM HAD RAISED MY SISTER AND I WITH THOSE DESTINIES IN MIND...
I WAS NEVER CONTENT TO PLAY BY THE RULES, ESPECIALLY DURING THE AUDITIONS EVERY LOS ANGELES KID TRIES ONCE IN HIS OR HER ADOLESCENCE...
I WANNA SAY THE LINES FROM CURLY SUE!
AGAIN, WHEN I WAS EIGHT...
HE IS DELICIOUS! I CAN GET HIM CAST!
NAH...
BUT SINA, DON'T YOU WANT MONEY, AND FRIENDS?
YEAH, BUT I WANT MY FRIENDS TO LIKE ME FOR ME, NOT BECAUSE I'M FAMOUS.

I SUPPOSE A BOY CAN GET AWAY WITH SUCH PRECOCIOUS ASSUMPTIONS WHEN HE'S RAISED TO BELIEVE IN A GRAND FATE...

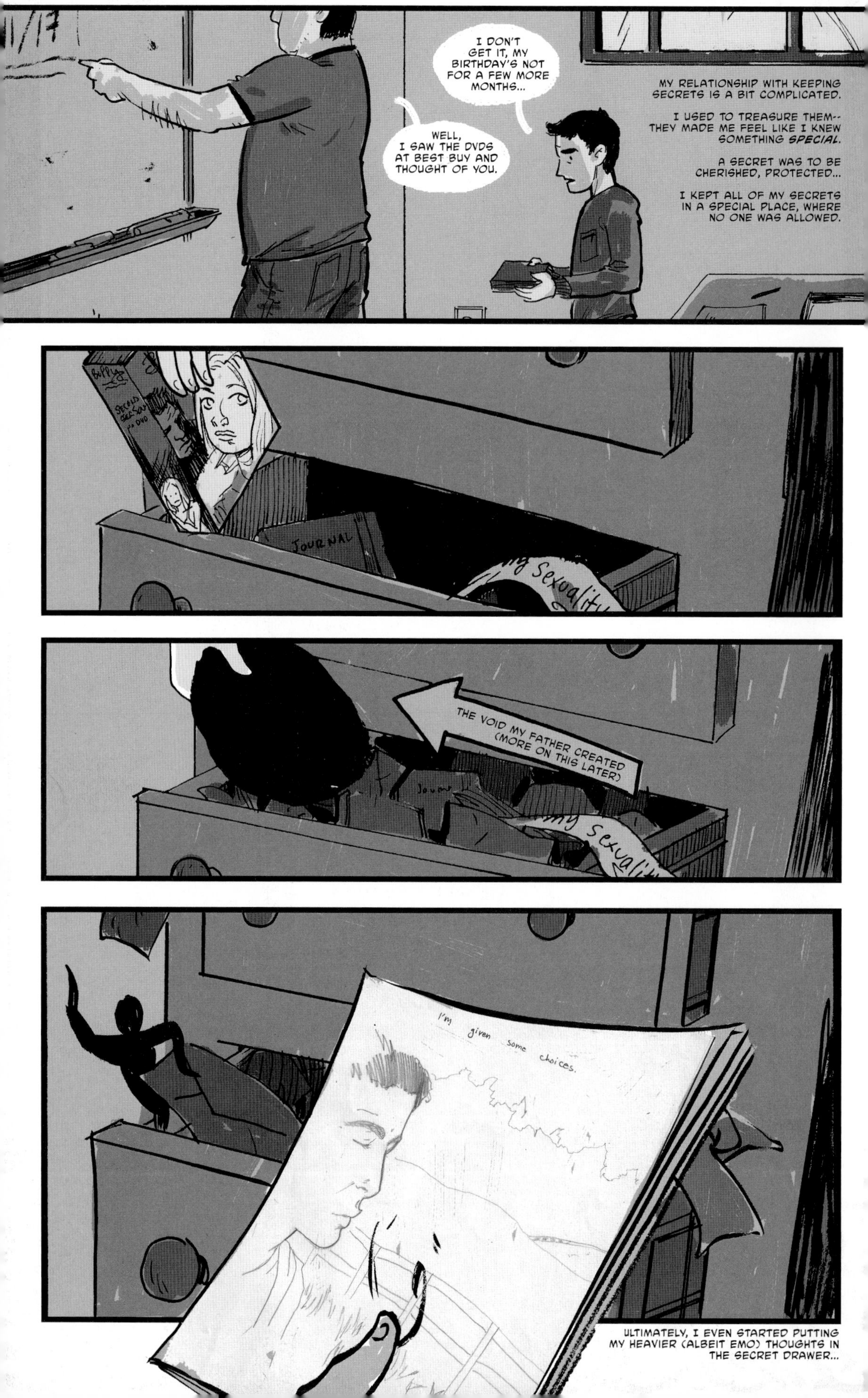
I DON'T GET IT, MY BIRTHDAY'S NOT FOR A FEW MORE MONTHS...
WELL, I SAW THE DVDS AT BEST BUY AND THOUGHT OF YOU.
MY RELATIONSHIP WITH KEEPING SECRETS IS A BIT COMPLICATED.
I USED TO TREASURE THEM-- THEY MADE ME FEEL LIKE I KNEW SOMETHING *SPECIAL*.
A SECRET WAS TO BE CHERISHED, PROTECTED...
I KEPT ALL OF MY SECRETS IN A SPECIAL PLACE, WHERE NO ONE WAS ALLOWED.
JOURNAL
THE VOID MY FATHER CREATED (MORE ON THIS LATER)
I'm given some choices.
ULTIMATELY, I EVEN STARTED PUTTING MY HEAVIER (ALBEIT EMO) THOUGHTS IN THE SECRET DRAWER...

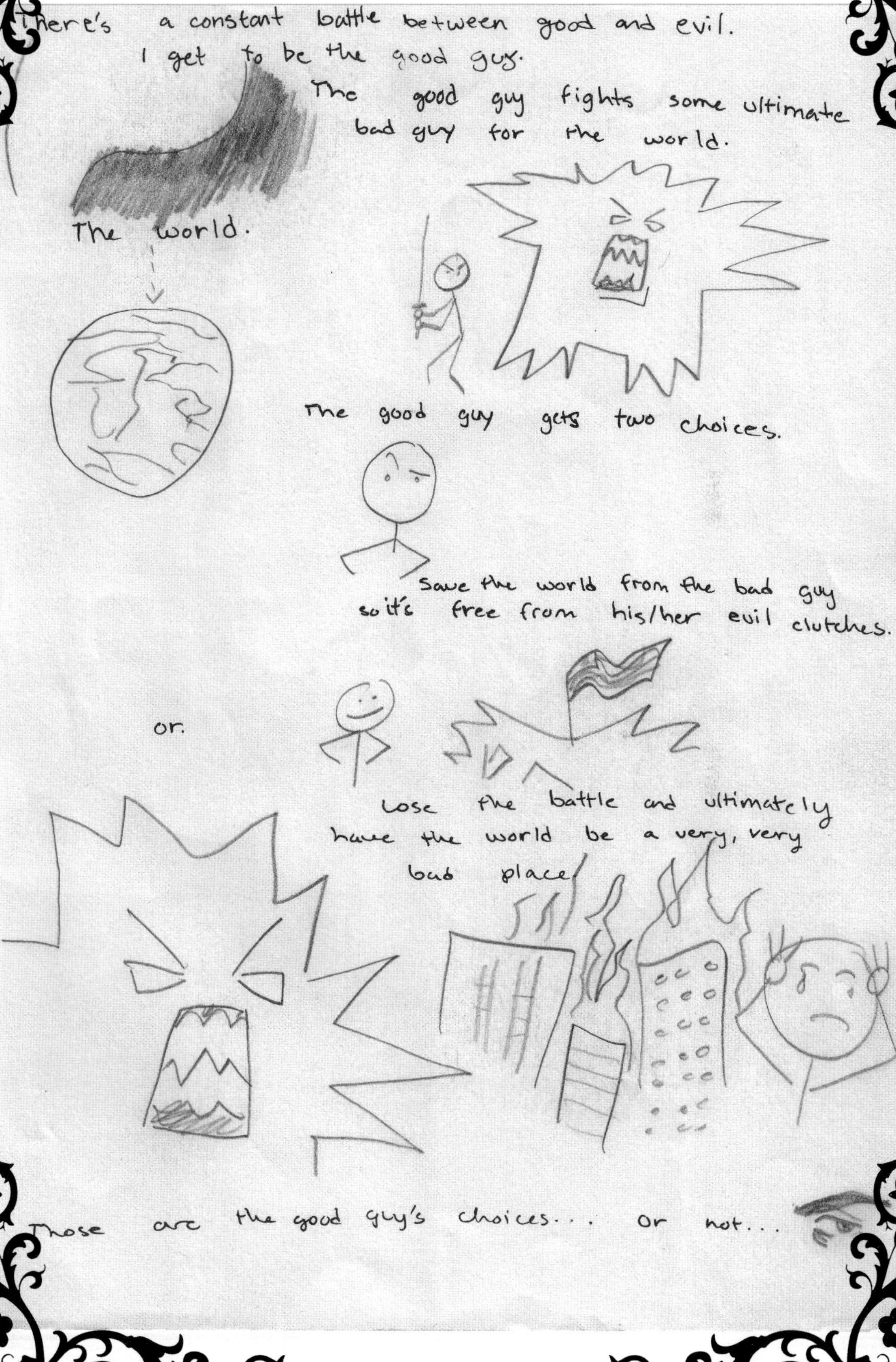
There's a constant battle between good and evil.
I get to be the good guy.
The good guy fights some ultimate bad guy for the world.
The world.
The good guy gets two choices.
Save the world from the bad guy so it's free from his/her evil clutches.
or.
Lose the battle and ultimately have the world be a very, very bad place!
Those are the good guy's choices... or not...

The bad guy needs some kind of threatening weapon. An A-bomb, some kind of ring, a burrito for all I care. The bad guy needs it. That's what the good guy and bad guy fight for. The bad guy will use the death toy, and the good guy will hide it or try desperately to destroy it. So, I'm the good guy, remember? I don't like these choices. I'm tired of choices. I'm tired of people relying on me to do the right thing. I'm tired of not knowing what the right thing is. If I stop the bad guy THIS time, what guarantees that it will be the very last time I have to save the world? The very last time I have to worry about billions of people. Billions of people who are most likely miserable. How many of these people want to live anyways? It's tiring, being the good guy. So I think to myself and ask "what about peace?" That's what the good guy wants. That's what I want. So here's my third choice. I win this object of apocalypse. And I use it. I end the world. No bullshit. Boom. The end. No more tears. No more people crying. I'm not sick. It's logical. The good guy wants the best ending. The ending where everything ends as well as it possibly can. The good guy just wants

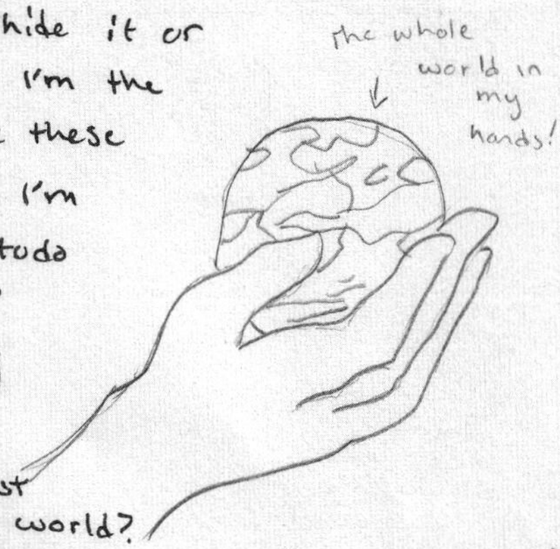
the whole world in my hands!

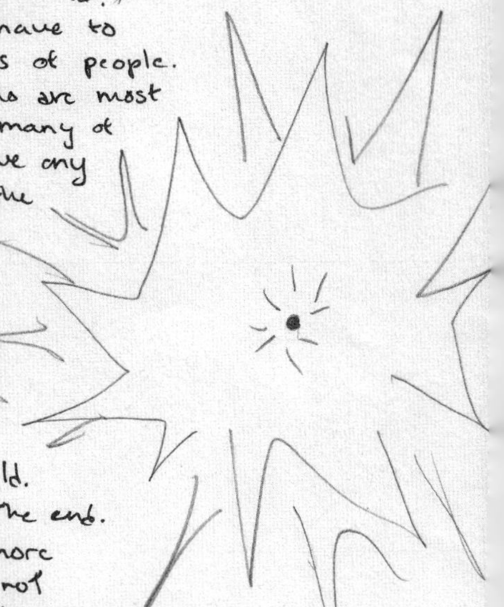

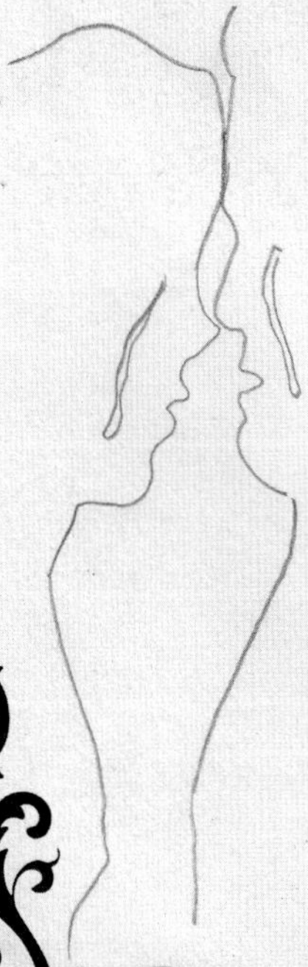

Peace.

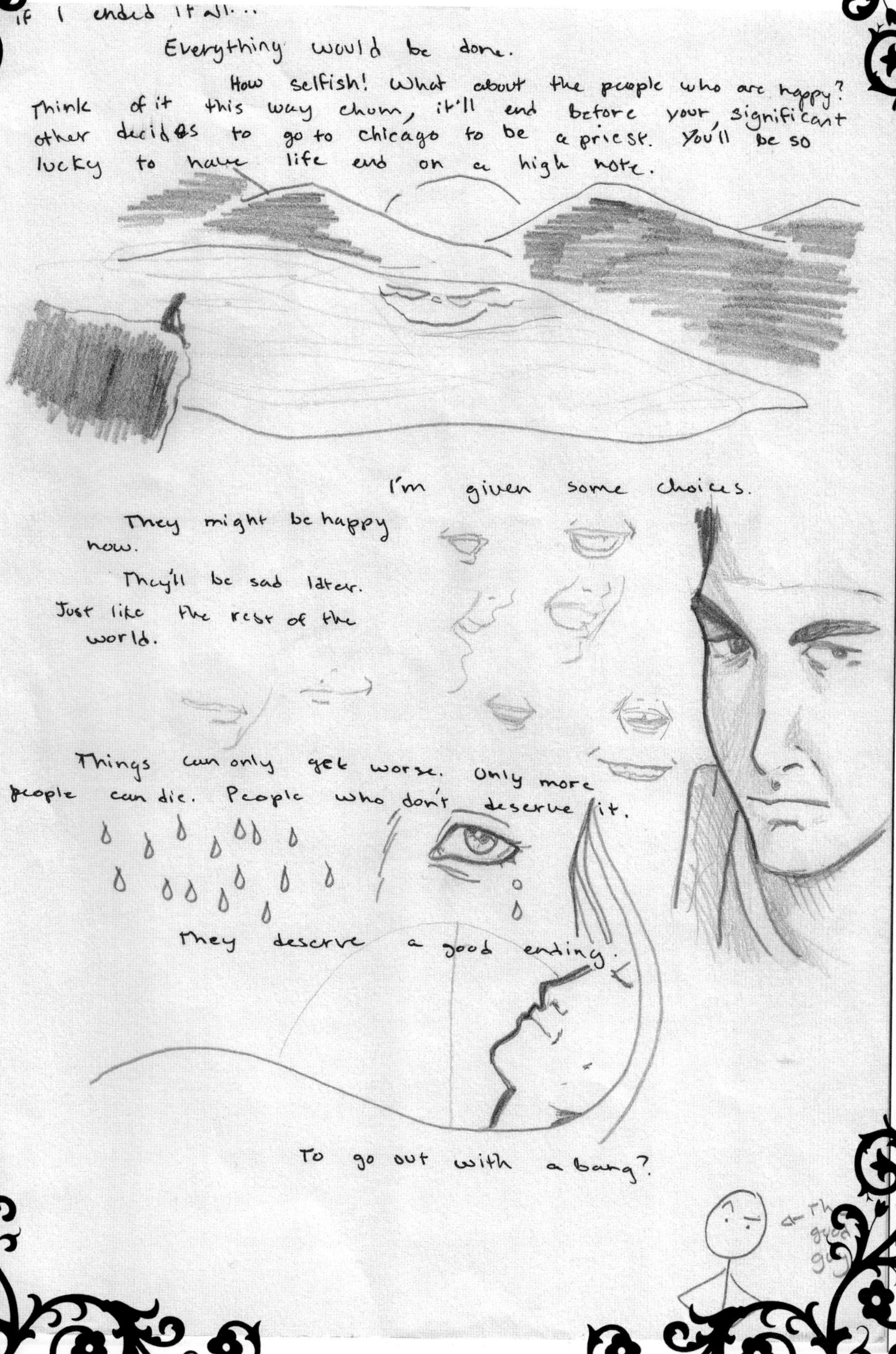
if I ended it all...
Everything would be done.
How selfish! What about the people who are happy?
Think of it this way chum, it'll end before your significant other decides to go to Chicago to be a priest. You'll be so lucky to have life end on a high note.
I'm given some choices.
They might be happy now.
They'll be sad later.
Just like the rest of the world.
Things can only get worse. Only more people can die. People who don't deserve it.
They deserve a good ending.
To go out with a bang?
← Th
goo
gu

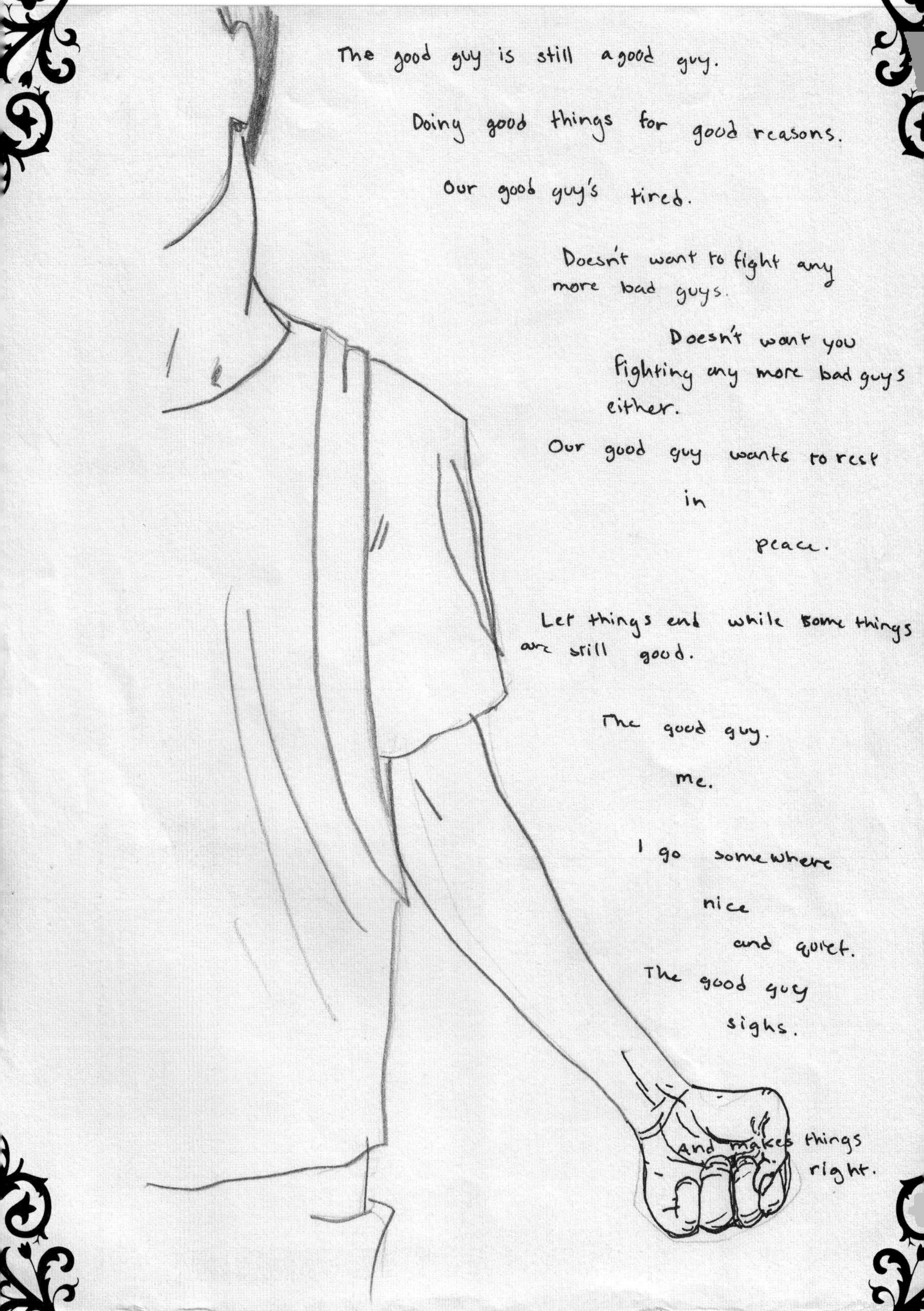
The good guy is still a good guy.
Doing good things for good reasons.
Our good guy's tired.
Doesn't want to fight any more bad guys.
Doesn't want you fighting any more bad guys either.
Our good guy wants to rest
in
peace.
Let things end while some things are still good.
The good guy.
me.
I go somewhere
nice
and quiet.
The good guy
sighs.
And makes things
right.

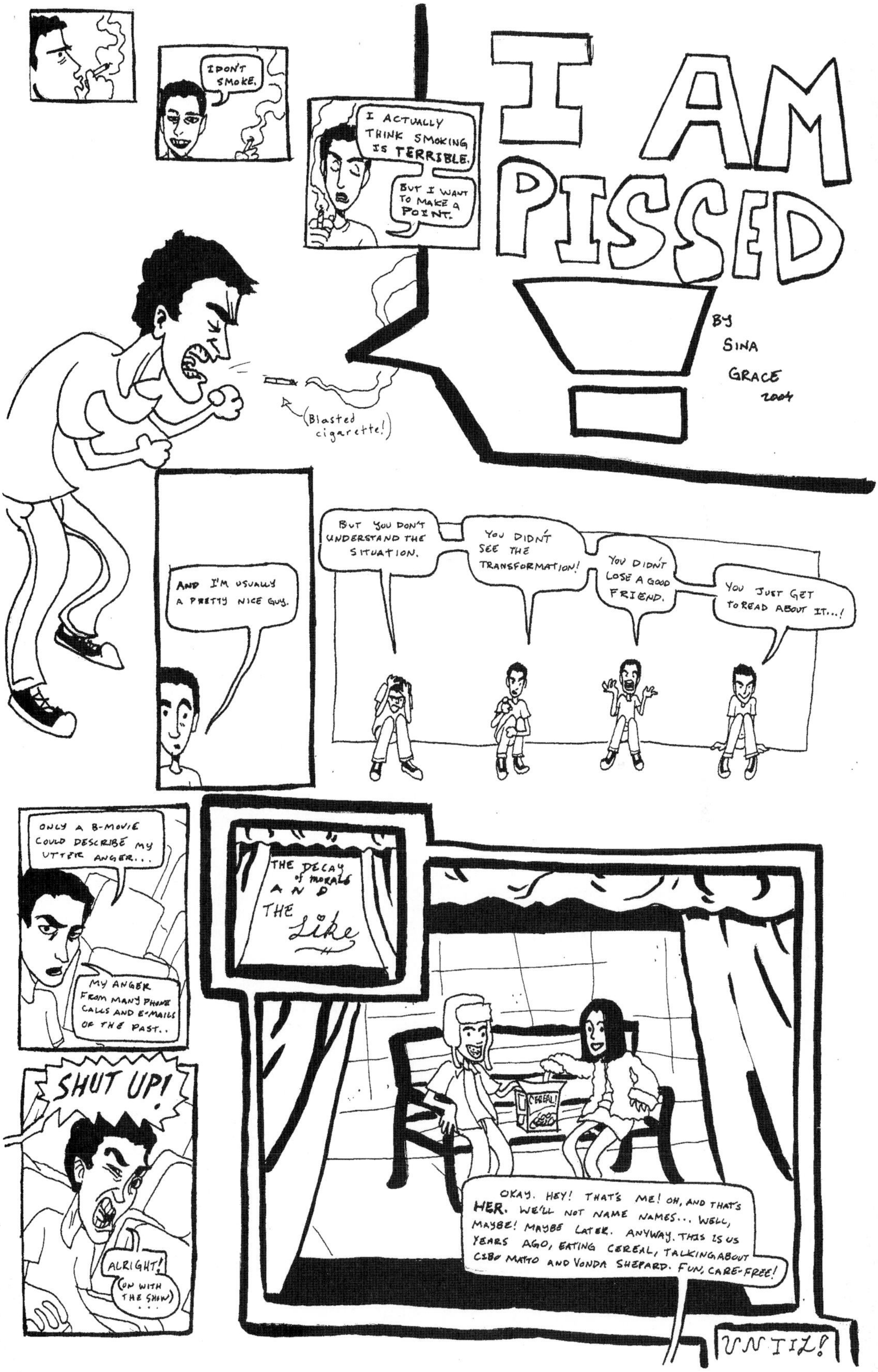
I DON'T SMOKE.
I ACTUALLY THINK SMOKING IS TERRIBLE.
BUT I WANT TO MAKE A POINT.
I AM PISSED!
BY SINA GRACE 2004
(Blasted cigarette!)
AND I'M USUALLY A PRETTY NICE GUY.
BUT YOU DON'T UNDERSTAND THE SITUATION.
YOU DIDN'T SEE THE TRANSFORMATION!
YOU DIDN'T LOSE A GOOD FRIEND.
YOU JUST GET TO READ ABOUT IT...!
ONLY A B-MOVIE COULD DESCRIBE MY UTTER ANGER...
MY ANGER FROM MANY PHONE CALLS AND E-MAILS OF THE PAST..
SHUT UP!
ALRIGHT!
(ON WITH THE SHOW)...
THE DECAY of morals AND THE Like
CEREAL!
OKAY. HEY! THAT'S ME! OH, AND THAT'S HER. WE'LL NOT NAME NAMES... WELL, MAYBE! MAYBE LATER. ANYWAY. THIS IS US YEARS AGO, EATING CEREAL, TALKING ABOUT CIBO MATTO AND VONDA SHEPARD. FUN, CARE-FREE!
UNTIL!

UNTIL SHE GOT---

---A BAND!

Bass

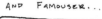

B-A-D-B-A-D-B...

WHAT!

WHAT WERE YOU EXPECTING!

TEEN PREGNANCY!?

AS IF!!

I SHOULD HAVE LISTENED TO LAUREN...

DUDE, SHE'S A SPOILED BABY.

BUT I KEPT GIVING THE PAST WE HAD A SECOND CHANCE...

WHAT UP, SINAW?!

(ELVIS COSTELLO GLASSES)

So THEY GOT FAMOUS...

AND FAMOUSER...

AND EVEN **FAMOUSER!**

HOLY SHIT, A DOUBLE-PAGER!

DAMN!

Interview

...PLAYING WITH ELVIS COSTELLO!?

OH FOR SURE YOU CAN THANK THEIR **DADS.**

THEY'VE GOT A CONTRACT WITH DREAMWORK RECORDS?!

AND SHE MADE ME FEEL SMALL...

AND SMALLER...

AND EVEN SMALLER!

COLD SHOULDERS & ATTITUDE PROBLEMS.

MISSED MEETINGS.

HAVING TO LISTEN ABOUT HOW "COOL" AND "CUTE" THE MOST VAPID AND SHALLOW OF PEOPLE ARE!

yay...

SO... WHAT BECAME OF THIS YEAR'S GIRL?

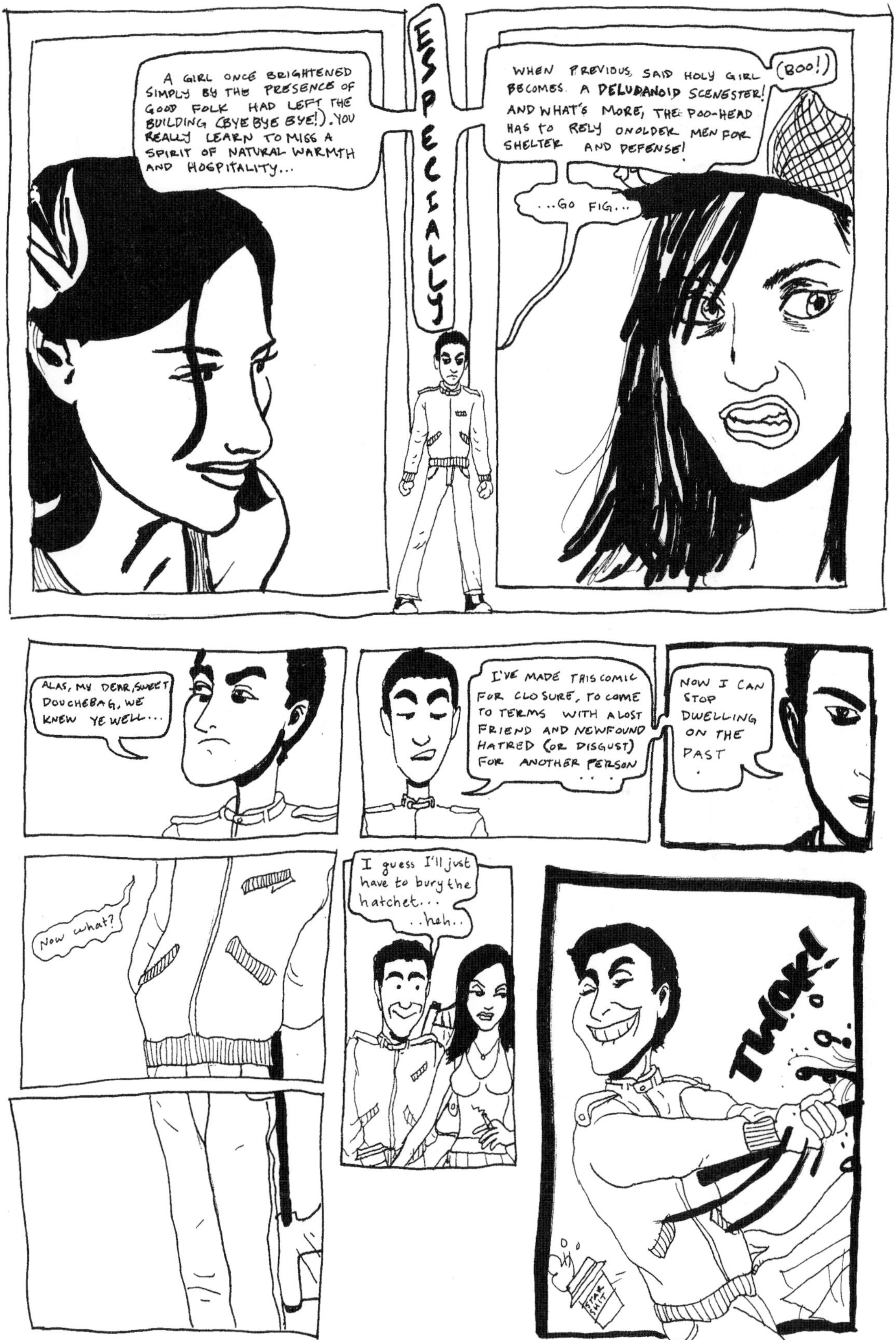

A GIRL ONCE BRIGHTENED SIMPLY BY THE PRESENCE OF GOOD FOLK HAD LEFT THE BUILDING (BYE BYE BYE!). YOU REALLY LEARN TO MISS A SPIRIT OF NATURAL WARMTH AND HOSPITALITY...
ESPECIALLY
WHEN PREVIOUS, SAID HOLY GIRL BECOMES A DELUDANOID SCENESTER! AND WHAT'S MORE, THE POO-HEAD HAS TO RELY ON OLDER MEN FOR SHELTER AND DEFENSE!
(BOO!)
...GO FIG...
ALAS, MY DEAR, SWEET DOUCHEBAG, WE KNEW YE WELL...
I'VE MADE THIS COMIC FOR CLOSURE, TO COME TO TERMS WITH A LOST FRIEND AND NEWFOUND HATRED (OR DISGUST) FOR ANOTHER PERSON...
NOW I CAN STOP DWELLING ON THE PAST.
Now what?
I guess I'll just have to bury the hatchet... ..heh..
THOK!
STAR SHIT

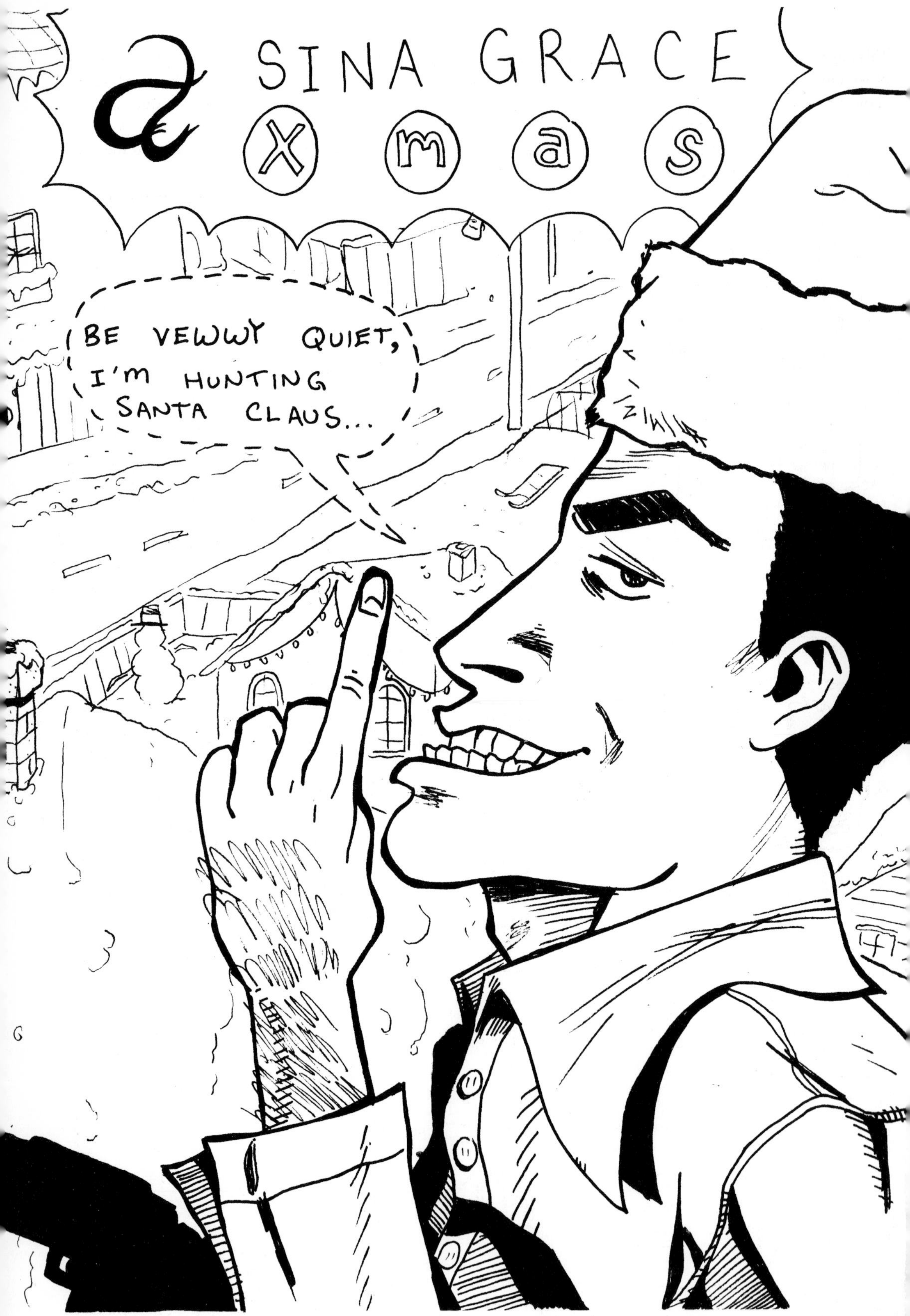
a SINA GRACE xmas
BE VEWWY QUIET, I'M HUNTING SANTA CLAUS...

This page and the next were taken from a holiday comic/zine I made my first winter back from college. Totally broke but wanting to give, I made 50 of these bad boys for extended family and friends. Pretty much everything about this comic makes me cringe, but I wanted to give you all a glimpse into my family life and introduce you to my Aunt Ginger (who never shows up in this book again).
Seriously... I went on lettering without a straight edge for like two more years after this until someone told me how ugly my pages looked. Yeesh.

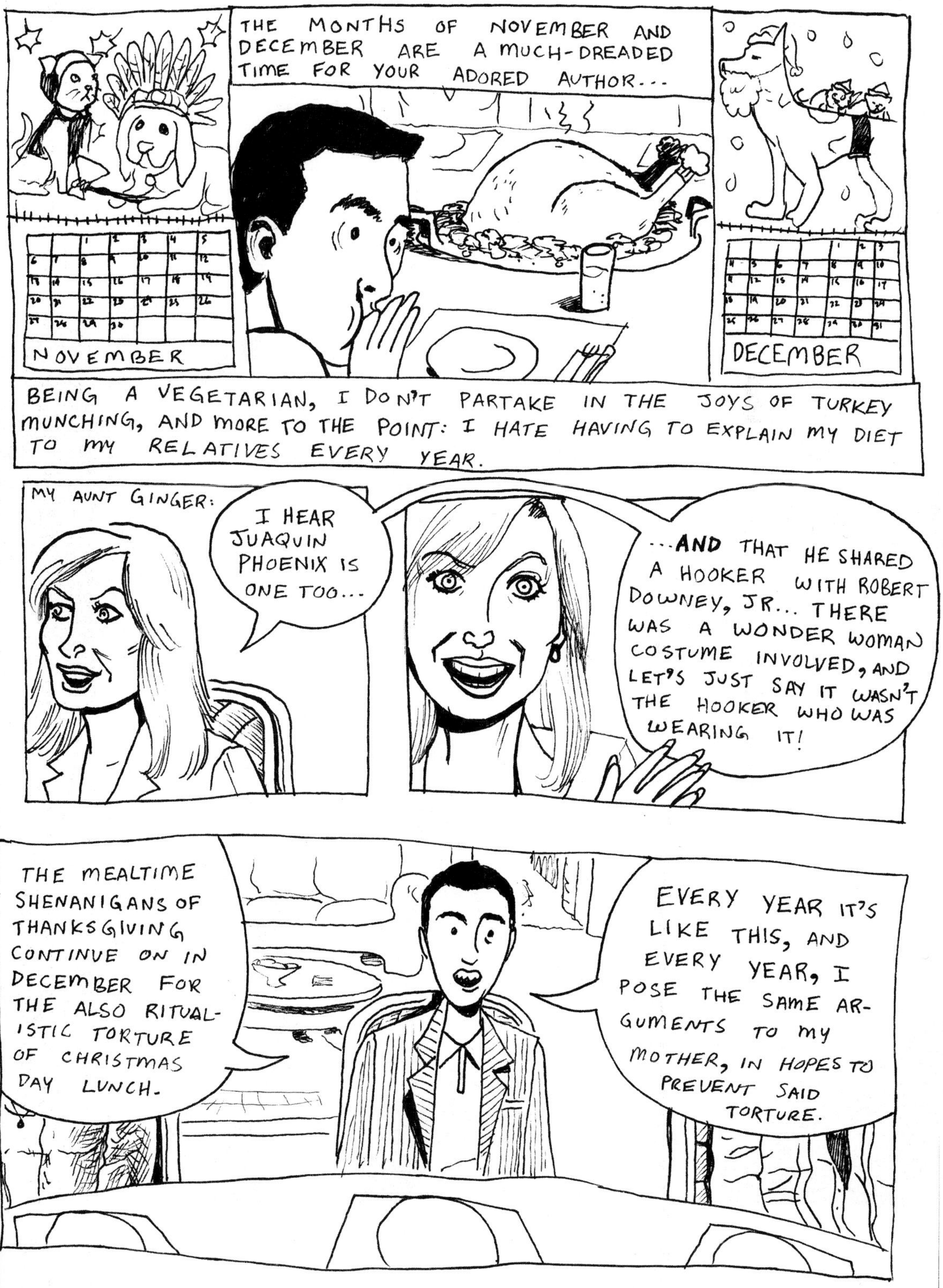
THE MONTHS OF NOVEMBER AND DECEMBER ARE A MUCH-DREADED TIME FOR YOUR ADORED AUTHOR...
NOVEMBER
DECEMBER
BEING A VEGETARIAN, I DON'T PARTAKE IN THE JOYS OF TURKEY MUNCHING, AND MORE TO THE POINT: I HATE HAVING TO EXPLAIN MY DIET TO MY RELATIVES EVERY YEAR.
MY AUNT GINGER:
I HEAR JUAQUIN PHOENIX IS ONE TOO...
...AND THAT HE SHARED A HOOKER WITH ROBERT DOWNEY, JR... THERE WAS A WONDER WOMAN COSTUME INVOLVED, AND LET'S JUST SAY IT WASN'T THE HOOKER WHO WAS WEARING IT!
THE MEALTIME SHENANIGANS OF THANKSGIVING CONTINUE ON IN DECEMBER FOR THE ALSO RITUAL-ISTIC TORTURE OF CHRISTMAS DAY LUNCH.
EVERY YEAR IT'S LIKE THIS, AND EVERY YEAR, I POSE THE SAME AR-GUMENTS TO MY MOTHER, IN HOPES TO PREVENT SAID TORTURE.

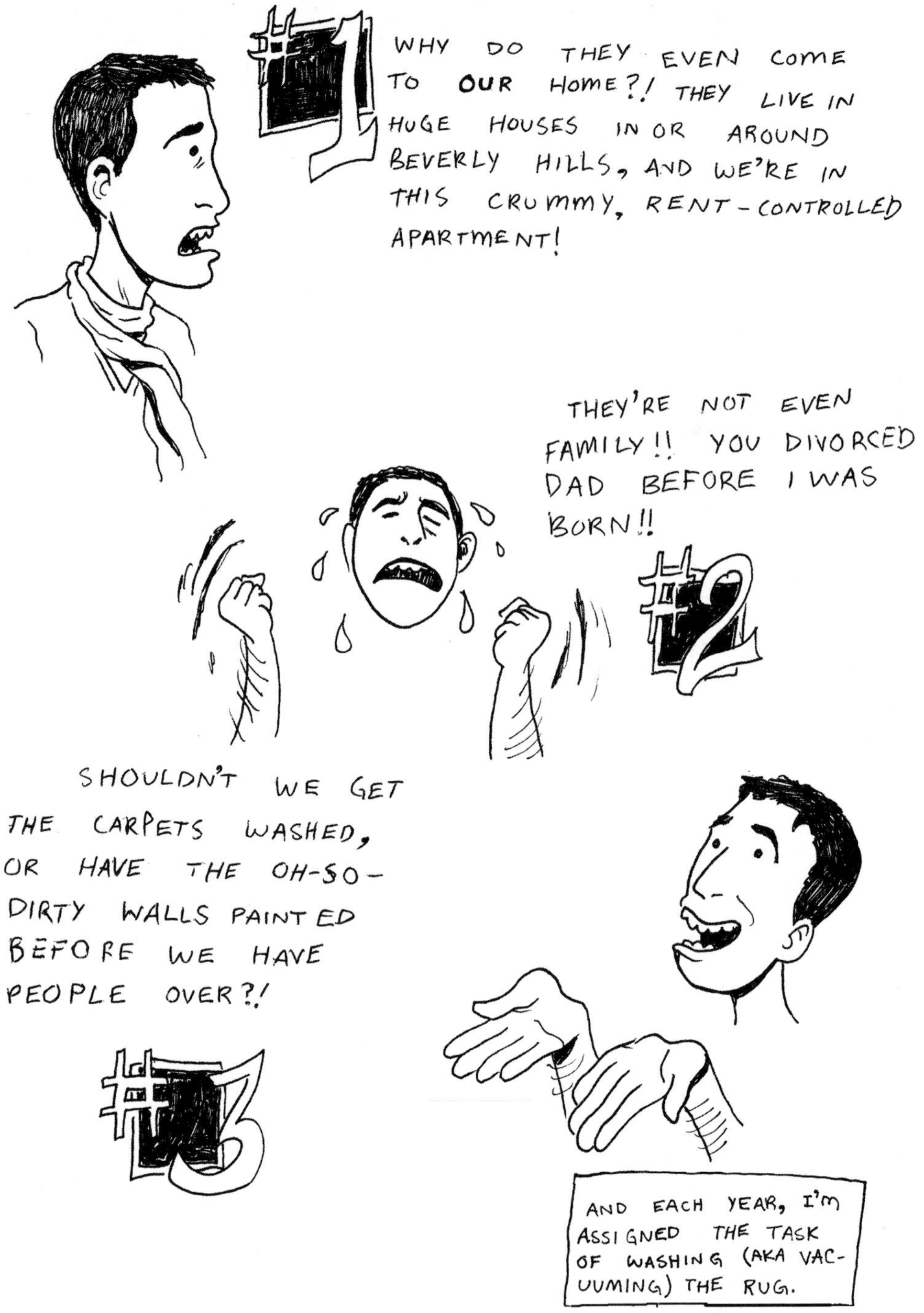
#1
WHY DO THEY EVEN COME TO OUR HOME?! THEY LIVE IN HUGE HOUSES IN OR AROUND BEVERLY HILLS, AND WE'RE IN THIS CRUMMY, RENT-CONTROLLED APARTMENT!
THEY'RE NOT EVEN FAMILY!! YOU DIVORCED DAD BEFORE I WAS BORN!!
#2
SHOULDN'T WE GET THE CARPETS WASHED, OR HAVE THE OH-SO-DIRTY WALLS PAINTED BEFORE WE HAVE PEOPLE OVER?!
#3
AND EACH YEAR, I'M ASSIGNED THE TASK OF WASHING (AKA VACUUMING) THE RUG.

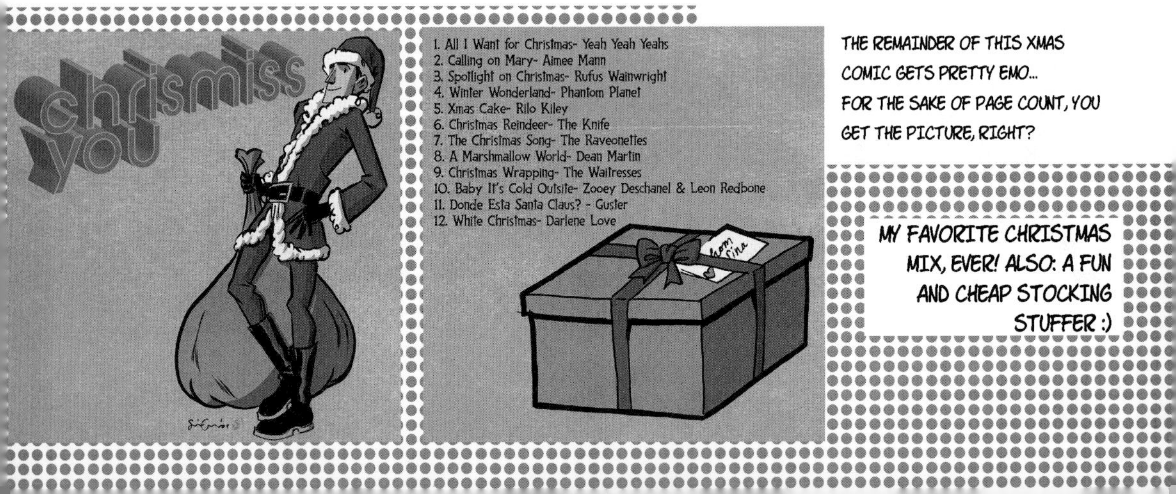
chrismiss you
1. All I Want for Christmas- Yeah Yeah Yeahs
2. Calling on Mary- Aimee Mann
3. Spotlight on Christmas- Rufus Wainwright
4. Winter Wonderland- Phantom Planet
5. Xmas Cake- Rilo Kiley
6. Christmas Reindeer- The Knife
7. The Christmas Song- The Raveonettes
8. A Marshmallow World- Dean Martin
9. Christmas Wrapping- The Waitresses
10. Baby It's Cold Outsite- Zooey Deschanel & Leon Redbone
11. Donde Esta Santa Claus? - Guster
12. White Christmas- Darlene Love
THE REMAINDER OF THIS XMAS COMIC GETS PRETTY EMO... FOR THE SAKE OF PAGE COUNT, YOU GET THE PICTURE, RIGHT?
MY FAVORITE CHRISTMAS MIX, EVER! ALSO: A FUN AND CHEAP STOCKING STUFFER :)

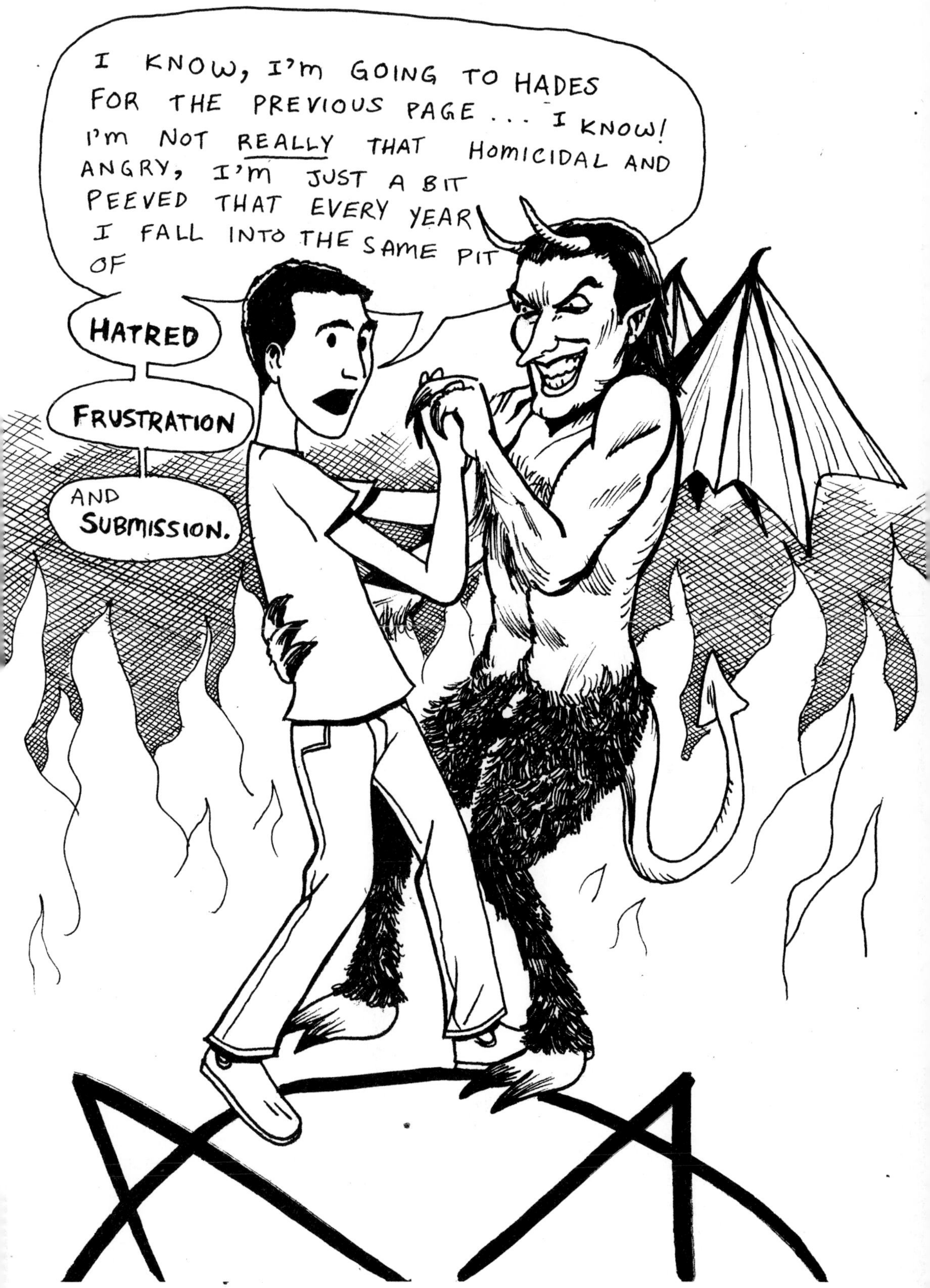
I KNOW, I'M GOING TO HADES FOR THE PREVIOUS PAGE... I KNOW! I'M NOT REALLY THAT HOMICIDAL AND ANGRY, I'M JUST A BIT PEEVED THAT EVERY YEAR I FALL INTO THE SAME PIT OF
HATRED
FRUSTRATION
AND SUBMISSION.

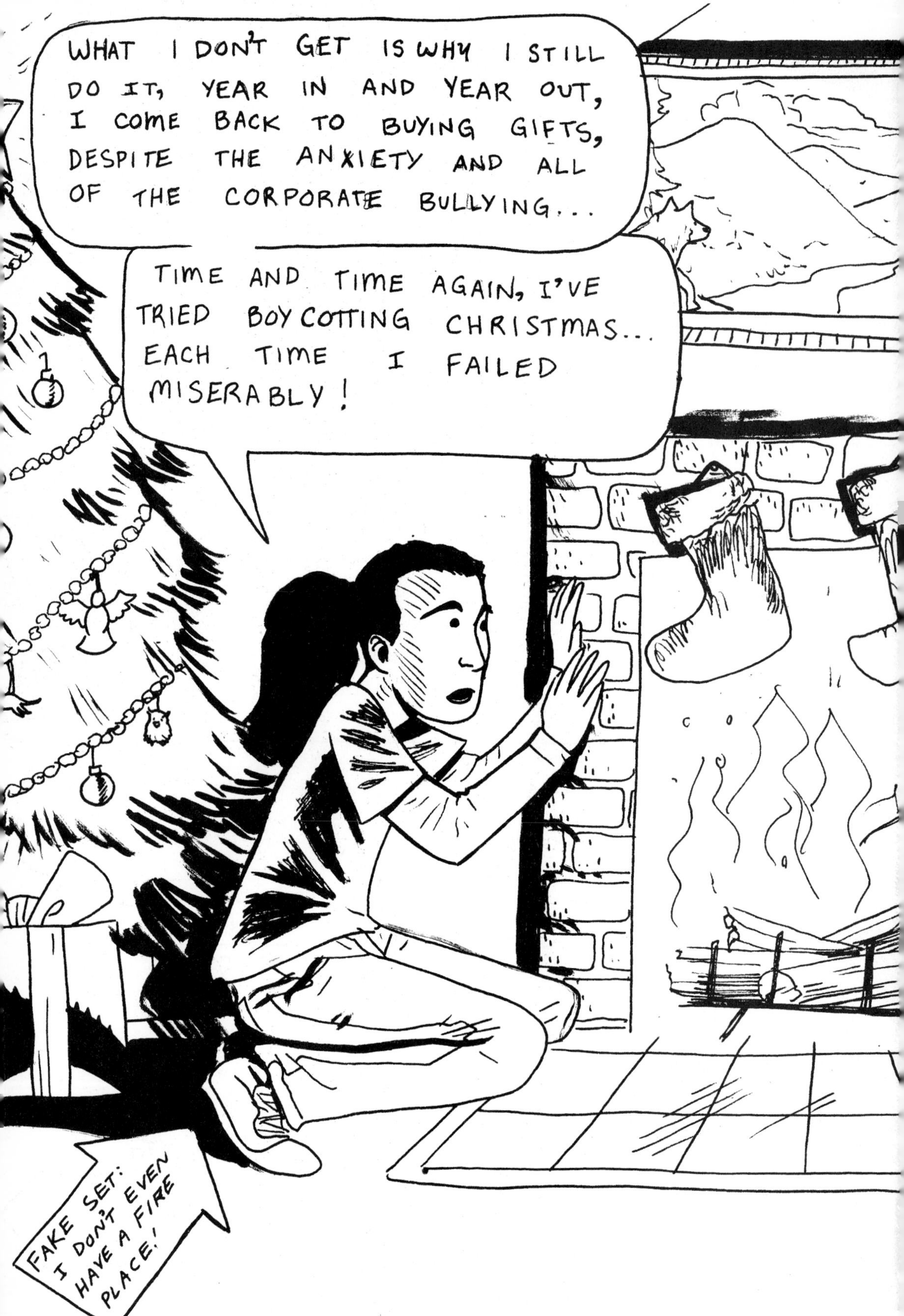
WHAT I DON'T GET IS WHY I STILL DO IT, YEAR IN AND YEAR OUT, I COME BACK TO BUYING GIFTS, DESPITE THE ANXIETY AND ALL OF THE CORPORATE BULLYING...
TIME AND TIME AGAIN, I'VE TRIED BOYCOTTING CHRISTMAS... EACH TIME I FAILED MISERABLY!
FAKE SET: I DON'T EVEN HAVE A FIRE PLACE!

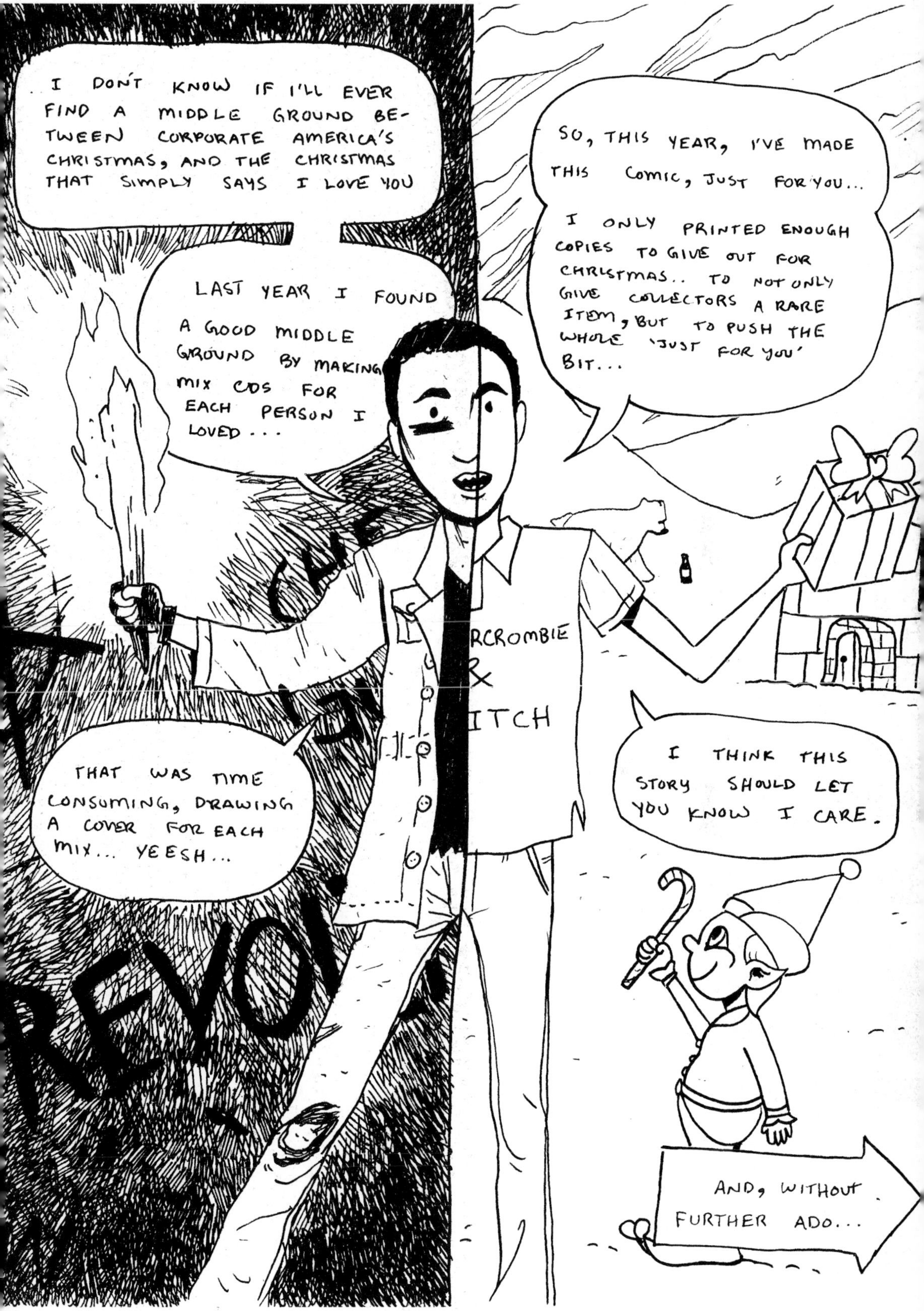
I DON'T KNOW IF I'LL EVER FIND A MIDDLE GROUND BETWEEN CORPORATE AMERICA'S CHRISTMAS, AND THE CHRISTMAS THAT SIMPLY SAYS I LOVE YOU
LAST YEAR I FOUND A GOOD MIDDLE GROUND BY MAKING MIX CDS FOR EACH PERSON I LOVED...
THAT WAS TIME CONSUMING, DRAWING A COVER FOR EACH MIX... YEESH...
SO, THIS YEAR, I'VE MADE THIS COMIC, JUST FOR YOU...
I ONLY PRINTED ENOUGH COPIES TO GIVE OUT FOR CHRISTMAS.. TO NOT ONLY GIVE COLLECTORS A RARE ITEM, BUT TO PUSH THE WHOLE 'JUST FOR YOU' BIT...
I THINK THIS STORY SHOULD LET YOU KNOW I CARE.
AND, WITHOUT FURTHER ADO...

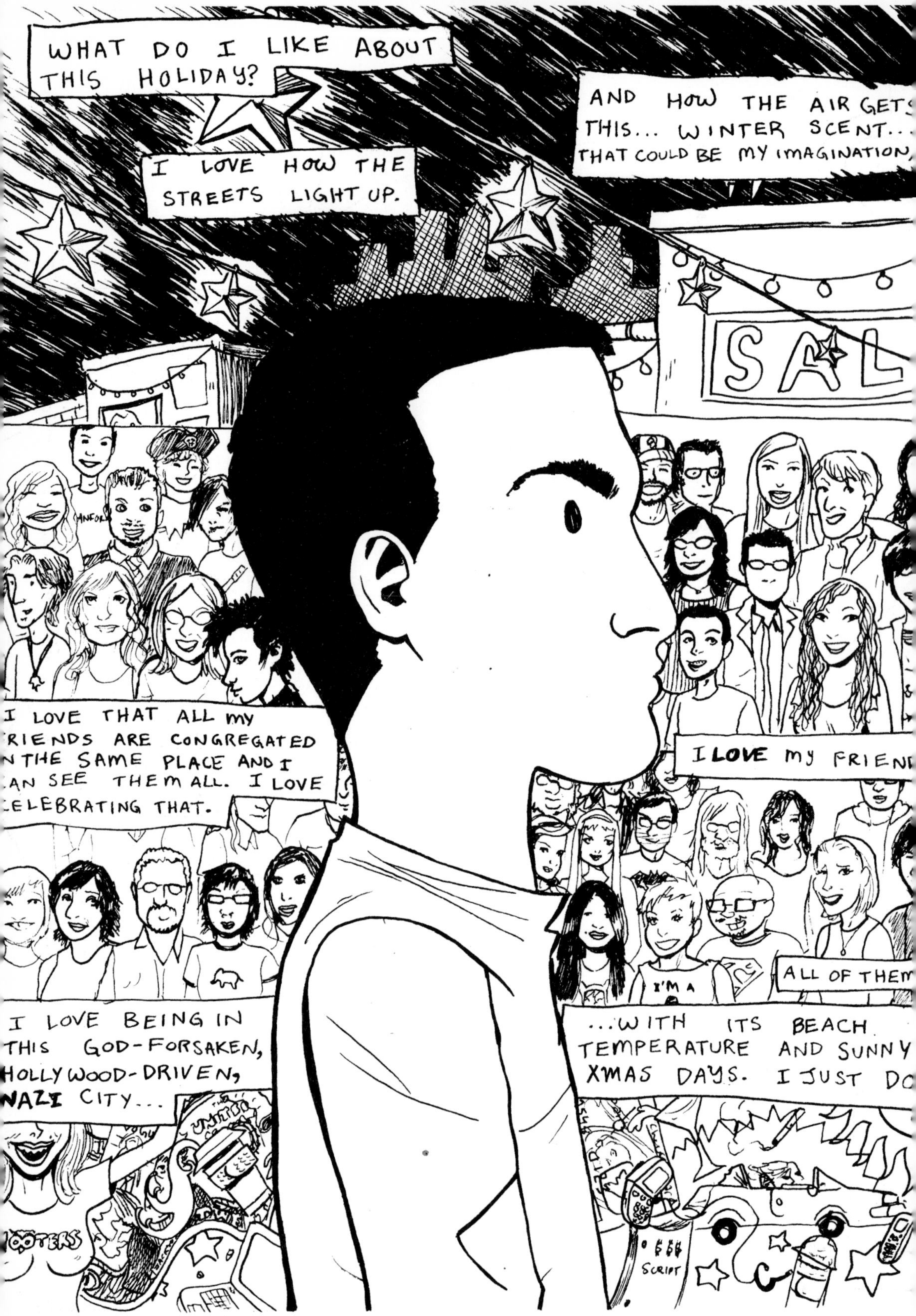
WHAT DO I LIKE ABOUT THIS HOLIDAY?
I LOVE HOW THE STREETS LIGHT UP.
AND HOW THE AIR GETS THIS... WINTER SCENT... THAT COULD BE MY IMAGINATION,
SAL
I LOVE THAT ALL MY FRIENDS ARE CONGREGATED IN THE SAME PLACE AND I CAN SEE THEM ALL. I LOVE CELEBRATING THAT.
I LOVE MY FRIEN
ALL OF THEM
I LOVE BEING IN THIS GOD-FORSAKEN, HOLLYWOOD-DRIVEN, NAZI CITY...
...WITH ITS BEACH TEMPERATURE AND SUNNY XMAS DAYS. I JUST DO
I'M A
SCRIPT

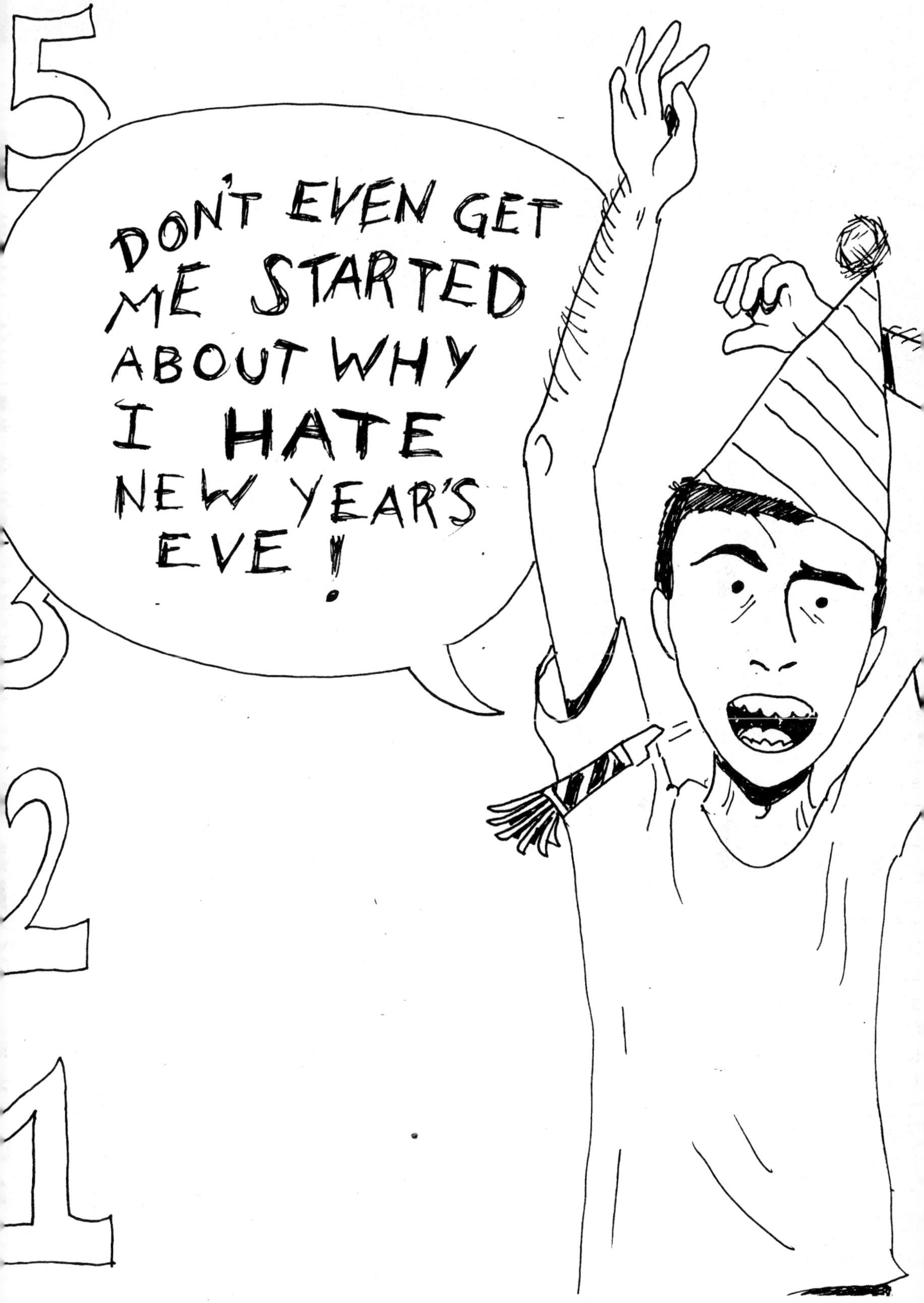
5
DON'T EVEN GET ME STARTED ABOUT WHY I HATE NEW YEAR'S EVE!
2
1

This little gag appeared in Top Cow's
The Magdalena, volume 2, issue 3

"STILL BAD-ASS AFTER ALL THESE YEARS"_

SINA GRACE_

INTERN(TAINER)/PUNK-ASS_

LATEST COW SIGHTING_
08/09/03_
03:07:38 PM_
SANTA MONICA POLICE LINEUP_

BE ON THE LOOKOUT_
KNOW YOUR COWS_

HAVE YOU SEEN THIS BOY?

SINA GRACE
[Editorial Intern / Punk-ass]

MEET YOUR COWS.
TOP COW

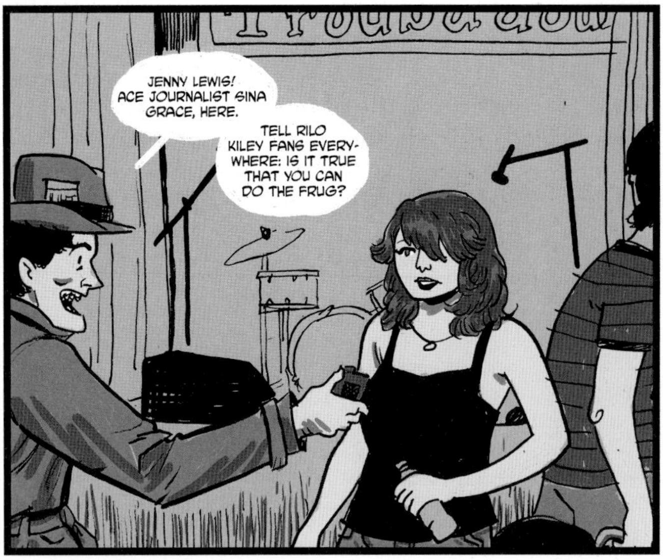
JENNY LEWIS! ACE JOURNALIST SINA GRACE, HERE.
TELL RILO KILEY FANS EVERYWHERE: IS IT TRUE THAT YOU CAN DO THE FRUG?

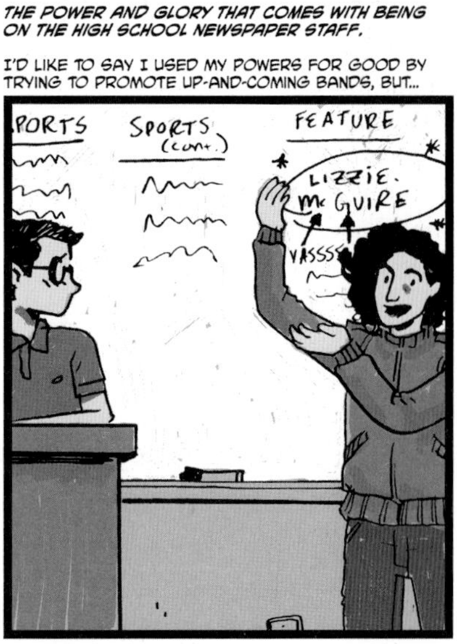
THE POWER AND GLORY THAT COMES WITH BEING ON THE HIGH SCHOOL NEWSPAPER STAFF.
I'D LIKE TO SAY I USED MY POWERS FOR GOOD BY TRYING TO PROMOTE UP-AND-COMING BANDS, BUT...
PORTS
SPORTS (cont.)
FEATURE
LIZZIE McGUIRE

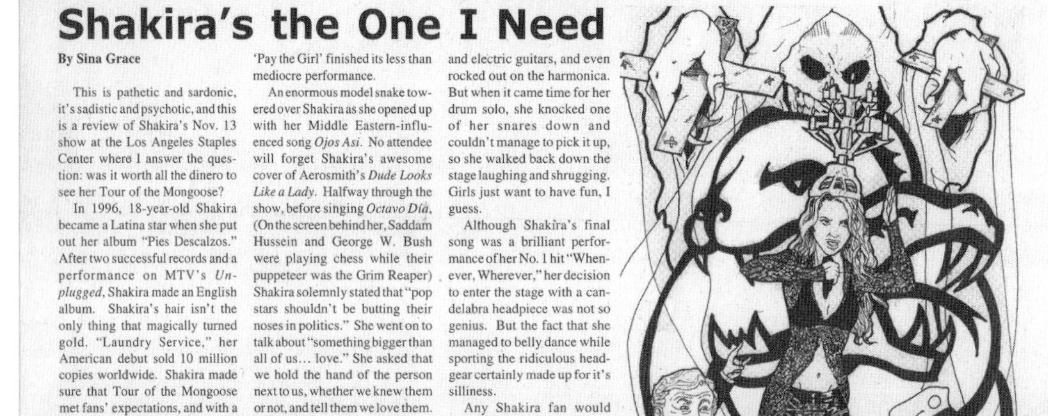
I MAY HAVE BEEN OVER-INDULGED, TO BE HONEST...

Feature

Shakira's the One I Need

By Sina Grace

This is pathetic and sardonic, it's sadistic and psychotic, and this is a review of Shakira's Nov. 13 show at the Los Angeles Staples Center where I answer the question: was it worth all the dinero to see her Tour of the Mongoose?

In 1996, 18-year-old Shakira became a Latina star when she put out her album "Pies Descalzos." After two successful records and a performance on MTV's *Unplugged*, Shakira made an English album. Shakira's hair isn't the only thing that magically turned gold. "Laundry Service," her American debut sold 10 million copies worldwide. Shakira made sure that Tour of the Mongoose met fans' expectations, and with a price tag of $40-$90 a ticket, it had better meet expectations!

Before Shakira came out, two flamboyant male fans had a dance-off. It was hilarious to watch thousands of people turn their heads from corner to corner of the arena to see which dancing queen would reign supreme. The "ShakHEra" wannabes were much needed entertainment after the opening band 'Pay the Girl' finished its less than mediocre performance.

An enormous model snake towered over Shakira as she opened up with her Middle Eastern-influenced song *Ojos Asi*. No attendee will forget Shakira's awesome cover of Aerosmith's *Dude Looks Like a Lady*. Halfway through the show, before singing *Octavo Día*, (On the screen behind her, Saddam Hussein and George W. Bush were playing chess while their puppeteer was the Grim Reaper) Shakira solemnly stated that "pop stars shouldn't be butting their noses in politics." She went on to talk about "something bigger than all of us… love." She asked that we hold the hand of the person next to us, whether we knew them or not, and tell them we love them. Fans rejoiced when Shaki sang the lyrics "To buy more thongs, and write more happy songs," in order to boost morale during these times of conflict.

When Shakira wasn't shaking her booty or singing her *corazón* out, she tried to play the many instruments she has learned through the years. She did do a splendid job playing the acoustic and electric guitars, and even rocked out on the harmonica. But when it came time for her drum solo, she knocked one of her snares down and couldn't manage to pick it up, so she walked back down the stage laughing and shrugging. Girls just want to have fun, I guess.

Although Shakira's final song was a brilliant performance of her No. 1 hit "Whenever, Wherever," her decision to enter the stage with a candelabra headpiece was not so genius. But the fact that she managed to belly dance while sporting the ridiculous headgear certainly made up for it's silliness.

Any Shakira fan would have been in ecstacy. Overpriced water ($3.75) and stolen Shakira posters could not hinder my happiness. If I ever got the chance to meet Shakira, I'd tell her that I'd love her for free and that I am not her mother.

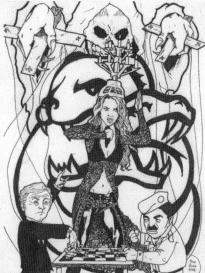

Pigs:Pets and Food!

By Carl Lisberger

Pork is not the only way we use

'Young Life' Helping Teens

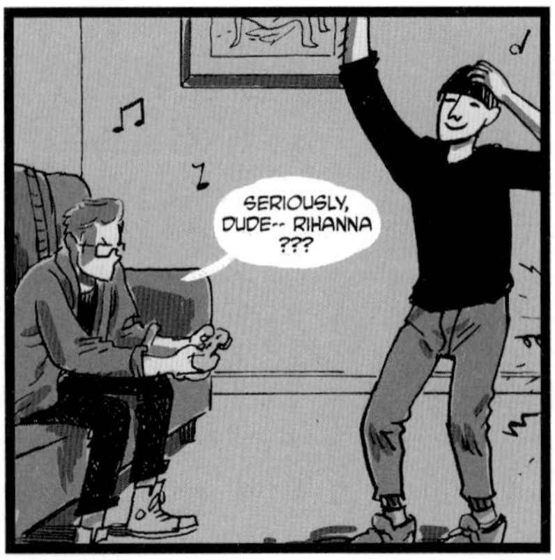
SERIOUSLY, DUDE-- RIHANNA ???

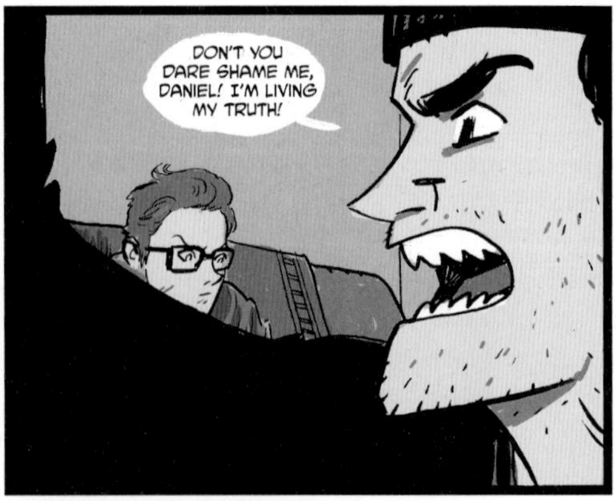
DON'T YOU DARE SHAME ME, DANIEL! I'M LIVING MY TRUTH!

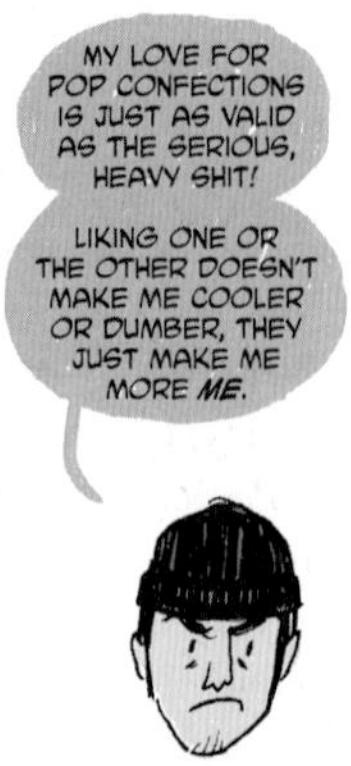
MY LOVE FOR POP CONFECTIONS IS JUST AS VALID AS THE SERIOUS, HEAVY SHIT!
LIKING ONE OR THE OTHER DOESN'T MAKE ME COOLER OR DUMBER, THEY JUST MAKE ME MORE ME.

The Lizzie McGuire Movie Is Actually Really Good

ne of the few times I played hooky in high school was to see The Lizzie McGuire Movie. For some reason, I had his elaborate plan where I had a fake note and a fake call from my mom to get me out of school for a "doctor's ppointment," all so I could meet my high school crush Rachel McNevin (cough) at the promenade to watch the ovie during a school day. She had done the easier thing and just not gone to school. We went into the theatre, oth packing candy from the liquor store, and had our lives changed. That movie had EVERYTHING.

ow, I know I'm not unique in this situation. Just a few days later, my friends (who were seniors) got wasted and w the movie, and had an equally spectacular time. Let me break it down for you why it's a modern asterpiece…

"...A perfect pop confection to be adored, laughed at, laughed with, and sung along to."

et me clarify one thing, the movie is not actually good. It doesn't deserve an Oscar, and we all know it was eant to be a vehicle for Hilary Duff's singing career. There may be a drinking game out there for how many mes she's FORCED to sing even though she's so not a singer. I meeeeeannn. But Disney didn't have to hire lex Borstein to play a campy dictator high school principal guiding the kids on a graduation trip, they didn't ave to make genuine efforts for the plot to make sense enough that we believe some bitch from the Midwest can ake being an Italian superstar… they could have shat out an oversized episode, but they didn't. They made a erfect pop confection to be adored, laughed at, laughed with, and sung along to.

ll one needs to know going in is that Lizzie McGuire is way too young to be in Italy barely supervised, and way oo pretty to be the loser underdog who ruined middle school graduation. Also, the entire movie is White Girl roblems. A dreamy pre-Bieber Italian pop star named Paolo Valisari discovers lowly Lizzie on the street, and nlists her to help him out while his musical partner is MIA due to "creative differences." You see, Lizzie looks ke a blonde version of Paolo's singing partner/ ex-girlfriend, Isabella Parigi. It's remarkably uncanny. Our rotagonist has to learn to sing and dance for some sort of weird Euro VMAs (held in an old coliseum???), go rough a bunch of travel and fashion montages (this movie really loves montages), AND pretend she's sick to over her adventures up from previously mentioned principal. Thank god her longtime best friend is the world's iggest monkey wrench and is willing to do anything to help Lizzie. Otherwise, she would have been SO busted.

o, throughout the whole film there's this tension that another chick who looks like Lizzie exists and may or may ot be effing Paolo over. It's not enough of course that we get to MEET Isabella (HilDuff in a brunette wig and ith a ghetto Italian accent), nor is it the biggest deal in the movie that she may not be the talentless hack that aolo made her out to be, but of course in the third act she and Lizzie sing TOGETHER. In true Euro trash MA style, there's back-up dancers, laser lights, and Alex Borstein doing the robot. Disney did the third act ght: twists, turns, surprises, and love interests galore. I know you think I'm giving away spoilers, but you have o clue what outfit either of them is wearing during this number, so trust me… you've got plenty of surprises aiting for you.

emember when I said this was a vehicle for Hilary Duff's music career? There is NOTHING better than atching a fourteen year old magically belt out a song she just learned, whilst matching pitch with her Italian iva doppelgänger. The movie also opens with her "goofily" crooning "The Tide is High" into her hairbrush she's just like us!), while her little brother secretly video tapes her. This throwaway #dickmove comes back in he third act… did I mention this movie has an airtight script? With lyrics like "Yesterday my life was duller/ ow everything's technicolor" you can trust that there is not a single wasted moment in this 94 minute gem. o this day, I still honor Hilary Duff's greatest achievement in cinema history. Literally ten years later I can still o the Paolo/ Lizzie duet with my friend Lauren (she was one of the drunkard seniors… we're still pals) without eeding to look up the lyrics. When I find my true love, we'll be watching this movie annually, celebrating the nniversary of when we both realized we loved The Lizzie McGuire Movie over a glass of wine at some cute Silver ake candlelit restaurant. We'll even try in vain to watch Raise Your Voice, or Cadet Kelly on Netflix… but it on't be the same. This, to me, is what dreams are made of.

Sina Grace

COMPOSITES

THIS DOESN'T *REALLY* MAKE SENSE WHEN YOU THINK ABOUT IT.

EVEN IF CARRIE WAS CHANGING THE NAMES OF HER FRIENDS, PEOPLE WOULD STILL FIGURE OUT WHO THEY ARE WHEN SHE'S BRINGING THEM OUT TO PARTIES.

I ALWAYS ASSUMED THAT THEY WERE COMPOSITES OF MULTIPLE PEOPLE.

OH MY GOD...

SO MANY TEETH...

YOU'RE IMAGINING ALL OF THE "SEX AND THE CITY" GIRLS AS ONE BIG BLOB OF A WOMAN, AREN'T YOU?

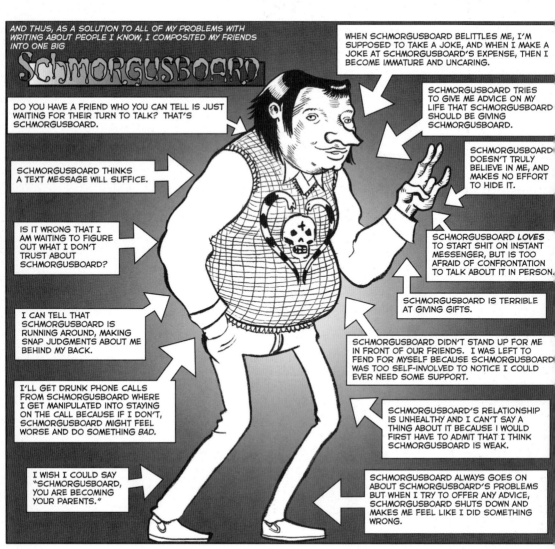

AND THUS, AS A SOLUTION TO ALL OF MY PROBLEMS WITH WRITING ABOUT PEOPLE I KNOW, I COMPOSITED MY FRIENDS INTO ONE BIG

Schmorgusboard

DO YOU HAVE A FRIEND WHO YOU CAN TELL IS JUST WAITING FOR THEIR TURN TO TALK? THAT'S SCHMORGUSBOARD.

SCHMORGUSBOARD THINKS A TEXT MESSAGE WILL SUFFICE.

IS IT WRONG THAT I AM WAITING TO FIGURE OUT WHAT I DON'T TRUST ABOUT SCHMORGUSBOARD?

I CAN TELL THAT SCHMORGUSBOARD IS RUNNING AROUND, MAKING SNAP JUDGMENTS ABOUT ME BEHIND MY BACK.

I'LL GET DRUNK PHONE CALLS FROM SCHMORGUSBOARD WHERE I GET MANIPULATED INTO STAYING ON THE CALL BECAUSE IF I DON'T, SCHMORGUSBOARD MIGHT FEEL WORSE AND DO SOMETHING *BAD*.

I WISH I COULD SAY "SCHMORGUSBOARD, YOU ARE BECOMING YOUR PARENTS."

WHEN SCHMORGUSBOARD BELITTLES ME, I'M SUPPOSED TO TAKE A JOKE, AND WHEN I MAKE A JOKE AT SCHMORGUSBOARD'S EXPENSE, THEN I BECOME IMMATURE AND UNCARING.

SCHMORGUSBOARD TRIES TO GIVE ME ADVICE ON MY LIFE THAT SCHMORGUSBOARD SHOULD BE GIVING SCHMORGUSBOARD.

SCHMORGUSBOARD DOESN'T TRULY BELIEVE IN ME, AND MAKES NO EFFORT TO HIDE IT.

SCHMORGUSBOARD *LOVES* TO START SHIT ON INSTANT MESSENGER, BUT IS TOO AFRAID OF CONFRONTATION TO TALK ABOUT IT IN PERSON.

SCHMORGUSBOARD IS TERRIBLE AT GIVING GIFTS.

SCHMORGUSBOARD DIDN'T STAND UP FOR ME IN FRONT OF OUR FRIENDS. I WAS LEFT TO FEND FOR MYSELF BECAUSE SCHMORGUSBOARD WAS TOO SELF-INVOLVED TO NOTICE I COULD EVER NEED SOME SUPPORT.

SCHMORGUSBOARD'S RELATIONSHIP IS UNHEALTHY AND I CAN'T SAY A THING ABOUT IT BECAUSE I WOULD FIRST HAVE TO ADMIT THAT I THINK SCHMORGUSBOARD IS WEAK.

SCHMORGUSBOARD ALWAYS GOES ON ABOUT SCHMORGUSBOARD'S PROBLEMS BUT WHEN I TRY TO OFFER ANY ADVICE, SCHMORGUSBOARD SHUTS DOWN AND MAKES ME FEEL LIKE I DID SOMETHING WRONG.

RE YOU THINKING WHAT I'M THINKING?

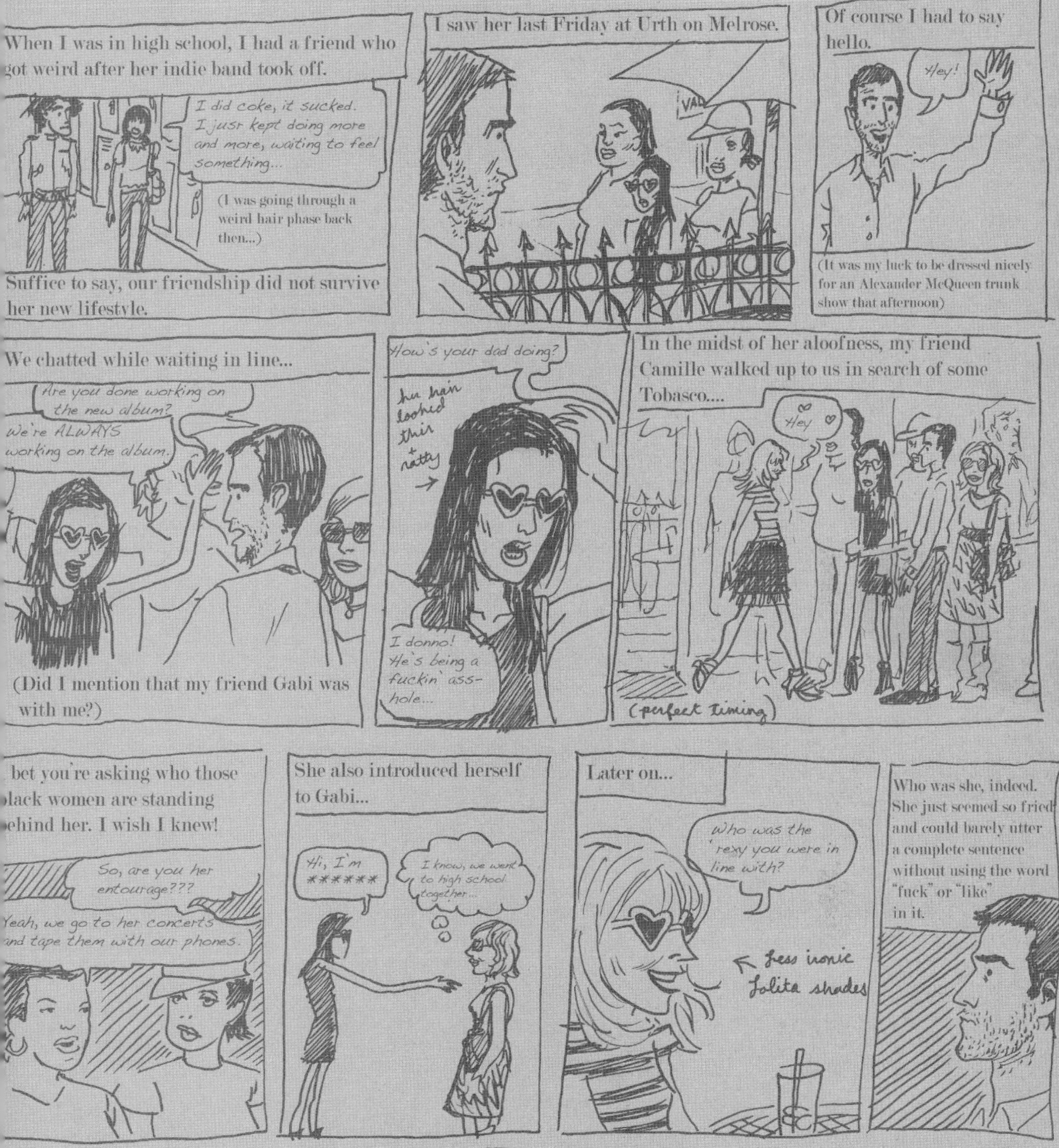

When I was in high school, I had a friend who got weird after her indie band took off.
I did coke, it sucked. I just kept doing more and more, waiting to feel something...
(I was going through a weird hair phase back then...)
Suffice to say, our friendship did not survive her new lifestyle.
I saw her last Friday at Urth on Melrose.
Of course I had to say hello.
Hey!
(It was my luck to be dressed nicely for an Alexander McQueen trunk show that afternoon)
We chatted while waiting in line...
Are you done working on the new album?
We're ALWAYS working on the album.
(Did I mention that my friend Gabi was with me?)
How's your dad doing?
her hair looked thin + ratty
I donno! He's being a fuckin' ass-hole...
In the midst of her aloofness, my friend Camille walked up to us in search of some Tobasco....
Hey
(perfect timing)
bet you're asking who those black women are standing behind her. I wish I knew!
So, are you her entourage???
Yeah, we go to her concerts and tape them with our phones.
She also introduced herself to Gabi...
Hi, I'm *****
I know, we went to high school together...
Later on...
Who was the sexy you were in line with?
less ironic Lolita shades
Who was she, indeed. She just seemed so fried and could barely utter a complete sentence without using the word "fuck" or "like" in it.
wasn't jealous of her, or interested in getting back in touch with an old friend...
just felt kind of bad that the lifestyle she indulged in had made her look like such a mess... Oh well.
Seriously! What the fuck were those Queen Latifahs doing with her???
I really want a mannequin
THE END
ditor's Note: Camille guessed and confirmed two days later that they were rehab nurses/ assistants.
uffice to say, I felt like a major asshole after posting this with her name on it a few days ago.

SINA GRACE

IN...

HOW I MET YOUR WIZARD

Part One of Two

IT ALL HAPPENED ONE NIGHT WHEN I WAS WORKING ON A SHORT STORY DUE FOR MY FICTION WORKSHOP...

I WAS WRITING THIS SAD, SAD STORY ABOUT A BI-POLAR ARTIST WHO WAS NEVER SATISFIED WITH HIS WORK.

IN HOMAGE TO SOME CHINESE FOLK TALE I HEARD, THE ENDING WAS PRETTY BRUTAL.

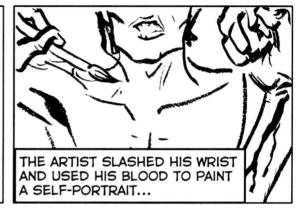

THE ARTIST SLASHED HIS WRIST AND USED HIS BLOOD TO PAINT A SELF-PORTRAIT...

THE STORY JUST WOULD NOT COME OUT OF MY FINGERS...

INSTEAD, MY HAND KEPT LINGERING OVER TO MY CELL PHONE...

I WALKED OUT OF LULU'S TO TALK TO MY FRIEND MIKAEL. AN IDEA CAME TO ME THEN...

I ENVISIONED HIM AS A DETECTIVE, UNEARTHING A DARK MYSTERY...

(THIS WOULD ULTIMATELY BECOME THE ENDING OF *CEDRIC HOLLOWS*)

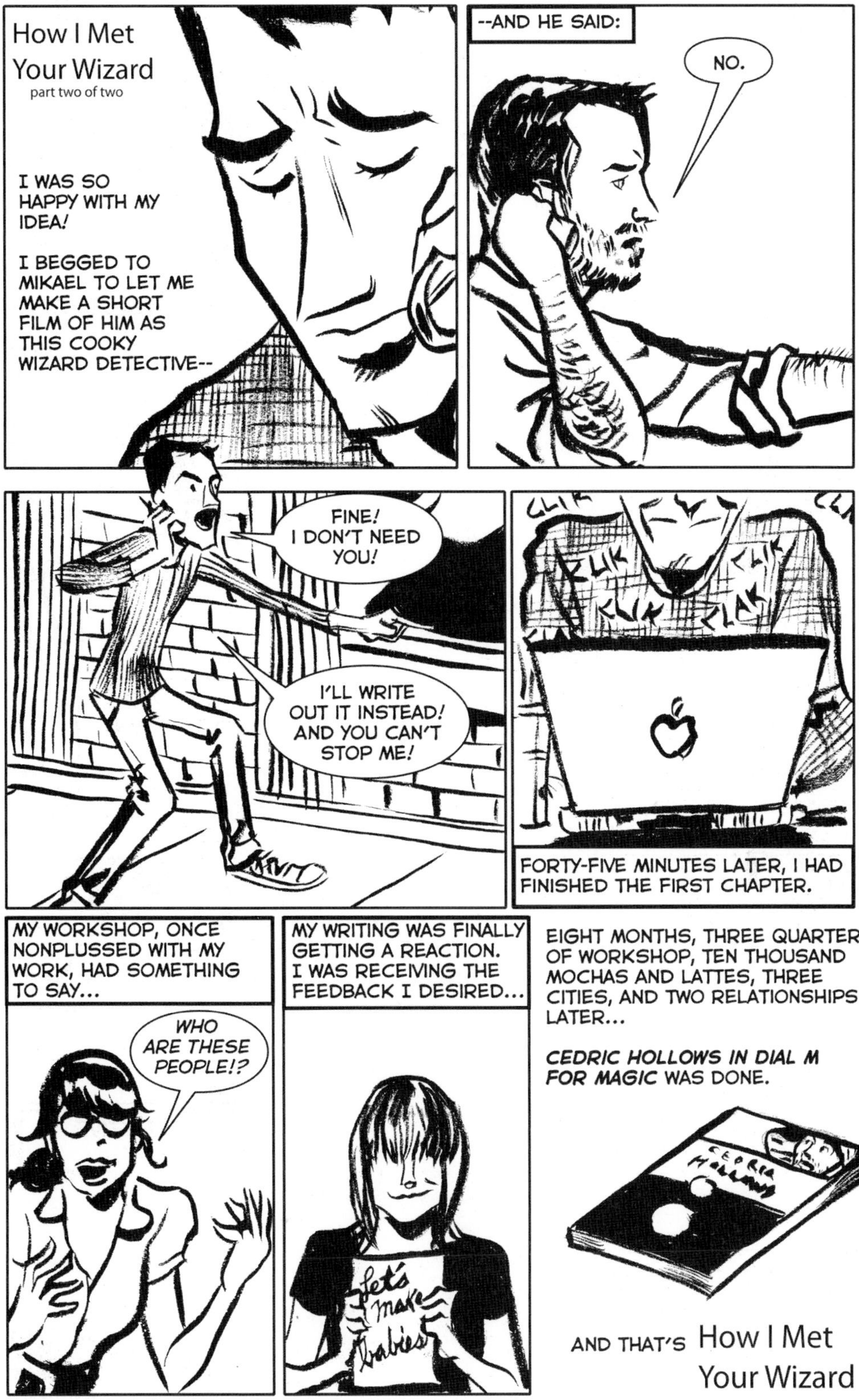
How I Met Your Wizard
part two of two
I WAS SO HAPPY WITH MY IDEA!
I BEGGED TO MIKAEL TO LET ME MAKE A SHORT FILM OF HIM AS THIS COOKY WIZARD DETECTIVE--
--AND HE SAID:
NO.
FINE! I DON'T NEED YOU!
I'LL WRITE OUT IT INSTEAD! AND YOU CAN'T STOP ME!
FORTY-FIVE MINUTES LATER, I HAD FINISHED THE FIRST CHAPTER.
MY WORKSHOP, ONCE NONPLUSSED WITH MY WORK, HAD SOMETHING TO SAY...
WHO ARE THESE PEOPLE!?
MY WRITING WAS FINALLY GETTING A REACTION. I WAS RECEIVING THE FEEDBACK I DESIRED...
EIGHT MONTHS, THREE QUARTERS OF WORKSHOP, TEN THOUSAND MOCHAS AND LATTES, THREE CITIES, AND TWO RELATIONSHIPS LATER...
CEDRIC HOLLOWS IN DIAL M FOR MAGIC WAS DONE.
AND THAT'S How I Met Your Wizard

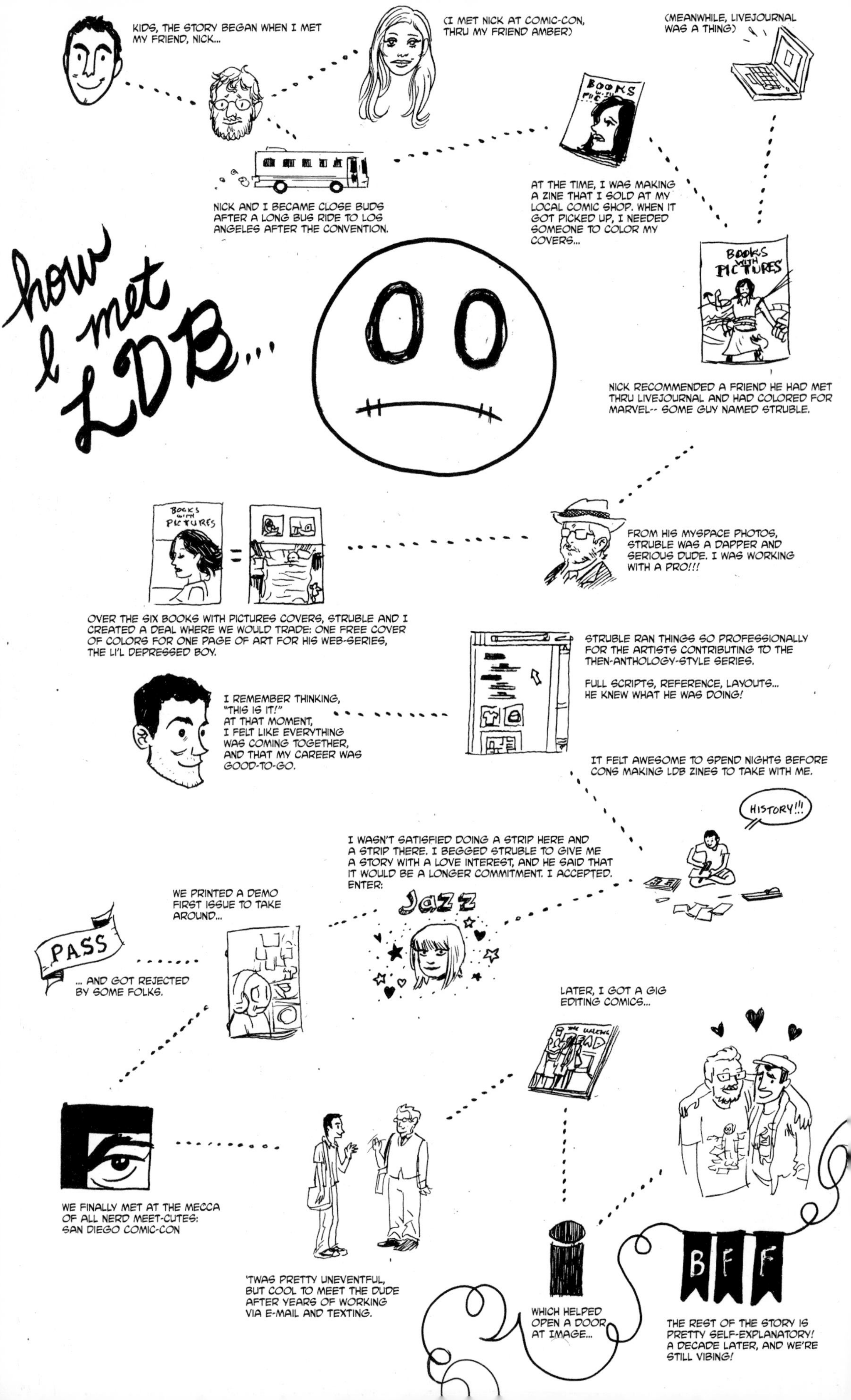
how I met LDB...
KIDS, THE STORY BEGAN WHEN I MET MY FRIEND, NICK...
(I MET NICK AT COMIC-CON, THRU MY FRIEND AMBER)
NICK AND I BECAME CLOSE BUDS AFTER A LONG BUS RIDE TO LOS ANGELES AFTER THE CONVENTION.
BOOKS WITH PICTURES
AT THE TIME, I WAS MAKING A ZINE THAT I SOLD AT MY LOCAL COMIC SHOP. WHEN IT GOT PICKED UP, I NEEDED SOMEONE TO COLOR MY COVERS...
(MEANWHILE, LIVEJOURNAL WAS A THING)
BOOKS WITH PICTURES
NICK RECOMMENDED A FRIEND HE HAD MET THRU LIVEJOURNAL AND HAD COLORED FOR MARVEL-- SOME GUY NAMED STRUBLE.
FROM HIS MYSPACE PHOTOS, STRUBLE WAS A DAPPER AND SERIOUS DUDE. I WAS WORKING WITH A PRO!!!
BOOKS WITH PICTURES
OVER THE SIX BOOKS WITH PICTURES COVERS, STRUBLE AND I CREATED A DEAL WHERE WE WOULD TRADE: ONE FREE COVER OF COLORS FOR ONE PAGE OF ART FOR HIS WEB-SERIES, THE LI'L DEPRESSED BOY.
STRUBLE RAN THINGS SO PROFESSIONALLY FOR THE ARTISTS CONTRIBUTING TO THE THEN-ANTHOLOGY-STYLE SERIES.
FULL SCRIPTS, REFERENCE, LAYOUTS... HE KNEW WHAT HE WAS DOING!
I REMEMBER THINKING, "THIS IS IT!" AT THAT MOMENT, I FELT LIKE EVERYTHING WAS COMING TOGETHER, AND THAT MY CAREER WAS GOOD-TO-GO.
IT FELT AWESOME TO SPEND NIGHTS BEFORE CONS MAKING LDB ZINES TO TAKE WITH ME.
HISTORY!!!
I WASN'T SATISFIED DOING A STRIP HERE AND A STRIP THERE. I BEGGED STRUBLE TO GIVE ME A STORY WITH A LOVE INTEREST, AND HE SAID THAT IT WOULD BE A LONGER COMMITMENT. I ACCEPTED. ENTER:
Jazz
WE PRINTED A DEMO FIRST ISSUE TO TAKE AROUND...
PASS
... AND GOT REJECTED BY SOME FOLKS.
LATER, I GOT A GIG EDITING COMICS...
WE FINALLY MET AT THE MECCA OF ALL NERD MEET-CUTES: SAN DIEGO COMIC-CON
'TWAS PRETTY UNEVENTFUL, BUT COOL TO MEET THE DUDE AFTER YEARS OF WORKING VIA E-MAIL AND TEXTING.
WHICH HELPED OPEN A DOOR AT IMAGE...
B F F
THE REST OF THE STORY IS PRETTY SELF-EXPLANATORY! A DECADE LATER, AND WE'RE STILL VIBING!

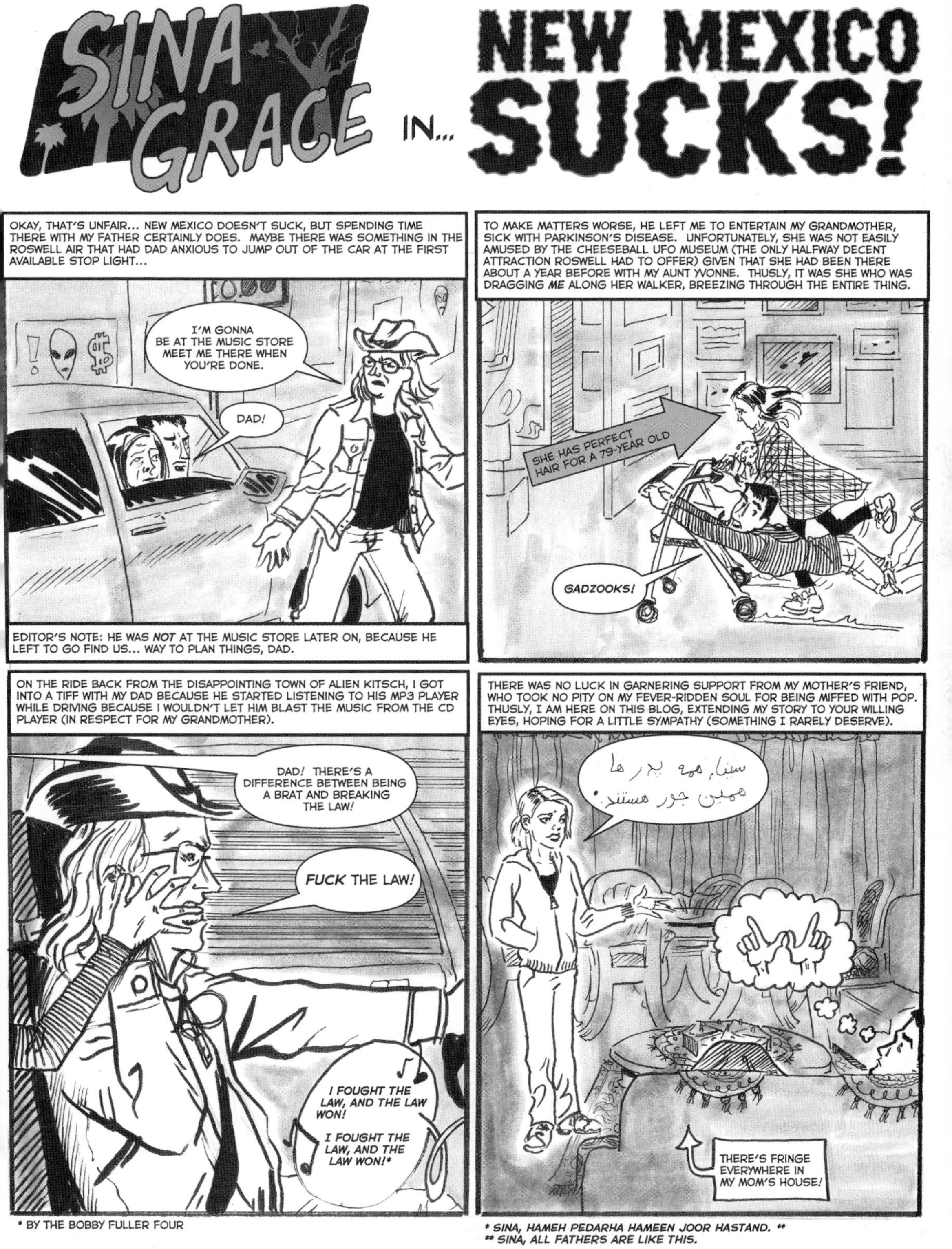
SINA GRACE
IN...
NEW MEXICO SUCKS!
OKAY, THAT'S UNFAIR... NEW MEXICO DOESN'T SUCK, BUT SPENDING TIME THERE WITH MY FATHER CERTAINLY DOES. MAYBE THERE WAS SOMETHING IN THE ROSWELL AIR THAT HAD DAD ANXIOUS TO JUMP OUT OF THE CAR AT THE FIRST AVAILABLE STOP LIGHT...
I'M GONNA BE AT THE MUSIC STORE MEET ME THERE WHEN YOU'RE DONE.
DAD!
EDITOR'S NOTE: HE WAS *NOT* AT THE MUSIC STORE LATER ON, BECAUSE HE LEFT TO GO FIND US... WAY TO PLAN THINGS, DAD.
TO MAKE MATTERS WORSE, HE LEFT ME TO ENTERTAIN MY GRANDMOTHER, SICK WITH PARKINSON'S DISEASE. UNFORTUNATELY, SHE WAS NOT EASILY AMUSED BY THE CHEESEBALL UFO MUSEUM (THE ONLY HALFWAY DECENT ATTRACTION ROSWELL HAD TO OFFER) GIVEN THAT SHE HAD BEEN THERE ABOUT A YEAR BEFORE WITH MY AUNT YVONNE. THUSLY, IT WAS SHE WHO WAS DRAGGING *ME* ALONG HER WALKER, BREEZING THROUGH THE ENTIRE THING.
SHE HAS PERFECT HAIR FOR A 79-YEAR OLD
GADZOOKS!
ON THE RIDE BACK FROM THE DISAPPOINTING TOWN OF ALIEN KITSCH, I GOT INTO A TIFF WITH MY DAD BECAUSE HE STARTED LISTENING TO HIS MP3 PLAYER WHILE DRIVING BECAUSE I WOULDN'T LET HIM BLAST THE MUSIC FROM THE CD PLAYER (IN RESPECT FOR MY GRANDMOTHER).
DAD! THERE'S A DIFFERENCE BETWEEN BEING A BRAT AND BREAKING THE LAW!
FUCK THE LAW!
I FOUGHT THE LAW, AND THE LAW WON!
*I FOUGHT THE LAW, AND THE LAW WON!**
THERE WAS NO LUCK IN GARNERING SUPPORT FROM MY MOTHER'S FRIEND, WHO TOOK NO PITY ON MY FEVER-RIDDEN SOUL FOR BEING MIFFED WITH POP. THUSLY, I AM HERE ON THIS BLOG, EXTENDING MY STORY TO YOUR WILLING EYES, HOPING FOR A LITTLE SYMPATHY (SOMETHING I RARELY DESERVE).
سینا، همه پدرها
همین جور هستند.*
THERE'S FRINGE EVERYWHERE IN MY MOM'S HOUSE!

* BY THE BOBBY FULLER FOUR

** SINA, HAMEH PEDARHA HAMEEN JOOR HASTAND. ***
*** SINA, ALL FATHERS ARE LIKE THIS.*

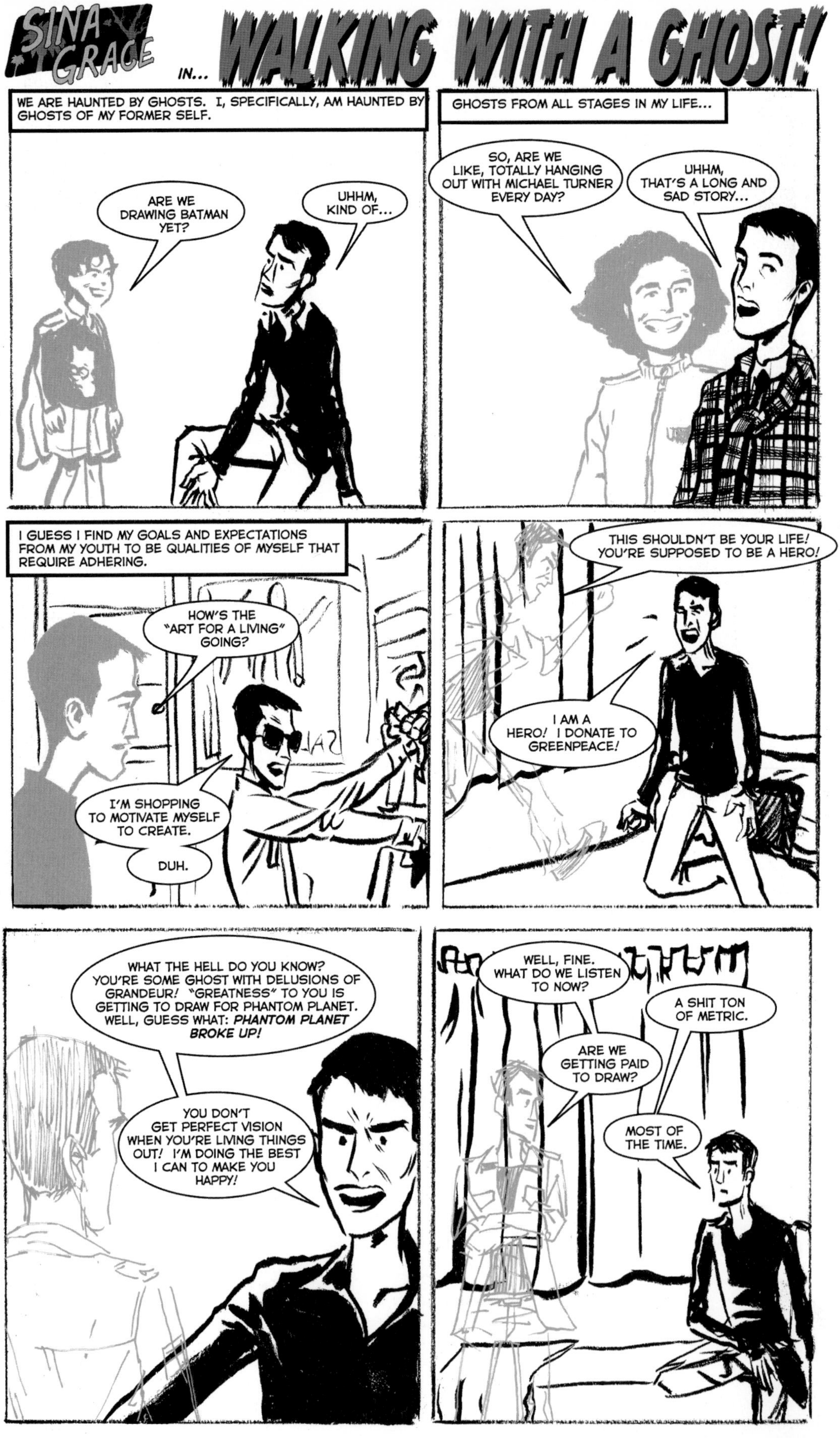
SINA GRACE
IN...
WALKING WITH A GHOST!
WE ARE HAUNTED BY GHOSTS. I, SPECIFICALLY, AM HAUNTED BY GHOSTS OF MY FORMER SELF.
ARE WE DRAWING BATMAN YET?
UHHM, KIND OF...
GHOSTS FROM ALL STAGES IN MY LIFE...
SO, ARE WE LIKE, TOTALLY HANGING OUT WITH MICHAEL TURNER EVERY DAY?
UHHM, THAT'S A LONG AND SAD STORY...
I GUESS I FIND MY GOALS AND EXPECTATIONS FROM MY YOUTH TO BE QUALITIES OF MYSELF THAT REQUIRE ADHERING.
HOW'S THE "ART FOR A LIVING" GOING?
I'M SHOPPING TO MOTIVATE MYSELF TO CREATE.
DUH.
THIS SHOULDN'T BE YOUR LIFE! YOU'RE SUPPOSED TO BE A HERO!
I AM A HERO! I DONATE TO GREENPEACE!
WHAT THE HELL DO YOU KNOW? YOU'RE SOME GHOST WITH DELUSIONS OF GRANDEUR! "GREATNESS" TO YOU IS GETTING TO DRAW FOR PHANTOM PLANET. WELL, GUESS WHAT: *PHANTOM PLANET BROKE UP!*
YOU DON'T GET PERFECT VISION WHEN YOU'RE LIVING THINGS OUT! I'M DOING THE BEST I CAN TO MAKE YOU HAPPY!
WELL, FINE. WHAT DO WE LISTEN TO NOW?
A SHIT TON OF METRIC.
ARE WE GETTING PAID TO DRAW?
MOST OF THE TIME.

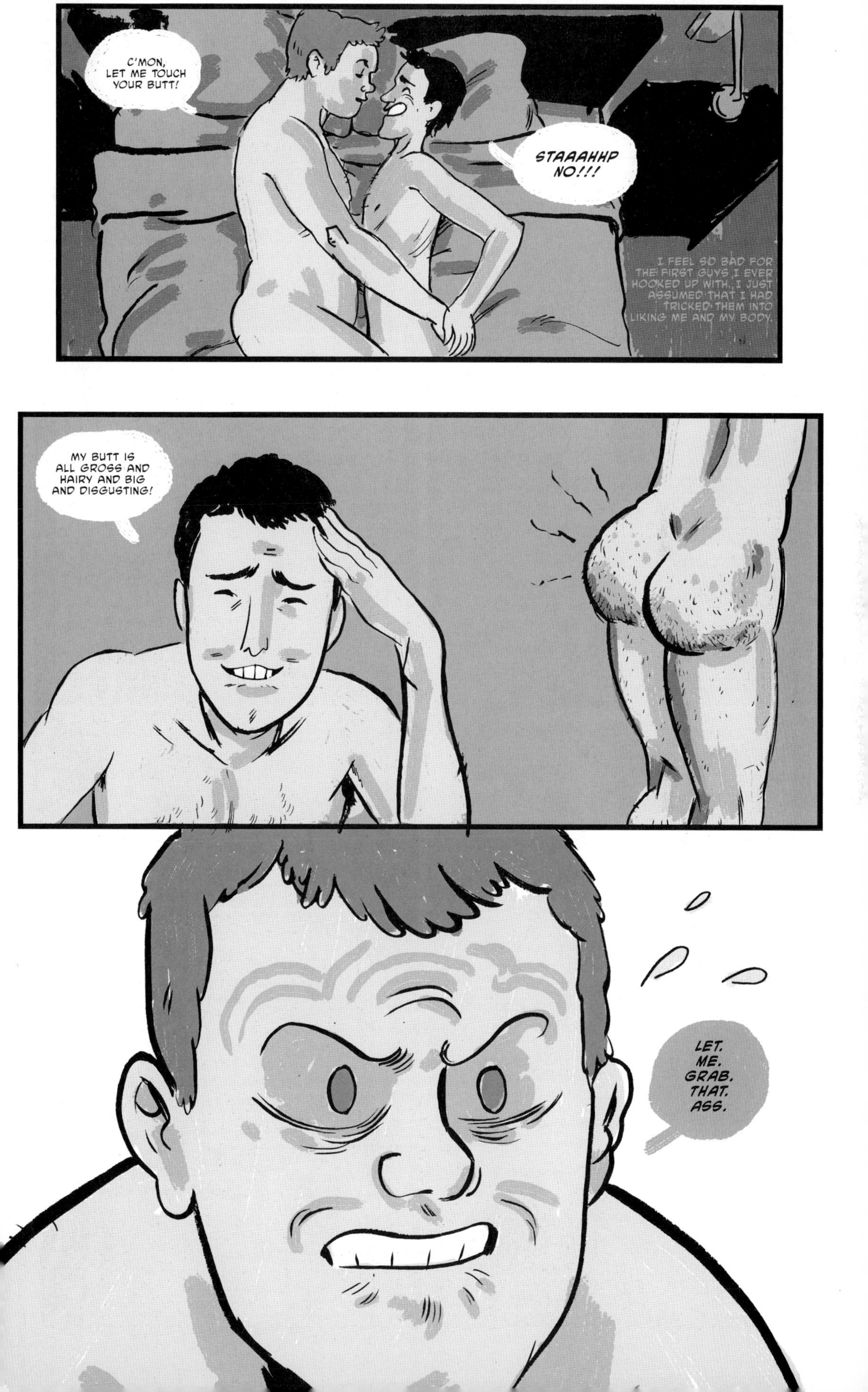
C'MON, LET ME TOUCH YOUR BUTT!
STAAAHHP NO!!!
I FEEL SO BAD FOR THE FIRST GUYS I EVER HOOKED UP WITH. I JUST ASSUMED THAT I HAD TRICKED THEM INTO LIKING ME AND MY BODY.
MY BUTT IS ALL GROSS AND HAIRY AND BIG AND DISGUSTING!
LET. ME. GRAB. THAT. ASS.

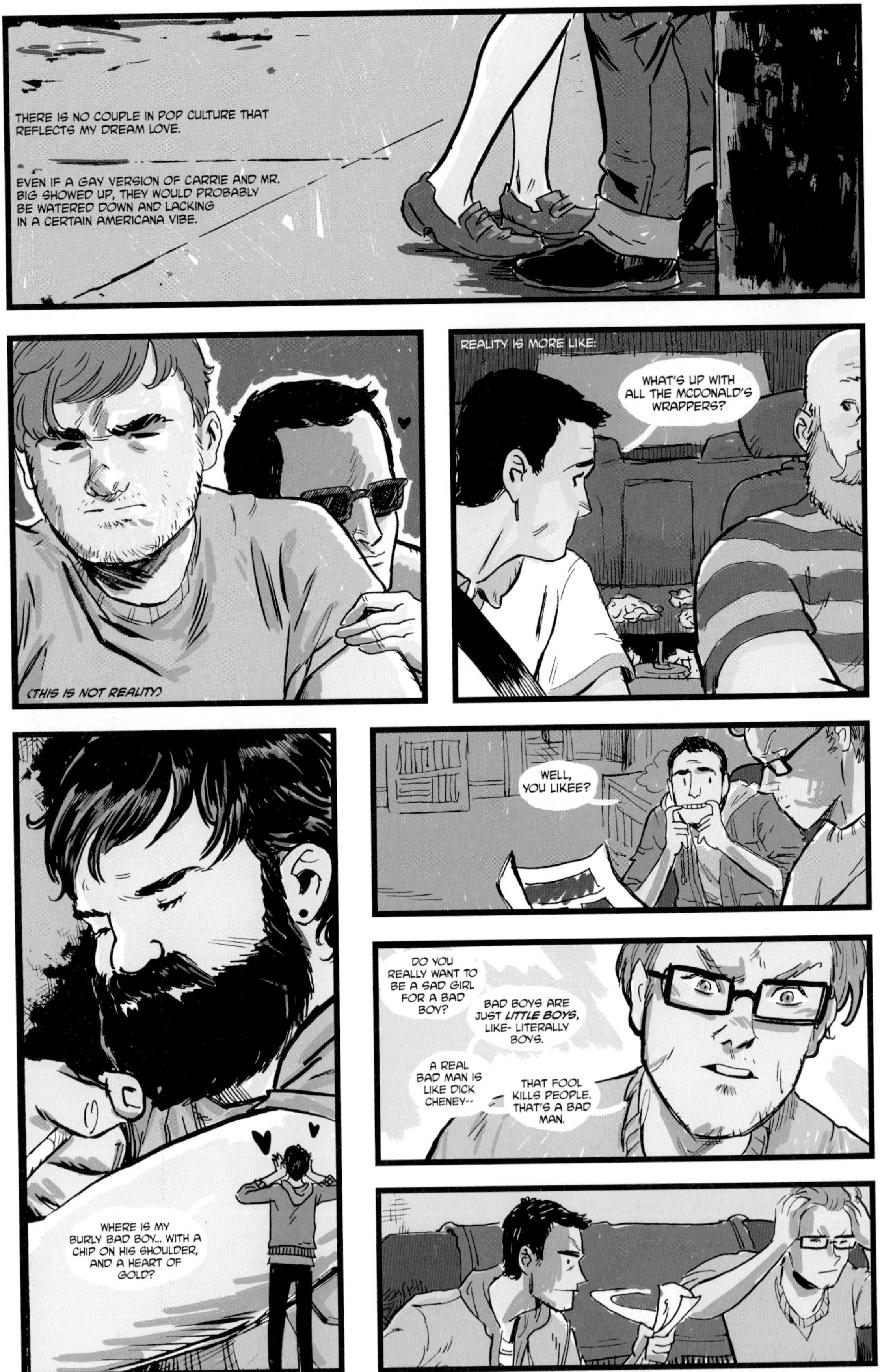
THERE IS NO COUPLE IN POP CULTURE THAT REFLECTS MY DREAM LOVE.
EVEN IF A GAY VERSION OF CARRIE AND MR. BIG SHOWED UP, THEY WOULD PROBABLY BE WATERED DOWN AND LACKING IN A CERTAIN AMERICANA VIBE.
(THIS IS NOT REALITY)
REALITY IS MORE LIKE:
WHAT'S UP WITH ALL THE MCDONALD'S WRAPPERS?
WHERE IS MY BURLY BAD BOY... WITH A CHIP ON HIS SHOULDER, AND A HEART OF GOLD?
WELL, YOU LIKEE?
DO YOU REALLY WANT TO BE A SAD GIRL FOR A BAD BOY?
BAD BOYS ARE JUST *LITTLE BOYS*, LIKE- LITERALLY BOYS.
A REAL BAD MAN IS LIKE DICK CHENEY--
THAT FOOL KILLS PEOPLE. THAT'S A BAD MAN.

I Like Big Gay Bears

an someone tell me when the general masses figured out what bears were (the subculture of obese hairy gay udes) and when they became a thing? Bears are my thing. There used to be a time when I had to feel mbarrassed by liking burly men with beards, and would have to tell my friends when I was dating a young John oodman, that his personality transcends the fact that he came to the restaurant already eating a donut. There as a time when I had to join random Yahoo groups because I couldn't readily find smut to my preference on ainstream sites. Now, if I show my straight friends a picture of whoever I'm going out with, their eyes light up d they gleefully inquire: "you like beeeeeeaaaaarrrrssss?" I'll tell you why this makes life harder for me.

"Why can't we just get rid of the clubhouse mentality? Gay people are supposed to have it better in that we're not obligated to do things the way straight people do-"

ow, I'm not mad at any of my friends for being not only pro-gay but pro-weird-dating-choices. It's not their ult that when I was young and dumb I was ashamed of anyone I was dating; that was my damage. What is so my damage is that I grew up without a father, probably felt some strange sense of comfort when a burly, rrel-chested swim instructor cradled me in his hairy arms as he taught me to float (#imagery), and I have been ying to recreate that feeling all these years later. I have no immediate, logical explanation for why I am tracted to bears, but it's my cross to ... bear. The only damage I have now is with this subculture I'm rticipating in. They can be some messy-ass bitches. If you're trying to feel safe and accepted for being the ay you are... you're not in the bear world.

r starters... everyone's still trying to prove something like any other scene. Usually if you spend your whole e feeling like the outcast because of your appearance, you've got such an inferiority complex that you let inny boys walk all over you, move in with you, and then relent to an open relationship because they've got "so uch love to give, and baby so do you." Gross. Those are the bears who got so big because they eat their feelings, n't respect themselves, and are aware that they can be replaced at the drop of a hat, so they buckle under the mands of their twinks. What's even #grosser is when these slobs have the perfect amount of facial hair, and eir BMI looks perfect in plaid. These guys- the model bears- they're the living worst. If you think the razor arp stare of an anorexic go-go dancer at Mickey's, is bad, just WAIT to see what happens when you hit on a ar who thinks his stock is more valuable than the likes of you... or better yet, if he's bear for bear. It's a mix the condescending "nice try" look and the equally brutal "you're not welcome here" glare.

's all one big mess. All my friends think it's like being the gay couple in Modern Family: that the gender roles e amplified, and the bear is either some kind of a wuvable oaf that nephews and nieces like to hug, or they're g rugged brawny men who want nothing but a new buck knife and homemade beard wax. Maybe the tter-than-thou bears are acting like assholes to make up for how shitty everyone was to them in grade school, nen we'd ask what those garish marks stretching up and down their bellies and backs were in the gym dressing om. Why can't we just get rid of the clubhouse mentality? Gay people are supposed to have it better in that e're not obligated to do things the way straight people do- we don't have to be bitchy at clubs... we don't have be demure or awkward about things. So why is it that an even smaller community has to play into the awful ind games created by our gay and straight forefathers?

goes this way because that's just the way boys- and bears- are. I react the way I do because of my upbringing d all the things my subconscious forces me to do, and they're acting their turdy way because of their equally eird backgrounds. The bear scene is not cute like on some NBC sitcom where the fat beast always messes things up by being an aloof pig, but then saves the day because he's got a heart of gold. No. These guys are just as fickle d taciturn if not more so than any fag hag's boyfriend du jour. It's just as brutal as it is for everyone else: if e guy knows he's "hot" by someone else's standards, he's gonna be a dick to those unworthy. To bring it back my point of why I'm mad that they've become popularized: this small ghetto has been empowered, and now ave to also deal with straight dudes dressing more like atypical bears because their girlfriends saw some shit tumblr and they want to be proud that their chubby-chasing tendencies are finally being rewarded. But, I ed to look on the bright side. When they make a Sex and the City adaptation of my life, no one will balk when ay I want that dude from The Guy Code to play my Mr. Big.

Sina Grace

SEX

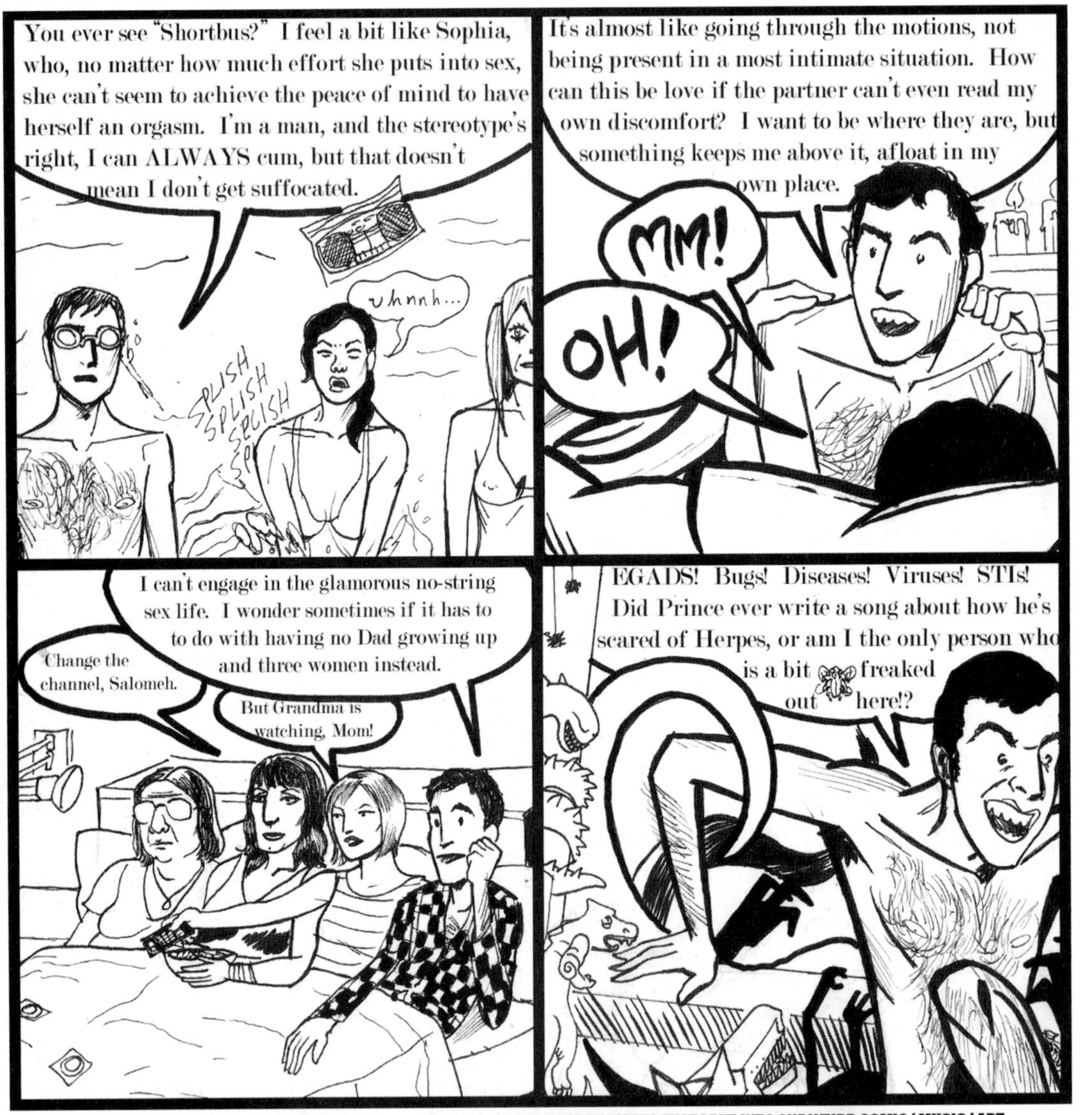
You ever see "Shortbus?" I feel a bit like Sophia, who, no matter how much effort she puts into sex, she can't seem to achieve the peace of mind to have herself an orgasm. I'm a man, and the stereotype's right, I can ALWAYS cum, but that doesn't mean I don't get suffocated.
uhnnh...
SPLISH SPLISH SPLISH
It's almost like going through the motions, not being present in a most intimate situation. How can this be love if the partner can't even read my own discomfort? I want to be where they are, but something keeps me above it, afloat in my own place.
MM!
OH!
I can't engage in the glamorous no-string sex life. I wonder sometimes if it has to to do with having no Dad growing up and three women instead.
Change the channel, Salomeh.
But Grandma is watching, Mom!
EGADS! Bugs! Diseases! Viruses! STIs! Did Prince ever write a song about how he's scared of Herpes, or am I the only person who is a bit freaked out here!?

THE NEXT FEW PAGES WERE ORIGINALLY PART OF TWO SEPARATE COLLEGE PROJECTS THAT I PUT INTO ONE WEIRD COMIC/ MUSIC/ ART OBJECT. I CAN'T REMEMBER NOW WHY I WAS ALLOWED TO DO THIS, BUT I MADE A MIX OF "MY 69 LOVE SONGS," PICKING MUSIC THAT TIED TO HOW I MEDIATED DESIRE... WHICH IS WHY THE MAGNETIC FIELDS AND RUFUS WAINWRIGHT GET A LOT OF PLAYTIME... I DON'T KNOW WHAT'S MORE EMBARRASSING, THE CONTENT OF THE STRIPS RELATED TO EACH DISC OF THE ALBUM, OR THE SONG CHOICES. EITHER WAY, THEY'RE HERE FOR YOUR AMUSEMENT.

01 BRING A BOOK - JERRI BLANK
02 SHAKE THAT ASS - THE LOVEMAKERS
03 VOULEZ VOUS - ABBA
04 CICATRIZ - SANAZ YAMIN
05 SEX SHOOTER - APOLLONIA 6
06 LET'S PRETEND WE'RE BUNNY RABBITS
07 GIRLS - DEATH IN VEGAS
08 I U SHE - PEACHES
09 BETWEEN MY LEGS - RUFUS WAINWRIGHT
10 INTERLUDE - INTERPOL
11 I WISH I HAD AN EVIL TWIN - THE MAGNETIC FIELDS
12 MY BEAT - SALOMEH GRACE
13 LET'S CALL IT LOVE - SLEATER-KINNEY
14 NIGHT LIGHT - SLEATER-KINNEY
15 SHAVE 'EM DRY - LUCILLE BOGAN
16 YOU MAKE ME FEEL (MIGHTY REAL) SYLVESTER
17 MUSKET - JERRI BLANK
18 WORK IT - MISSY ELLIOT

SEX

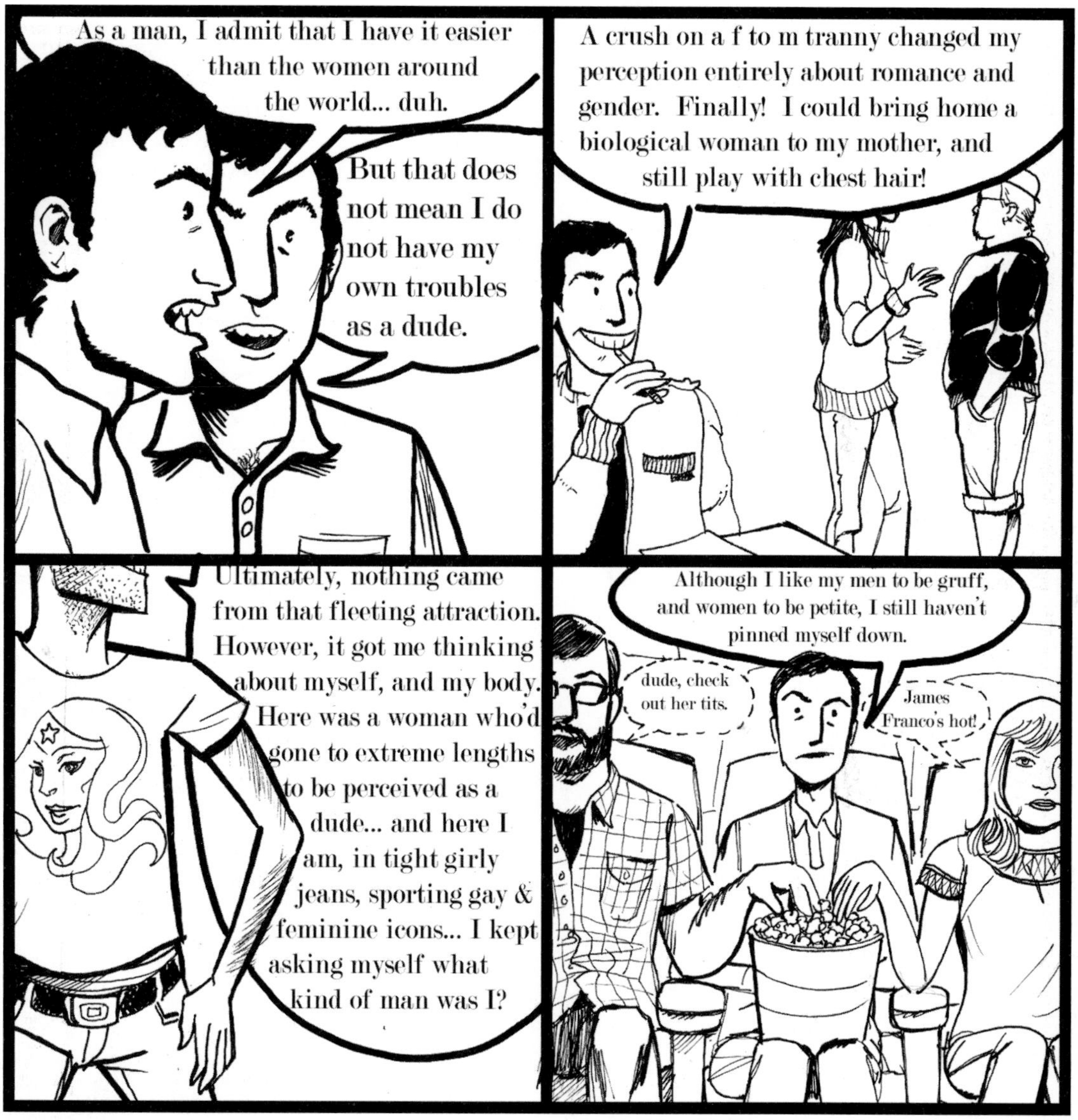

As a man, I admit that I have it easier than the women around the world... duh.
But that does not mean I do not have my own troubles as a dude.
A crush on a f to m tranny changed my perception entirely about romance and gender. Finally! I could bring home a biological woman to my mother, and still play with chest hair!
Ultimately, nothing came from that fleeting attraction. However, it got me thinking about myself, and my body. Here was a woman who'd gone to extreme lengths to be perceived as a dude... and here I am, in tight girly jeans, sporting gay & feminine icons... I kept asking myself what kind of man was I?
Although I like my men to be gruff, and women to be petite, I still haven't pinned myself down.
dude, check out her tits.
James Franco's hot!

01 OH WHAT A WORLD - RUFUS WAINWRIGHT
02 EVERYTHING - SLEATER-KINNEY
03 WALK ON THE WILD SIDE - LOU REED
04 BOYS WANNA BE HER - PEACHES
05 I STARTED SOMETHING I COULDN'T FINISH - THE SMITHS
06 LETS PLAY BOYS CHASE GIRLS - BLOW
07 OH! YOU PRETTY THINGS - DAVID BOWIE
08 ANGRY INCH - HEDWIG & THE ANGRY INCH
09 YOUR DICK IS MY GOD - VAMPHI
10 WHEN MY BOY WALKS DOWN THE STREET - THE MAGNETIC FIELDS
11 TIM I WISH YOU WERE BORN A GIRL - OF MONTREAL
12 CROWD SURF OFF A CLIFF - EMILY HAINES & THE SOFT SKELETON
13 ONE MAN GUY - RUFUS WAINWRIGHT
14 YOU ARE WHAT YOU LOVE (FALSE START) - JENNY LEWIS
15 YOU ARE WHAT YOU LOVE - JENNY LEWIS
16 VIZ - LE TIGRE
17 MY BODY IS A CAGE - ARCADE FIRE
18 PASSIVE MANIPULATION - THE WHITE STRIPES

LOVE

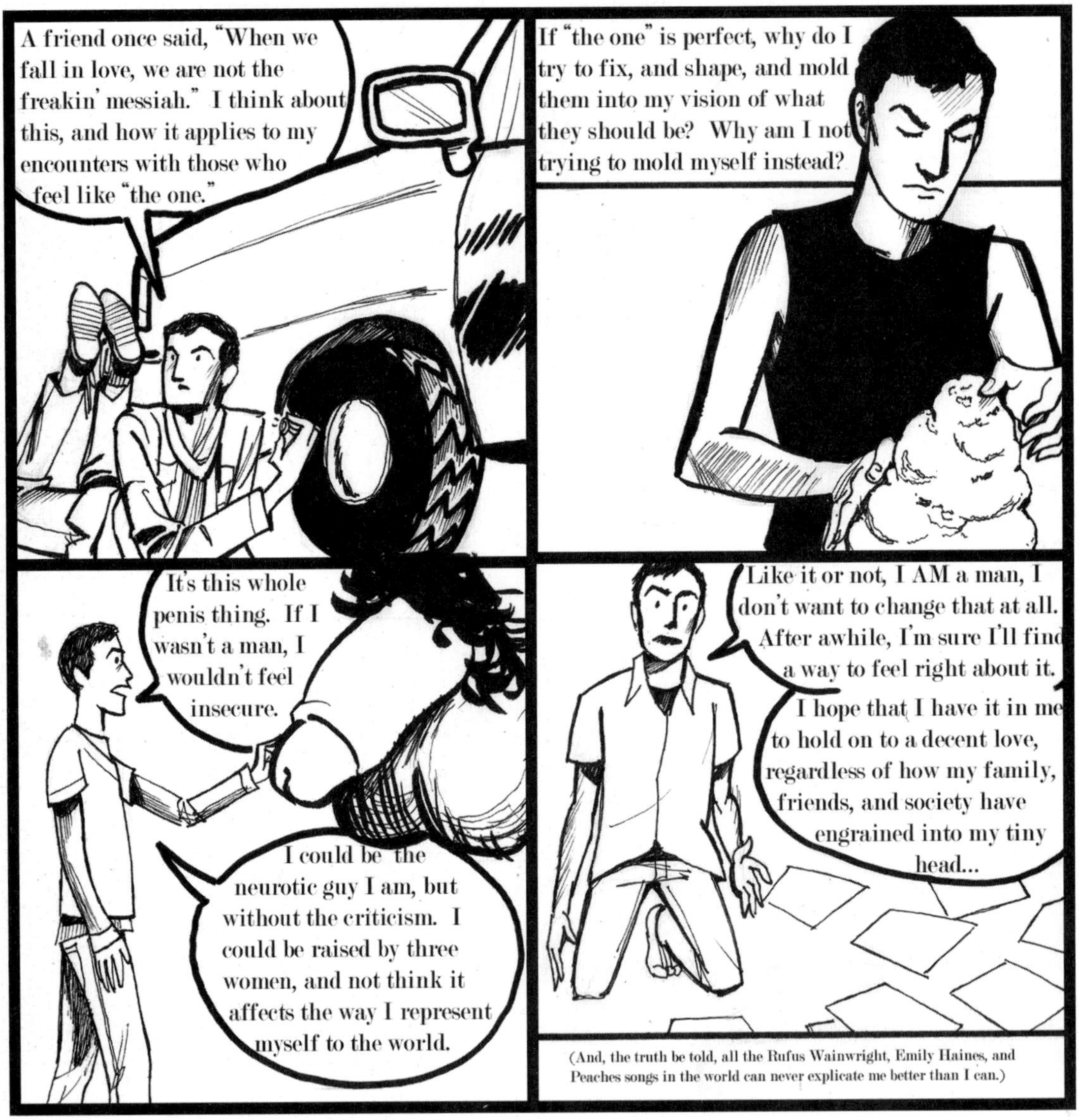
A friend once said, "When we fall in love, we are not the freakin' messiah." I think about this, and how it applies to my encounters with those who feel like "the one."
If "the one" is perfect, why do I try to fix, and shape, and mold them into my vision of what they should be? Why am I not trying to mold myself instead?
It's this whole penis thing. If I wasn't a man, I wouldn't feel insecure.
I could be the neurotic guy I am, but without the criticism. I could be raised by three women, and not think it affects the way I represent myself to the world.
Like it or not, I AM a man, I don't want to change that at all. After awhile, I'm sure I'll find a way to feel right about it.
I hope that I have it in me to hold on to a decent love, regardless of how my family, friends, and society have engrained into my tiny head...
(And, the truth be told, all the Rufus Wainwright, Emily Haines, and Peaches songs in the world can never explicate me better than I can.)

01 OUR HELL - EMILY HAINES & THE SOFT SKELETON
02 WALKIN' AFTER MIDNIGHT - PATSY CLINE
03 OUR DAY WILL COME - BLOSSOM DEARIE
04 FIDELITY - REGINA SPEKTOR
05 PARENTHESES - BLOW
06 LONG DISTANCES - TIMOTHY RABBIT
07 PORTIONS FOR FOXES (BAD NEWS) - RILO KILEY
08 THAT'S JUST WHAT YOU ARE - AIMEE MANN
09 MAPS - YEAH YEAH YEAHS
10 UNTITLED - JENNY LEWIS
11 ONE OF US - ABBA
12 THE BOOK OF LOVE - THE MAGNETIC FIELDS
13 LIMIT TO YOUR LOVE - FEIST
14 NOT READY TO LOVE - RUFUS WAINWRIGHT
15 YOU'VE REALLY GOT A HOLD ON ME - LAURA NYRO & LA BELLE
16 1234 - FEIST
17 I FOUND A REASON - CAT POWER

WANT

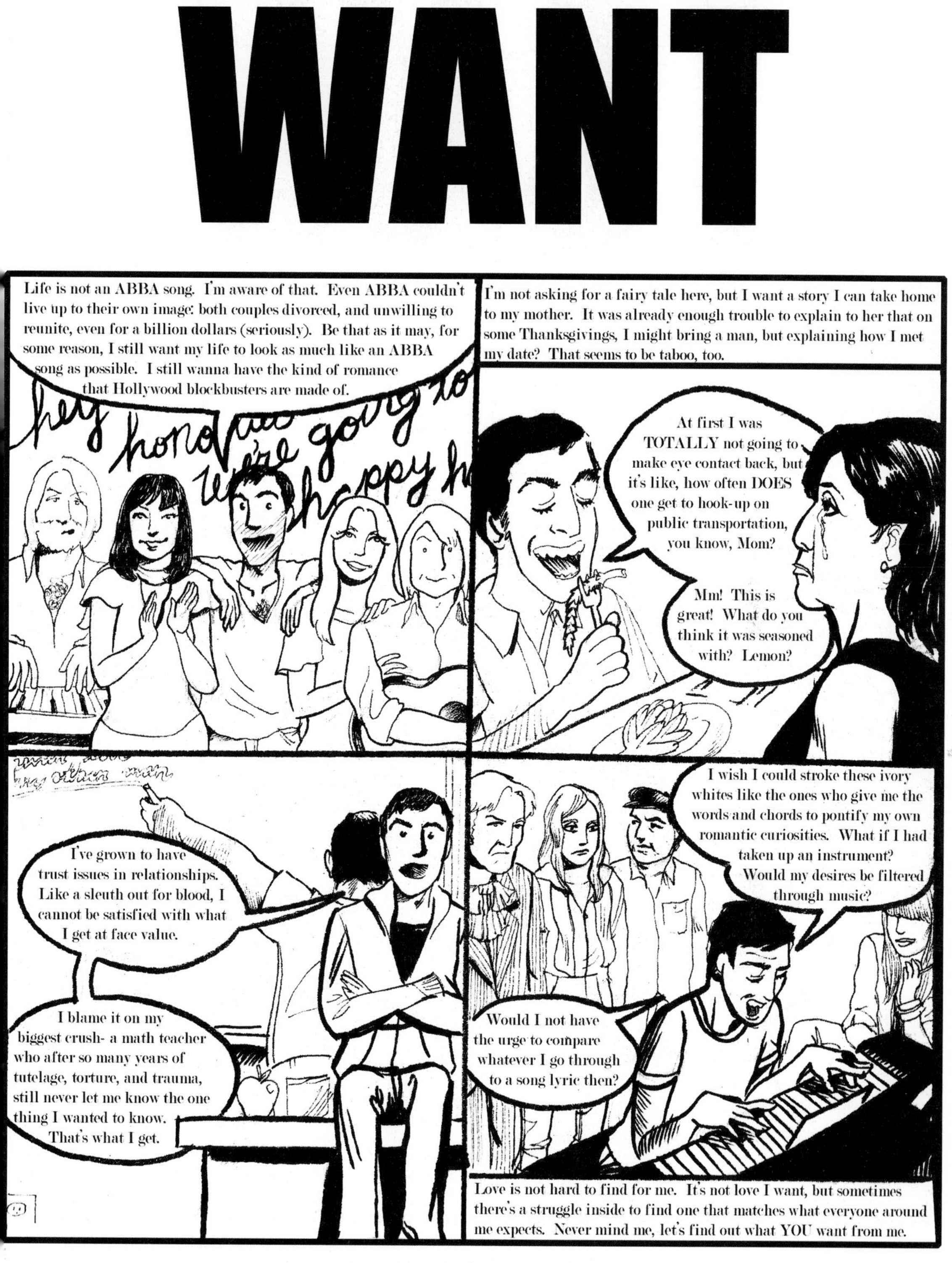
Life is not an ABBA song. I'm aware of that. Even ABBA couldn't live up to their own image: both couples divorced, and unwilling to reunite, even for a billion dollars (seriously). Be that as it may, for some reason, I still want my life to look as much like an ABBA song as possible. I still wanna have the kind of romance that Hollywood blockbusters are made of.
I'm not asking for a fairy tale here, but I want a story I can take home to my mother. It was already enough trouble to explain to her that on some Thanksgivings, I might bring a man, but explaining how I met my date? That seems to be taboo, too.
At first I was TOTALLY not going to make eye contact back, but it's like, how often DOES one get to hook-up on public transportation, you know, Mom?
Mm! This is great! What do you think it was seasoned with? Lemon?
I've grown to have trust issues in relationships. Like a sleuth out for blood, I cannot be satisfied with what I get at face value.
I blame it on my biggest crush- a math teacher who after so many years of tutelage, torture, and trauma, still never let me know the one thing I wanted to know. That's what I get.
I wish I could stroke these ivory whites like the ones who give me the words and chords to pontify my own romantic curiosities. What if I had taken up an instrument? Would my desires be filtered through music?
Would I not have the urge to compare whatever I go through to a song lyric then?
Love is not hard to find for me. It's not love I want, but sometimes there's a struggle inside to find one that matches what everyone around me expects. Never mind me, let's find out what YOU want from me.

01 WISH TO WANT - JERRI BLANK
02 THE GREATEST - CAT POWER
03 LIVING PROOF - CAT POWER
04 TELETHON - EMILY HAINES & THE SOFT SKELETON
05 I WILL INTERNALIZE - MARTHA WAINWRIGHT
06 FERNANDO - ABBA
07 WIRES AND WAVES - RILO KILEY
08 THE ART TEACHER - RUFUS WAINWRIGHT
09 THIS IS WHAT YOU GET - PHANTOM PLANET
10 I DON'T WANT TO GET OVER YOU - THE MAGNETIC FIELDS
11 MALE MODEL - SLEATER-KINNEY
12 WHEN I KISSED THE TEACHER - ABBA
13 HANDS CLEAN - ALANIS MORISSETTE
14 WANT - RUFUS WAINWRIGHT
15 THE HAPPY ENDING - AIMEE MANN
16 BEAUTIFUL - AIMEE MANN

On Being Self-Obsessed

illustrations by Emi Lenox

What better way to examine the life of a self-obsessed individual than to have it examined by another? Ryan O'Connell has made a name for himself over the years from his epic collection of Thought Catalog essays, recounting the pains and joys of being young, beautiful, and all too self-aware. The hard work of writing about himself in a tongue-in-cheek manner worked out: Ryan's now writing for TV and has a book coming out. I sat with Ryan and dished on what happens when you put your life story out into the world, and how being self-obsessed may be the key to getting through your 20s.

Sina Grace: Ryan, hey. So, I legitimately don't know the answer to this, but what did "breaking in" look like for you? From where I was standing, it was like: you were subletting with my friend in West Hollywood wearing chic loafers and short-shorts one day, and then the next my friends were sending me essays you wrote and telling me how this Ryan O'Connell guy is nailing it.

Ryan O'Connell: "Breaking in" for me involved being an unemployed 24 year old with lots and LOTS of feelings. I started writing these posts for Thought Catalog about what life looked like for me and my friends after graduation. Luckily, they found an audience and allowed me to get a full-time job as a writer. But it took a long time to think of myself as having broken into the biz. There was a part of me that was always waiting for the other shoe to drop and send me back to interning. I don't think it was until I got a job writing for television that I was like, "Okay, I don't think I'm ever going to have to bring a bossy 25-year-old named Liz her coffee again."

What about you? You are OWNING comics right now. Do you ever breathe a sigh of relief that you're not a Millennial casualty?

Sina: Hah! I'm glad it looks like I'm owning comics! I feel like I'm sort of almost keeping afloat.

Honestly, it wasn't until the beginning of this year that I realized, "Oh... I could stop doing odd jobs and freelance gigs now. I can maybe cover the bills with just comics." For the longest time, I've had this terrible delusion of success as being wardrobed entirely in endorsed clothes and getting some crazy Hollywood paychecks-- which, because of the city I live in is totally attainable, but not as a guy writing and drawing comics.

Sina Grace

I finally feel like I hit the point where after te years of climbing from an intern to a man o many zines to Somebody's Editor that I ca finally relax and do the work I've been dreamin of doing.

> **"For the longest time, I've had this terrible delusion of success as being wardrobed entirely in endorsed clothes and getting some crazy Hollywood paychecks--"**
> **Sina Grace**

You've made a career from writing work th hinges on your personal experience. You go in some pretty intimate details, dude... Maj props. What do you get from sharing the stories with hundreds of thousands of readers

Ryan: I get the comfort of knowing that I'm n completely psycho. People often like to thi that they're crazy for feeling the way they about relationships, family, or jobs and I'm the to show them that they're normal. It's ni Thought Catalog is like a little community weirdos who are going through all of li shitshows together.

When I was 24 or 25, I felt the need to expr my every thought or feeling because it helped make sense of what was going on around me.

But as I get older and feel more comfortable in my skin, the urge to share grows less and less. TV is the best format for me now because I can bring in my own point of view and sprinkle some of my life in the stories but the rest is fictionalized. Writing like I did on TC or Vice wasn't sustainable. I felt like a raw nerve and the more I wrote about my personal life, the less I had one. I'm finishing up my book now, which will be a memoir, and then I think that will be the end of confessional writing. I don't have anything left to say anymore. I'm much more interested in diving into other people's worlds than my own.

What about you? How personal would you consider your work? I know Not My Bag was based on your experiences in retail but how autobiographical do you want your comics to be? What pleasure do you get out of sharing?

Sina: It's funny that you bring up being a raw nerve. At face value, not my bag reads like confessions of a shopaholic or devil wears prada, but all the emotional stuff about relationships was like literally opening sealed boxes from the past and playing with emotional fire. Exploring the aspects of life where your hangups paralyze you isn't exactly fun-- but it is at the same time? Doing it in this format- collecting strips as they come along- is far safer for my sanity. I was working on pages to follow up not my bag, and it felt like I was purposely trying to be a Lana del Rey song... Like fiction Me wandering through a desert holding a lover I could soon no longer carry... Hah!

Ryan O'Connell

Gossip with me for a second, have you ever gotten a date from your Thought Catalog writing? For me, I think people read the fiction I do and go, "This guy is tight," then they read my autobio stuff and go "N/M DADDY ISSUES." I've been deprived of being able to bed a reader, but at least it makes things easier when I'm courting: "here are all of my issues. Read up and decide if you want in."

Ryan: I have hooked up with some groupies in my day. I'M NOT MADE OUT OF STONE, SINA. Two years ago, I went on a college speaking tour that took me to Yale, Princeton, UCLA, McGill, and University of Vermont. After I'd give my talk, I would have the hottest guys trying to pick me up, which was so surreal. I mean, I am very average-looking and not in great shape. I know I'm not a gargoyle but I'm realistic about the kind of guys I can attract. So to have boys who were legit on par with Ryan Gosling being like, "Hi, I'd like to see you naked...." I couldn't believe it! Of course, there was a part of me that found the whole thing gross. If these dudes weren't a fan of my writing, there was no way they'd ever give me a second look at a gay bar. But I have to admit, it felt nice to be wanted like that. None of them materialized into anything more than a hookup. Having an actual relationship with someone who's a fan of your work seems problematic at best.

I think that's also another reason why I want to step away from personal writing. I really want to get a boyfriend and be in a real relationship and I don't think that's possible to do when you're just live-blogging your life.

> "I would have the *hottest* guys trying to pick me up, which was so surreal. I mean, I am very average-looking and not in great shape. "
> **Ryan O'Connell**

Forgive me if this is a dumb question, I'm not too familiar with the comic book world, but are there a lot of gay men in your field? And if there are, are many of them writing about gay life like you are?

Sina: Haha, I had a friend who I had messed around with once, and- thinking I was adorable- I mentioned something about how he could end up being fodder for a comic, and he was NOT CHILL ABOUT IT. It's one of those moments where you realize that Carrie Bradshaw is Scary Sadshaw in reality. Most of my exes get a warning when they're being written about. I've had my website shut down once from not giving sufficient warning that I would be cartooning some realness on my blog.

There are a ton of wonderful queer creators, and I don't know how true this is, but my perception is that we're still being ghettoized. Alison Bechdel made some amazing graphic novels tied into her sexuality and identity, and there are some amazing resources for a bunch of emerging voices, but I don't know that we have the same platform that gay voices have in other fields. You were kind of one of the first to be recognized for being unabashedly gay and asking for love with no fear. I think I get away from being categorized as "Gay Cartoonist" because I was getting attention for my professional associations and love of good-looking indie bands. Do you ever feel like your work to date has pigeonholed you in any way?

Ryan: No, I don't think so and even if I was pigeonholed as a gay writer, I wouldn't care. My sexuality informs everything I do so if I'm known as that gay blogger who writes about being gay a lot then WTVR. I think when I started out I felt a lot of insecurity about not being a journalist because that to me was the definition of a real writer. Now I realize that the definition is so much more broad than that. I stand by everything I've ever written, even the stuff that is LOL terrible, because it's a part of who I am.

What is your ultimate career dream? Like, what will be the thing that makes you feel like you've achieved what you've sought out to do?

Sina: I feel you on standing by everything you've done... They're like tattoos: you gotta live with immortalizing your state-of-mind, even an emo 19 year-old state of mind.

"There are a ton of wonderful queer creators, and I don't know how true this is, but my perception is that we're still being ghettoized."
Sina Grace

There's a book I have in my head... It's what I think will be my biggest and best project yet, but it's one of those projects that I know would be a couple-year commitment and would require me giving 125% to it. I'm scared to dive into something of that scale... It will be my dream to not have that fear and try to do something that could potentially be bigger than me.

What do you think "There" will feel like for you?

Ryan: I want to see a gay disabled character on TV. I want to be a showrunner. I want a house in Laurel Canyon and "fuck you" money.

But honestly, I think my greatest achievem will be finding a husband?!!!! Okay, I know, g me, but here's the thing: I understand car stuff. I know what I have to do to get there. not so worried about it. Relationships, on other hand, have eluded me.

"I stand by everything I've ever written, even the stuff that is LOL terrible, because it's a part of who I am."
Ryan O'Connell

Okay, last question: What is your dream da (This is getting so gay.)

Sina: Lee Pace as a Gay Ned from Push daisies! You?!

Ryan: My dream date involves making out two hours with some guy with a nice ass w listening to Slowdive.

Ryan O'Connell writes for TV shows, books, and th Internet. He's less #dark in person.

Follow him on twitter @ryanoconn

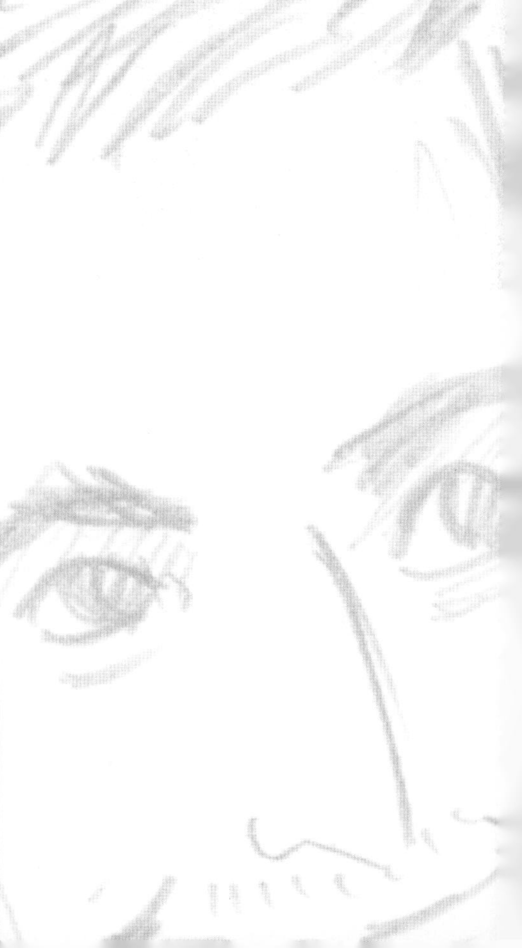

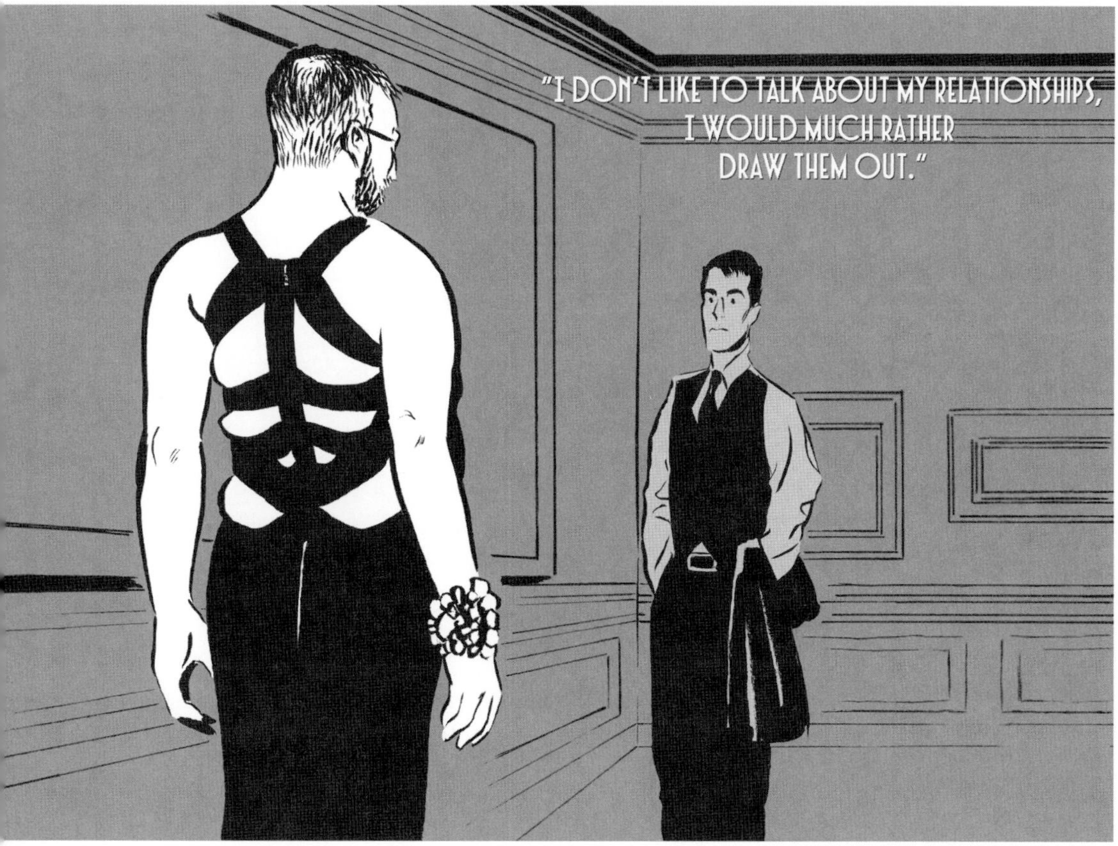
"I DON'T LIKE TO TALK ABOUT MY RELATIONSHIPS,
I WOULD MUCH RATHER
DRAW THEM OUT."

HOW I WISH MY BREAK-UPS WENT...

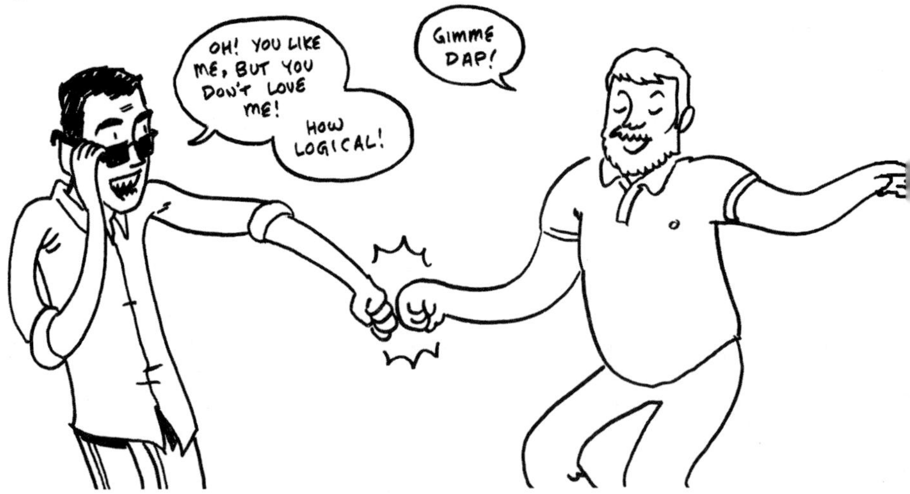

OH! YOU LIKE ME, BUT YOU DON'T LOVE ME!
HOW LOGICAL!
GIMME DAP!

SYMPATHY

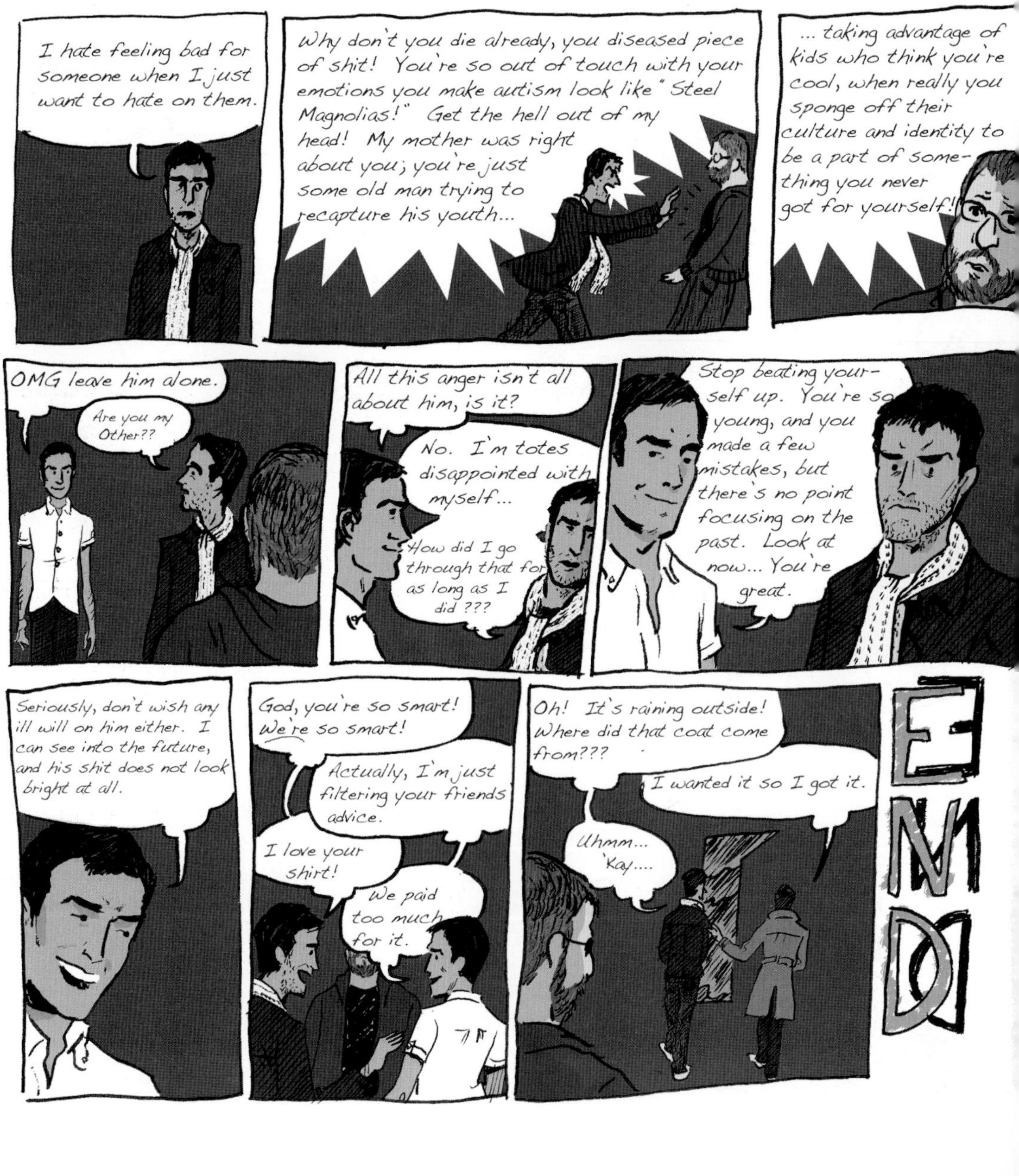

I hate feeling bad for someone when I just want to hate on them.
Why don't you die already, you diseased piece of shit! You're so out of touch with your emotions you make autism look like "Steel Magnolias!" Get the hell out of my head! My mother was right about you; you're just some old man trying to recapture his youth...
... taking advantage of kids who think you're cool, when really you sponge off their culture and identity to be a part of something you never got for yourself!
OMG leave him alone.
Are you my Other??
All this anger isn't all about him, is it?
No. I'm totes disappointed with myself...
How did I go through that for as long as I did ???
Stop beating yourself up. You're so young, and you made a few mistakes, but there's no point focusing on the past. Look at now... You're great.
Seriously, don't wish any ill will on him either. I can see into the future, and his shit does not look bright at all.
God, you're so smart! We're so smart!
Actually, I'm just filtering your friends' advice.
I love your shirt!
We paid too much for it.
Oh! It's raining outside! Where did that coat come from???
I wanted it so I got it.
Uhmm... 'Kay....
END

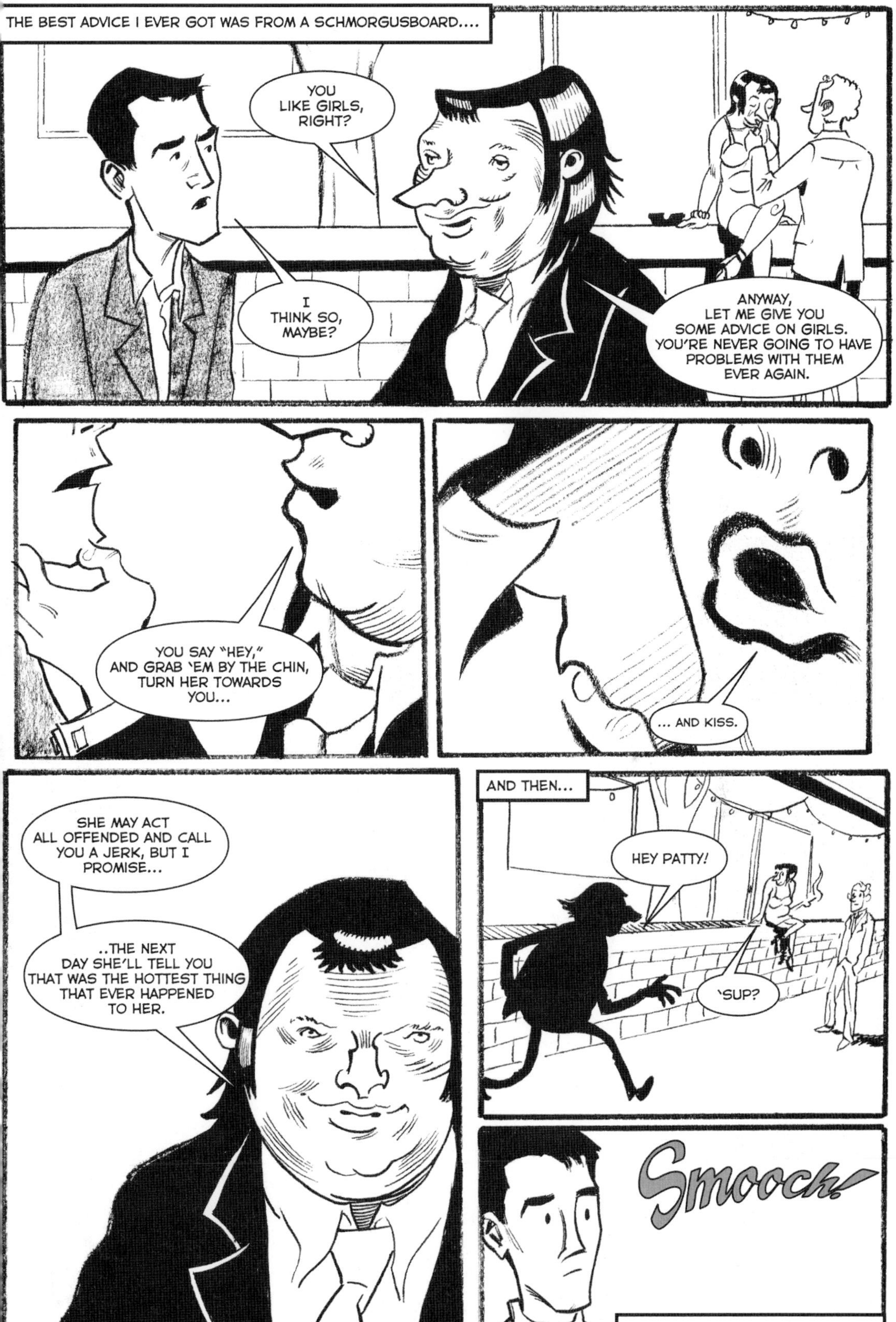
THE BEST ADVICE I EVER GOT WAS FROM A SCHMORGUSBOARD....
YOU LIKE GIRLS, RIGHT?
I THINK SO, MAYBE?
ANYWAY, LET ME GIVE YOU SOME ADVICE ON GIRLS. YOU'RE NEVER GOING TO HAVE PROBLEMS WITH THEM EVER AGAIN.
YOU SAY "HEY," AND GRAB 'EM BY THE CHIN, TURN HER TOWARDS YOU...
... AND KISS.
SHE MAY ACT ALL OFFENDED AND CALL YOU A JERK, BUT I PROMISE...
..THE NEXT DAY SHE'LL TELL YOU THAT WAS THE HOTTEST THING THAT EVER HAPPENED TO HER.
AND THEN...
HEY PATTY!
'SUP?
Smooch!
WHAT CAN I SAY? SCHMORGUSBOARD HAS CHUTZPAH.

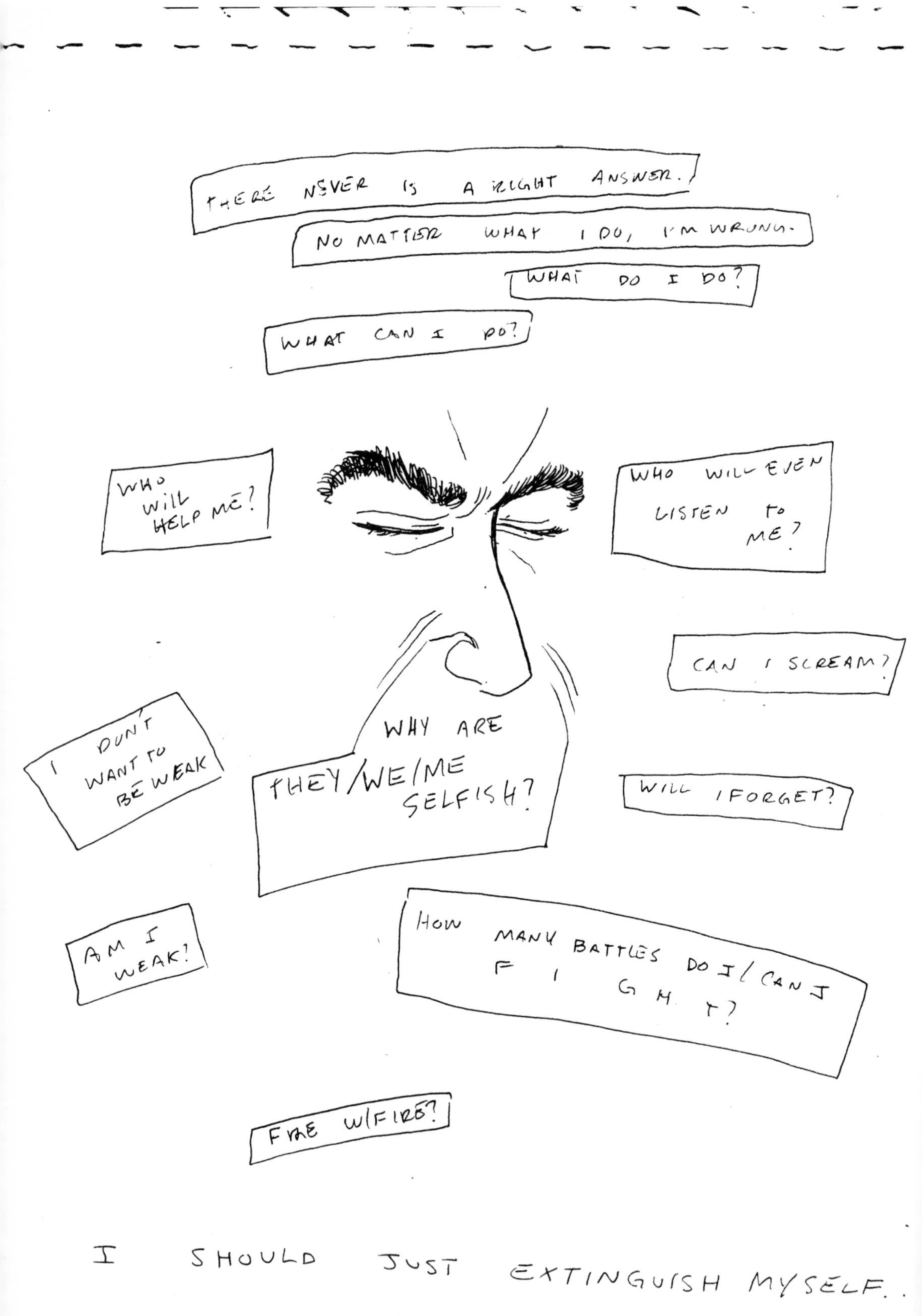
THERE NEVER IS A RIGHT ANSWER.
NO MATTER WHAT I DO, I'M WRONG.
WHAT DO I DO?
WHAT CAN I DO?
WHO WILL HELP ME?
WHO WILL EVEN LISTEN TO ME?
CAN I SCREAM?
I DON'T WANT TO BE WEAK
WHY ARE THEY/WE/ME SELFISH?
WILL I FORGET?
AM I WEAK?
HOW MANY BATTLES DO I/CAN I F I G H T?
FIRE W/FIRE?
I SHOULD JUST EXTINGUISH MYSELF..

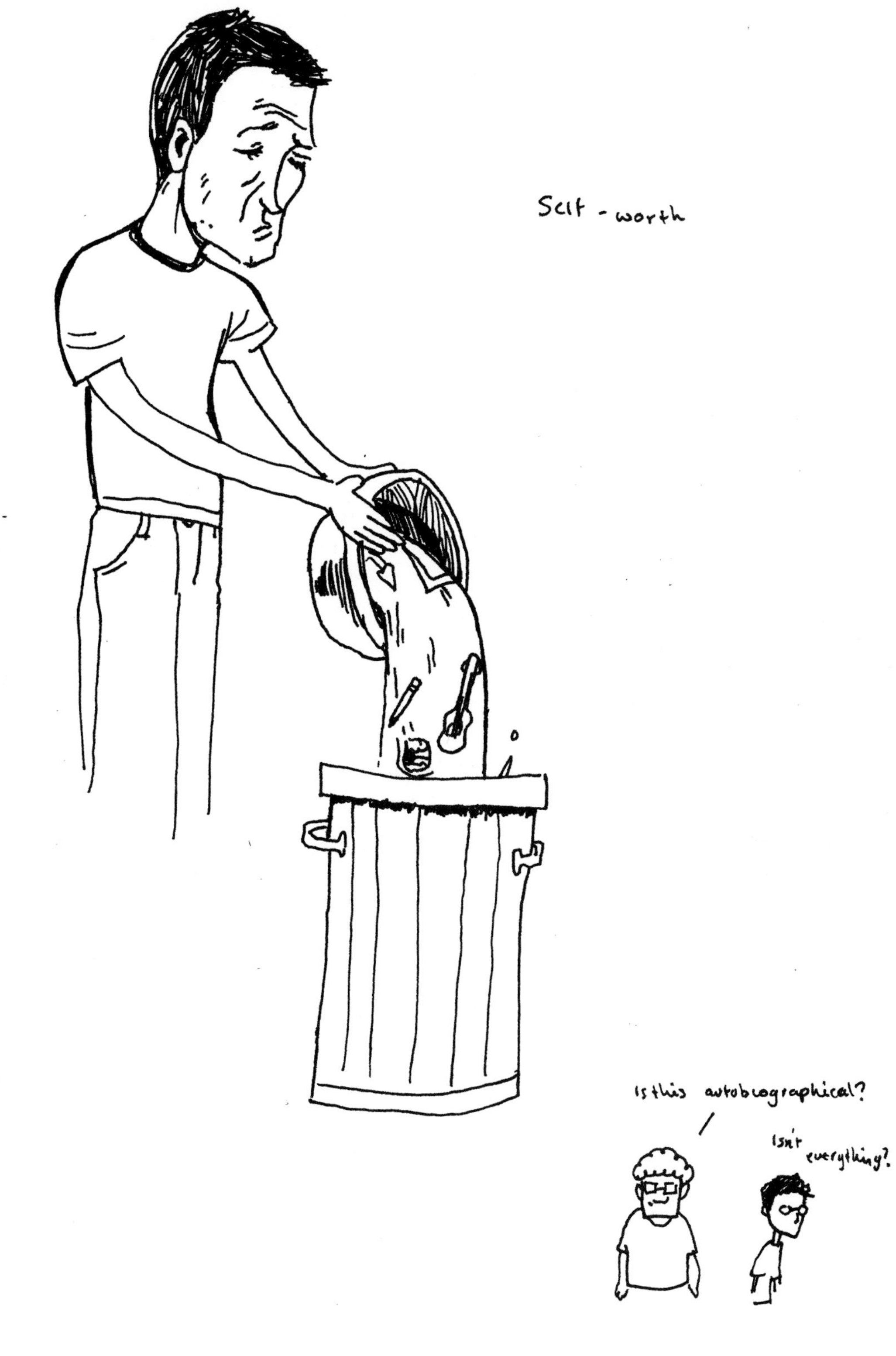
Self - worth
Is this autobiographical?
Isn't everything?

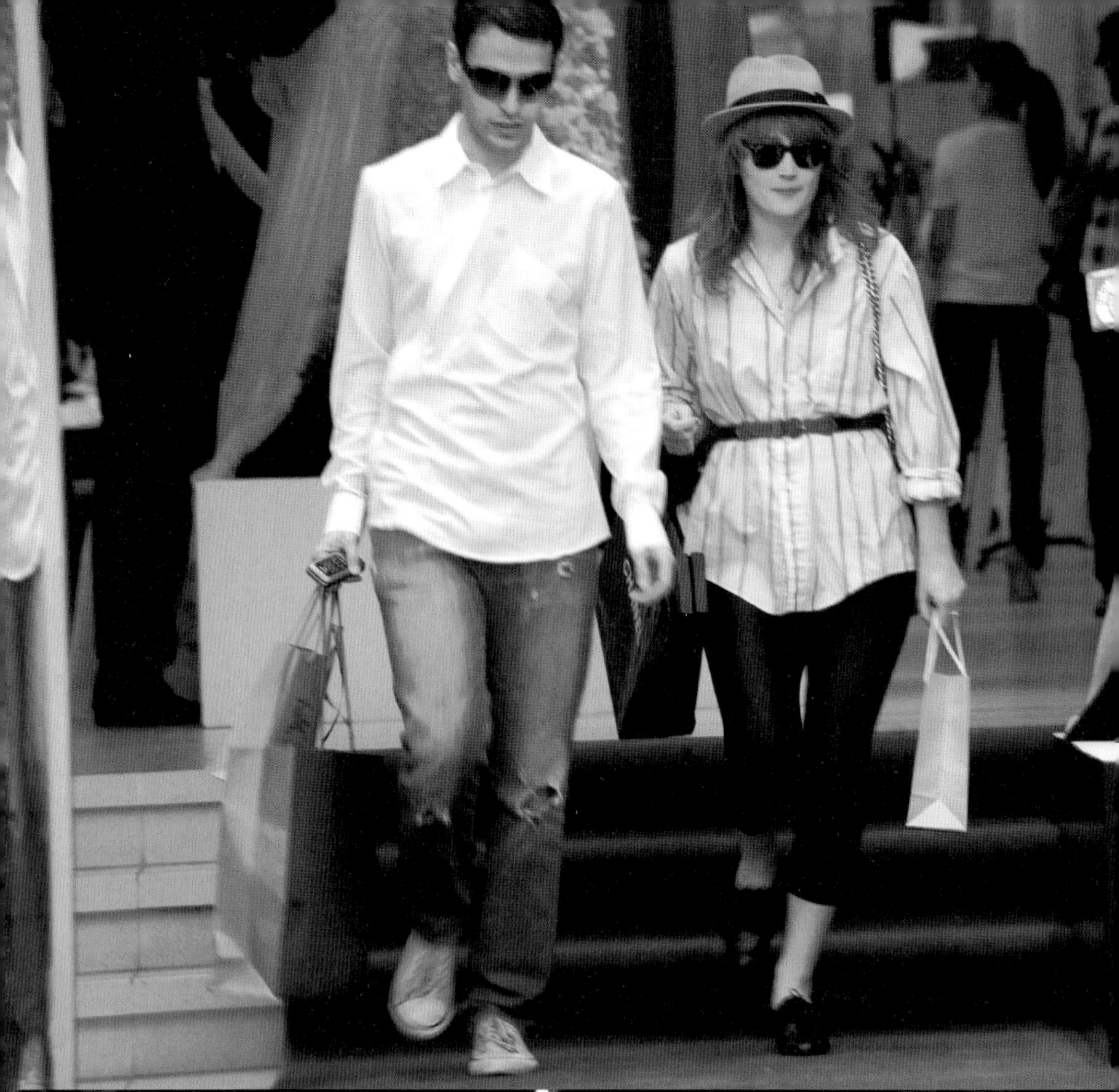
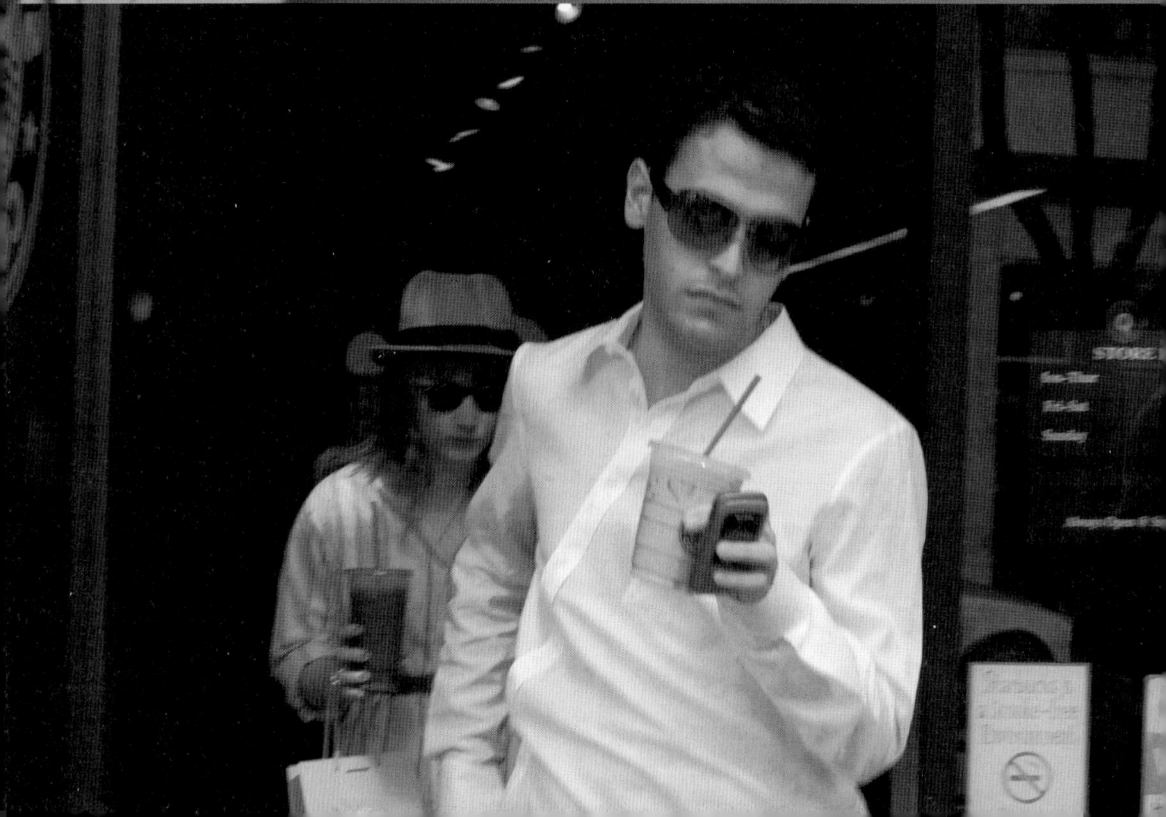

AUTHOR PHOTOS MY FAVE THING EVER

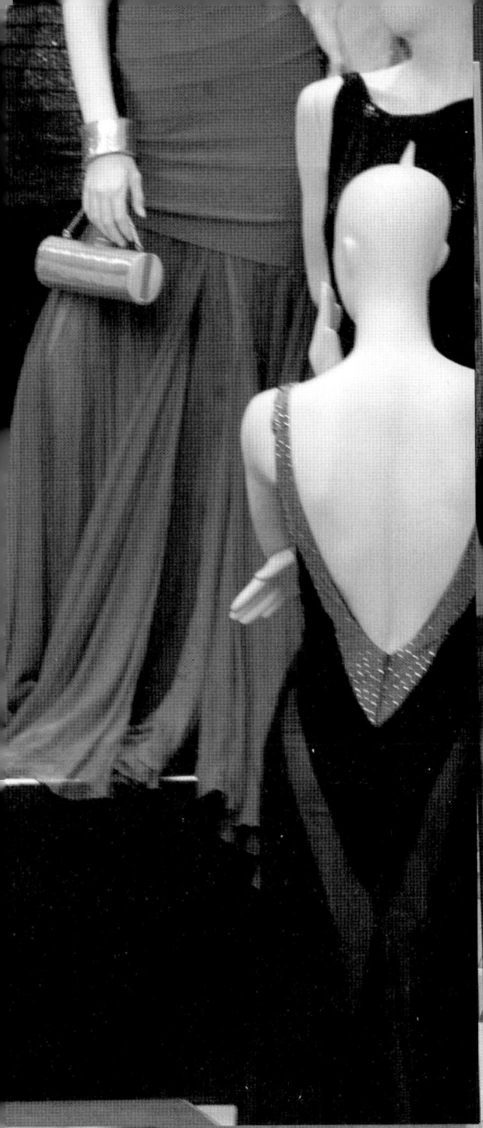

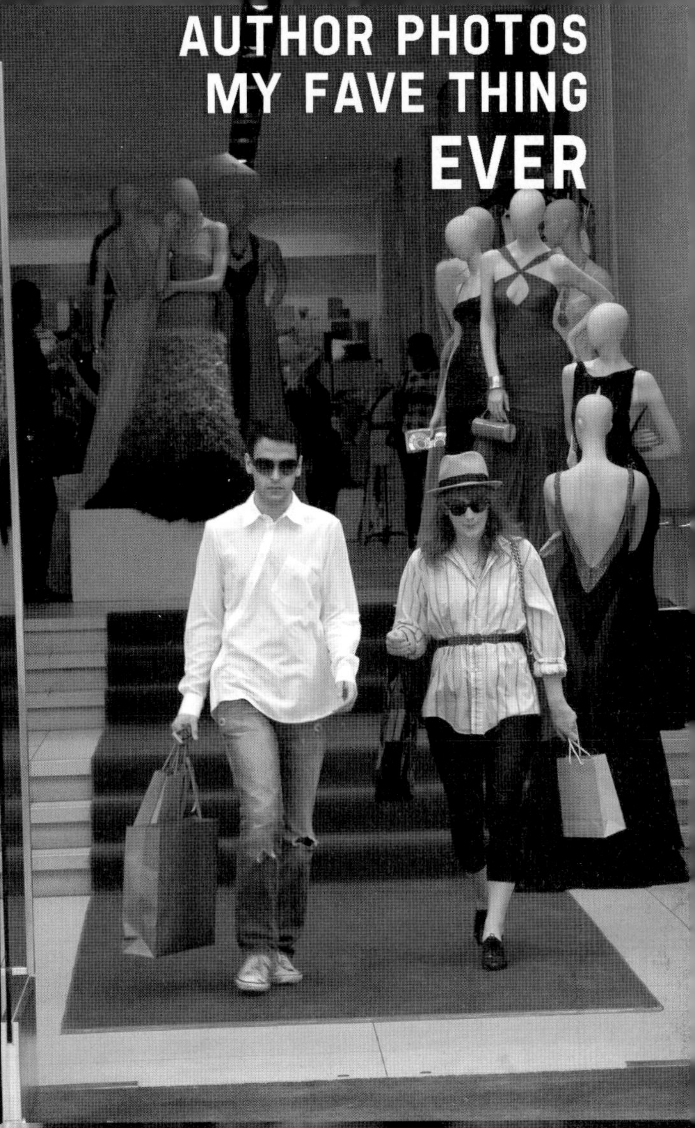

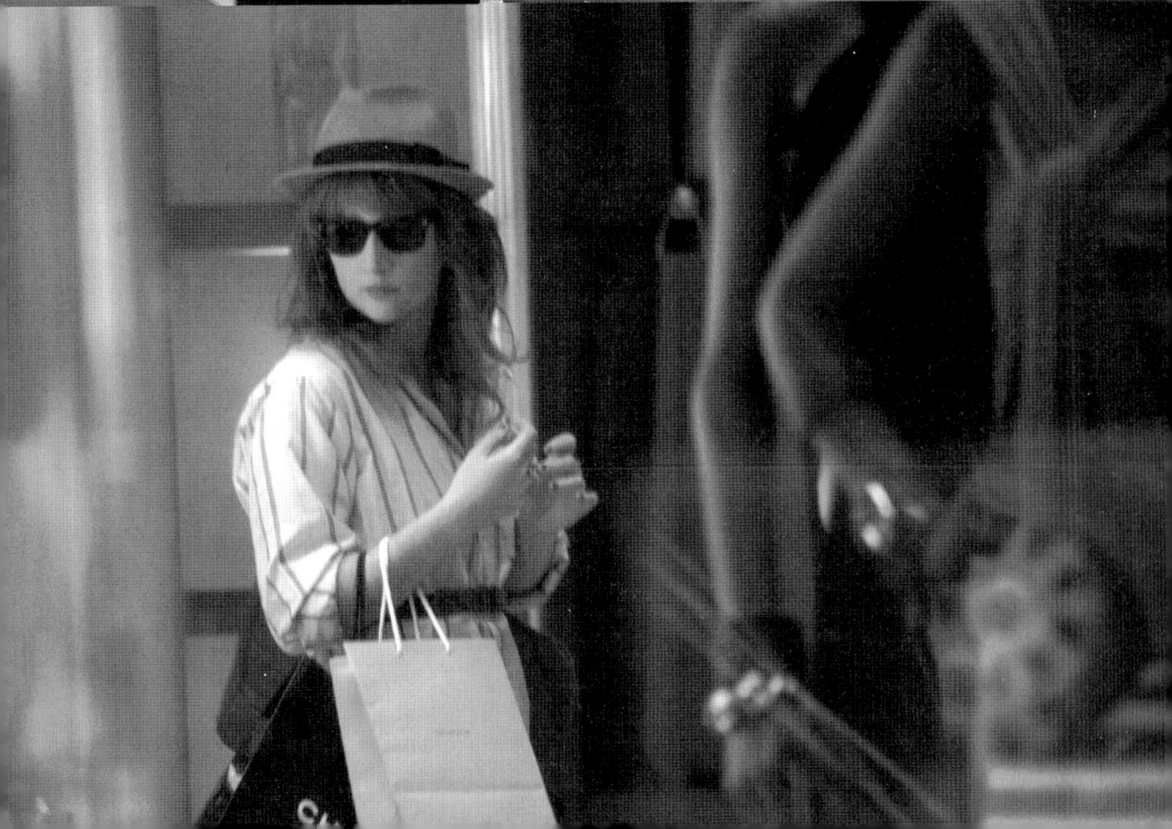

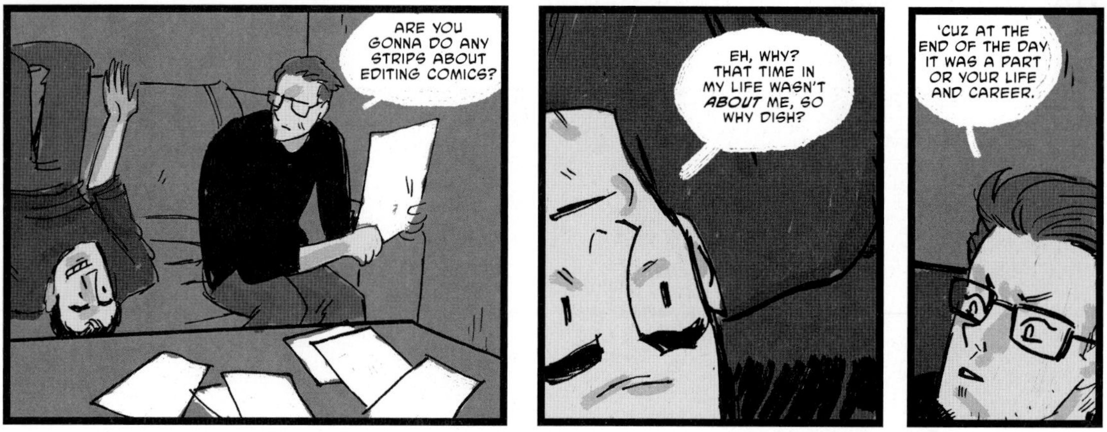
ARE YOU GONNA DO ANY STRIPS ABOUT EDITING COMICS?
EH, WHY? THAT TIME IN MY LIFE WASN'T *ABOUT* ME, SO WHY DISH?
'CUZ AT THE END OF THE DAY IT WAS A PART OR YOUR LIFE AND CAREER.

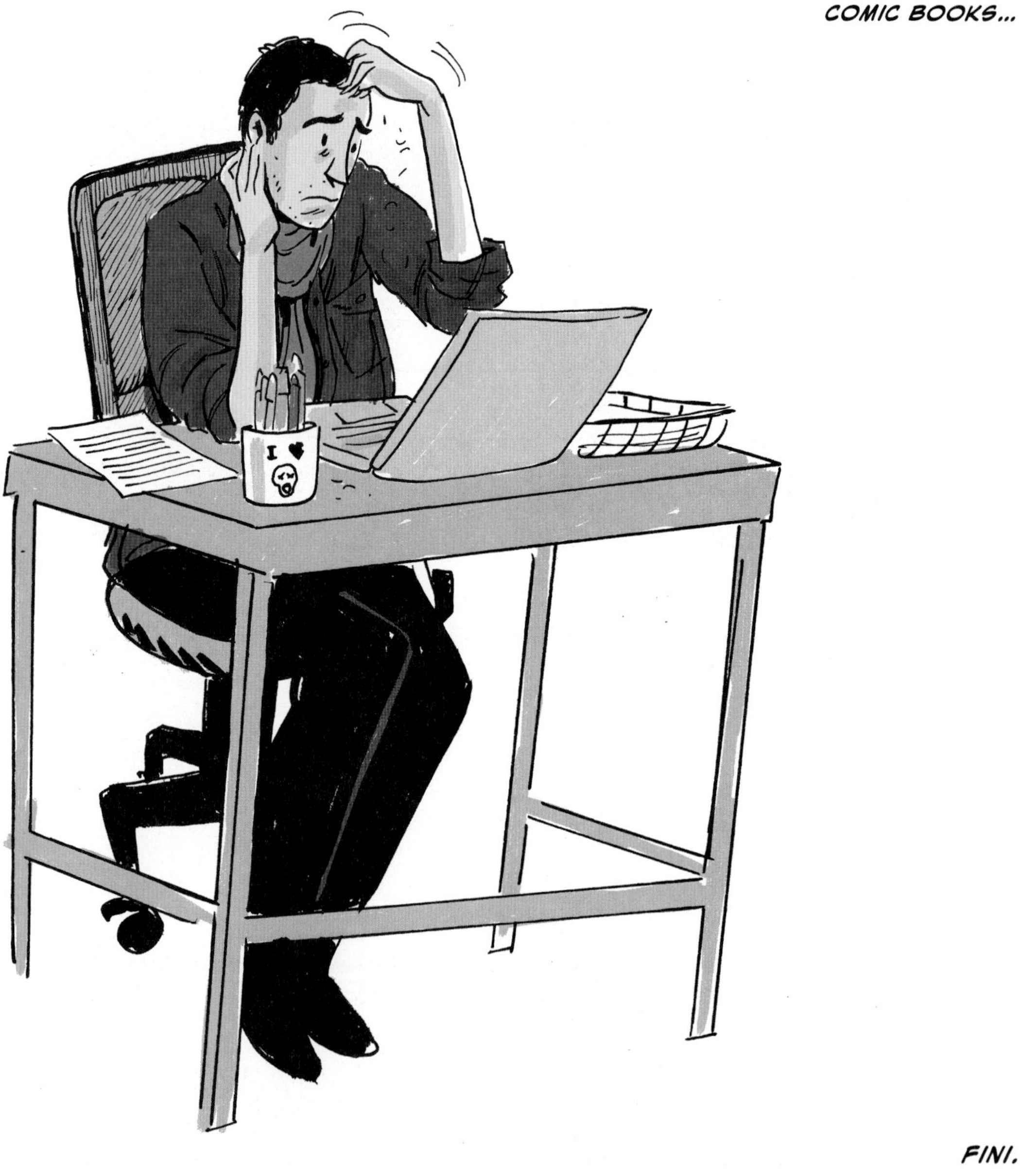
IN GRAND DETAIL, HERE IS A COMPLETE AND GRAPHIC DEPICTION OF EDITING COMIC BOOKS...
FINI.

THE THREE TIERS OF STRESS RELIEF

#1 - EATING

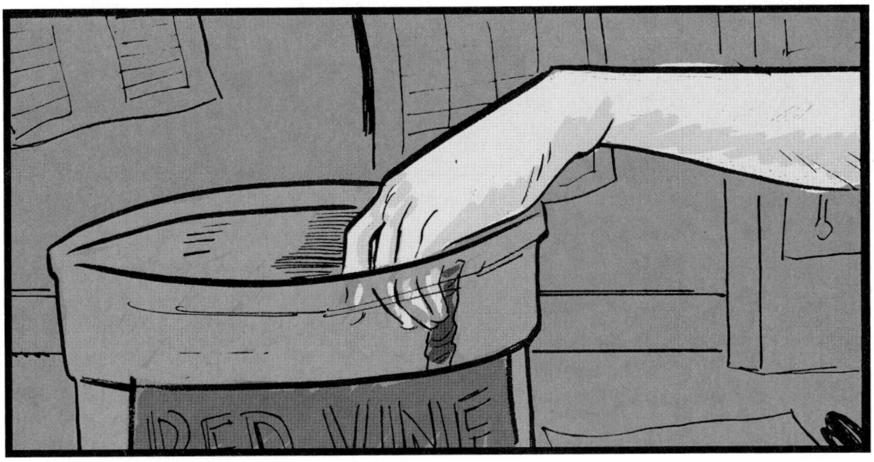

#2 - SHOPPING

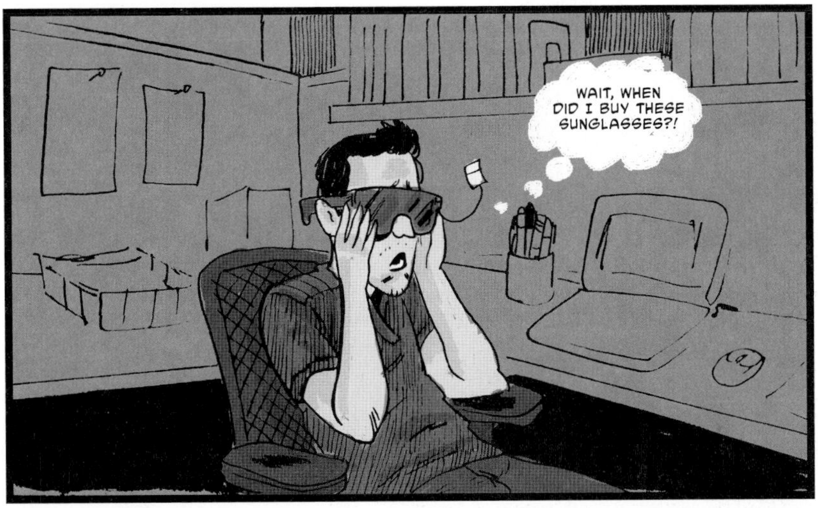
WAIT, WHEN DID I BUY THESE SUNGLASSES?!

#3 - HITTING UP DUDES WHO ARE BAD FOR ME

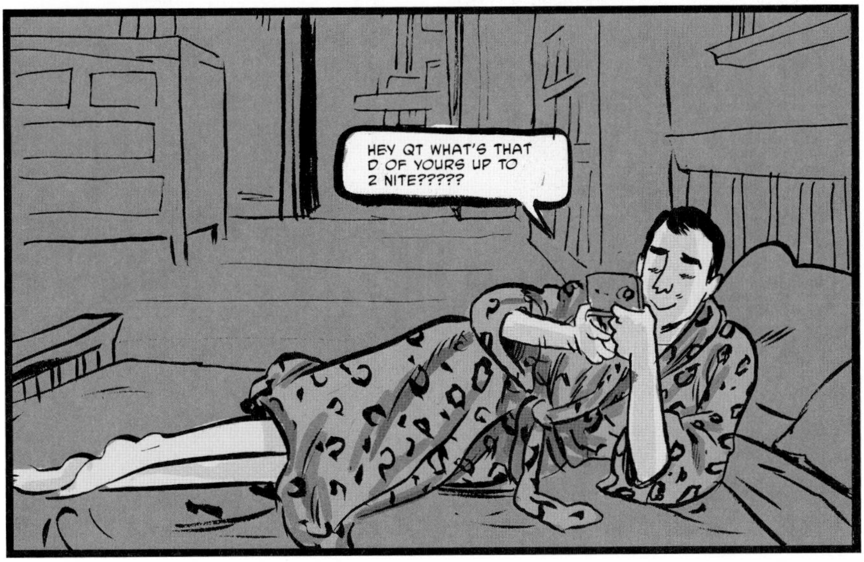
HEY QT WHAT'S THAT D OF YOURS UP TO 2 NITE?????

Dope Conversation

illustrations by Riley Rossmo

There's no original way to talk about how music affects the soul. Colleen Green's lo-fi rock offerings are deceptively simple, intensely personal, and all-around universal... like a great Ramones song. Her new album, I Want to Grow Up delivers 10 confections that feel as though they were in direct conversation with the strips in Self-Obsessed. Colleen was kind enough to hang for a minute and chat...

Sina Grace: Testing... I'm Sina, so you're Colleen?

Colleen Green: Yes.

SG: For the readers who may not be familiar with you, how did you get into music- how did you become Colleen Green?

CG: I just am Colleen Green... So, I always wanted to be a singer, I always wanted to play music and I played in bands since I was a teenager and just never stopped. Then one day I moved to L.A. and Colleen Green was born.

SG: What's funny is for me, y'know, for people who draw, we go and look at the people we admire and try to draw like them. And I would imagine, that's where everyone starts, is they try to emulate their heroes and somehow become heroes themselves. That's always fascinated me, at what point do we suddenly go from being like "Oh, so-and-so did that" to "this is how I do it."

CG: How do we get from "so-and-so did it like this" to "I did it like this?"

SG: Yeah.

CG: Well, my theory- and I've put thought into this- is that the new "original" is in application and interpretation. So, like, I feel like what I do is very referential and it's kind of just like me wanting to sound like all the sounds I ever loved, 'cuz that's the music that I loved. I'm always pulling stuff and referencing bands I really like just because that music is the best, why would I try to do something better than that? What I love is what I love, and that's what I do. Everything's already pretty much been done at this point, and it's more in how you interpret and present your influences, and still be creative under the umbrella of your influences.

SG: You used a really good word, "application" because at the end of the day I know I'm doi[ng] something someone else did... even today I'll p[ut] a so-and-so brush stroke.

CG: Yeah! There's nothing you can do that hasn['t] been done. It's like that Barenaked Ladies song[.]

SG: It's very recent for it to be okay to tip yo[ur] hat. I feel like before there had to be pretense, like the old Original was lying about there bein[g] reference. I know you're like, "I am Colle[en] Green," but there's the whole sunglasses thin[g,] I'm assuming your last name isn't Green?

CG: No, it is.

SG: Oh, it's real!? Like, the government say[s] you're Colleen Green?

CG: They do.

> **"What I love is what I love, and that's what I do."**
> **Colleen Green**

SG: Okay tight, I thought it was a stage nam[e.] What parts of you do you go, "Yeah, I wan[t] people to see that," to "...no."

CG: I don't think about everyone, I think abou[t] relationships I have on a person-to-person basi[s,] when you get to know someone you get to kno[w] stuff about them, and you don't just reveal ever[y] aspect of yourself to everyone in the world ever[y] time you meet... it takes time to get to kno[w] someone and eventually you get to learn mor[e] about them.

SG: But you give the world a part of you in [a] song. You wouldn't tell someone you met at [a] coffee house that you're still not over your ex o[r] "TV is my friend," you know? How do you mak[e] the decisions to draw the line?

It's a decision to be like, "I'm gonna talk abou[t] my feelings for the public" instead of, "I a[m] making a concept album and I only write abou[t] like- the weather."

CG: I don't know, I feel like I pretty much put it all out here in my songs, I feel like there isn't a dark subject that I haven't touched on. I felt like for this album that would make the most interesting lyrical content I could think of for myself. I'm really interested in psychology and the human brain and how our minds work, so it was just really interesting to me. I feel like I'm gonna talk about it all, and that's why people like me. I don't know!

CG: I always felt scared of telling anyone something legitimately personal... but now I realize if I tell everyone, no one person has power over me. No one can hold anything over my head if everyone gets it.

CG: Pretty much everyone is gonna get it. We're all the same. I feel the same as you where I'd be like, "Oh no, I can't tell anyone that about myself." But as I grew older, I was like: "Why? Why would I be ashamed of being a human?" We all go through the same shit and it's kind of sad that you feel that shame, so I was like, I'm gonna do the opposite of that."

Sina Grace

SG: How does your family feel about you being creative for a living?

CG: They support me. They're super proud of me. The first few years, my mom was like, "Okay that's great but did you find a job?" She was really concerned about me having health benefits because I have an autoimmune disease, but now I have California state health insurance and it's really great. But that was for the first few years. They're really proud of me.

SG: My mom doesn't understand why I don't just do Spider-Man... do they ever hit you with that? You do Rock, and that's not an easy genre to say you're making whatever dollars, and you have a home, and three dogs and nine kids and whatever. Did they ever want you to be Katy Perry?

CG: No, definitely not, because they love rock n' roll also.

SG: Lucky.

CG: They would always wanna know how much money I'm making. "Are they paying you well?"

SG: Have you ever been hit with your own personal walls? For me I get to those places where I don't know if I can keep pulling this off every year. I know I can, but I don't know if I can keep pulling this level of it off, where it's like you keep having to book your own events or gigs for you... and I have to sleep on a couch and carry my own shit around. You got gear and guitars... we got books. Have you ever been hit with that? From the outside looking in, it seems like a nice steady progression.

CG: I'm pretty spoiled, because I live with my brother for free, so I don't have many expenses. I don't have a car. I am OK, I don't have to sleep on a couch or sleep in a crazy house with a million people. I'm fine.

SG: Even when you're touring, are you like, "I want a real hotel room" have you ever been hit with that?

> "I always felt scared of telling anyone something legitimately personal... but now I realize if I tell everyone, no *one* person has power over me."
>
> Sina Grace

CG: You have to keep yourself sane, and comfortable and happy. Sometimes you sacrifice as much as you can for your art, but you should take some time to take care of yourself.

SG: Who taught you to do that? 'Cuz I'm figuring out who taught me that. To have self-nurture, not everyone has that in them. I always wonder who did that to my brain.

CG: I don't know. Maybe my parents? Maybe being a stoner, maybe being like "No bro, just eat the cheesecake, just do it." 'Cuz it'll be awesome and it's not the end of the world if you spend 50 bucks on a hotel room or something like that.

SG: It's the little things, you know. That's what they always say.

CG: If you want it, just fucking do it. You can always make more money, it's not like the end of the world if you're not starving or destitute or on the streets.

SG: And now I'm just asking questions: have you seen your friends not fucking cut it?

CG: I don't know if I would say "not cutting it," I've definitely seen people who were always playing in bands and always wanted to be musicians- I've seen them go the normal route and quit playing music and get a real job.

SG: Would that ever happen to you?

CG: To me? Yeah, maybe. I don't know. I think about that sometimes. Maybe I would just be normal. I think I could, but I don't know if I will. Sometimes I fantasize about being totally normal but I don't know if I can, because I like doing creative stuff too much, and it is who I am.

SG: Someone said that to me, they said I'd be a really good manager for actors, because I love putting people and projects together. I would do that... it'd be all business lunches. I could do that shit, but it's like, I'm doing the fucking thing I want to do. Being a manager would be helping other people's dreams come true and I'm like, "Yeah, that's a fine deed, but I'd rather make my dream come true, and that'll make people super happy in different ways."

> **"Sometimes I fantasize about being totally normal but I don't know if I can, because I like doing creative stuff too much, and it is who I am."**
>
> **Colleen Green**

CG: Creative people just need to do creative stuff. You need to get it out, you know?

SG: What made you decide to music for income?

CG: I always wanted to play music, and when I put out my tape (Milo Goes to Compton), Hardly Art

contacted me a few months later and said t wanted to work with me, and I was like, "Y obviously, I'll do that." Before that I just kine was going along with whatever, making mu and going on tour, and just trying to get music out there.

Colleen Green

SG: I used to do a lot of freelance editing, a this year I was like "dude, try to go the wh year taking art gigs or writing gigs." Pulling b from another job, and seeing if the money making doing the thing I love is enough to k me chill. You're lucky.

CG: I pretty much came to LA to make mu 'cuz i knew I'd be living for free, so I t advantage of the situation.

SG: That's rad, congrats.

CG: It's such bullshit though, it's so un-punk I mean whatever, I have a good excuse.

SG: We all have struggles, so you can still be pu in other ways.

CG: Totally.

SG: I'm taking your credentials away, you're i punk enough.

CG: Do you see this neighborhood (West Angeles)? It's punk as fuck.

SG: Some thug is always throwing a brick in window when I come here.

I Want to Grow Up is out now through Hardly Ar Records. For more information about Colleen, vis www.colleengreen.com

" and you all think I'm stupid
too nice, too aloof
There's no winning here at all
Been on the road for so long
singing Self-Obsessed songs
I'm always coming us
I'm going. "

Rilo Kiley
"Somebody Else's Clothes"

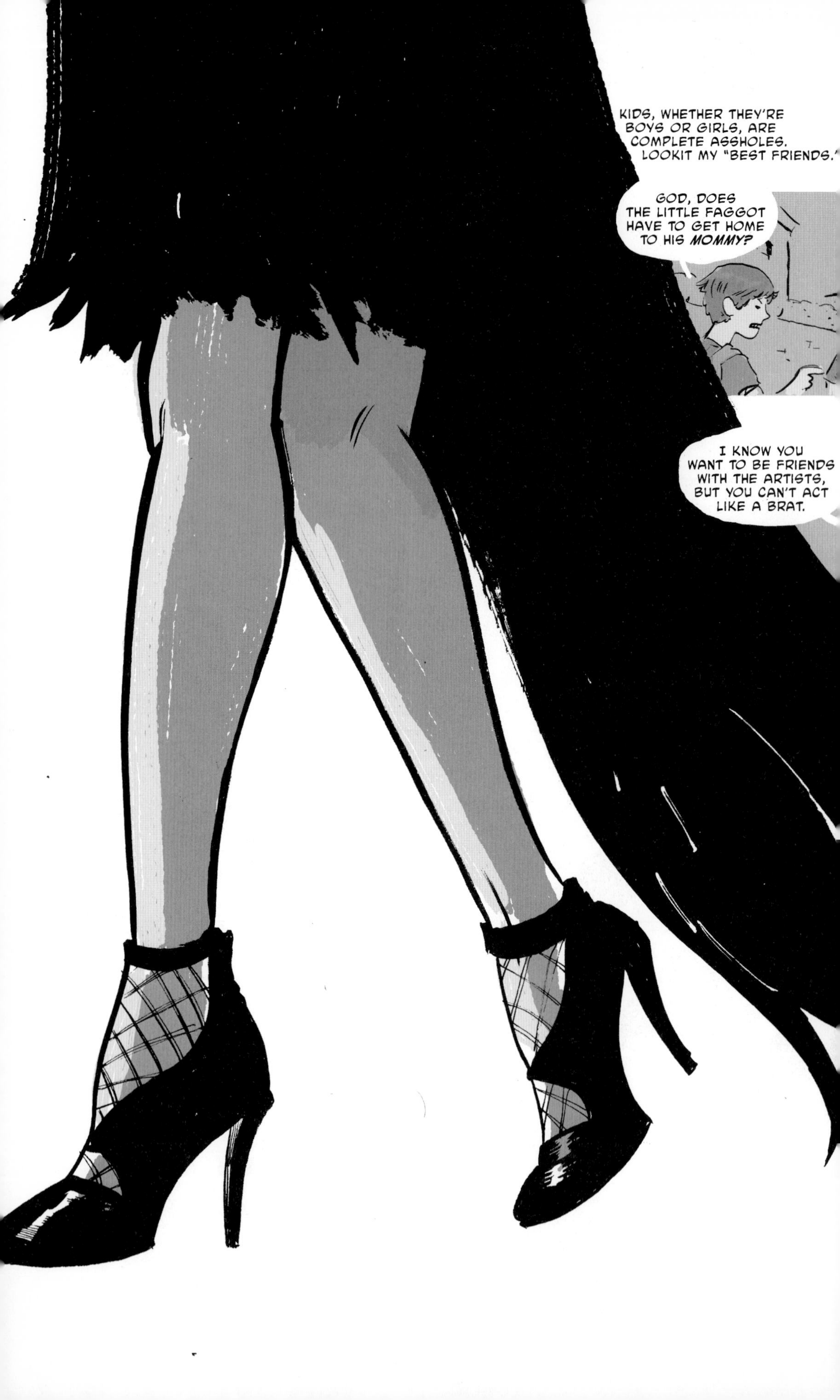
KIDS, WHETHER THEY'RE BOYS OR GIRLS, ARE COMPLETE ASSHOLES. LOOKIT MY "BEST FRIENDS."
GOD, DOES THE LITTLE FAGGOT HAVE TO GET HOME TO HIS *MOMMY?*
I KNOW YOU WANT TO BE FRIENDS WITH THE ARTISTS, BUT YOU CAN'T ACT LIKE A BRAT.

coat tails

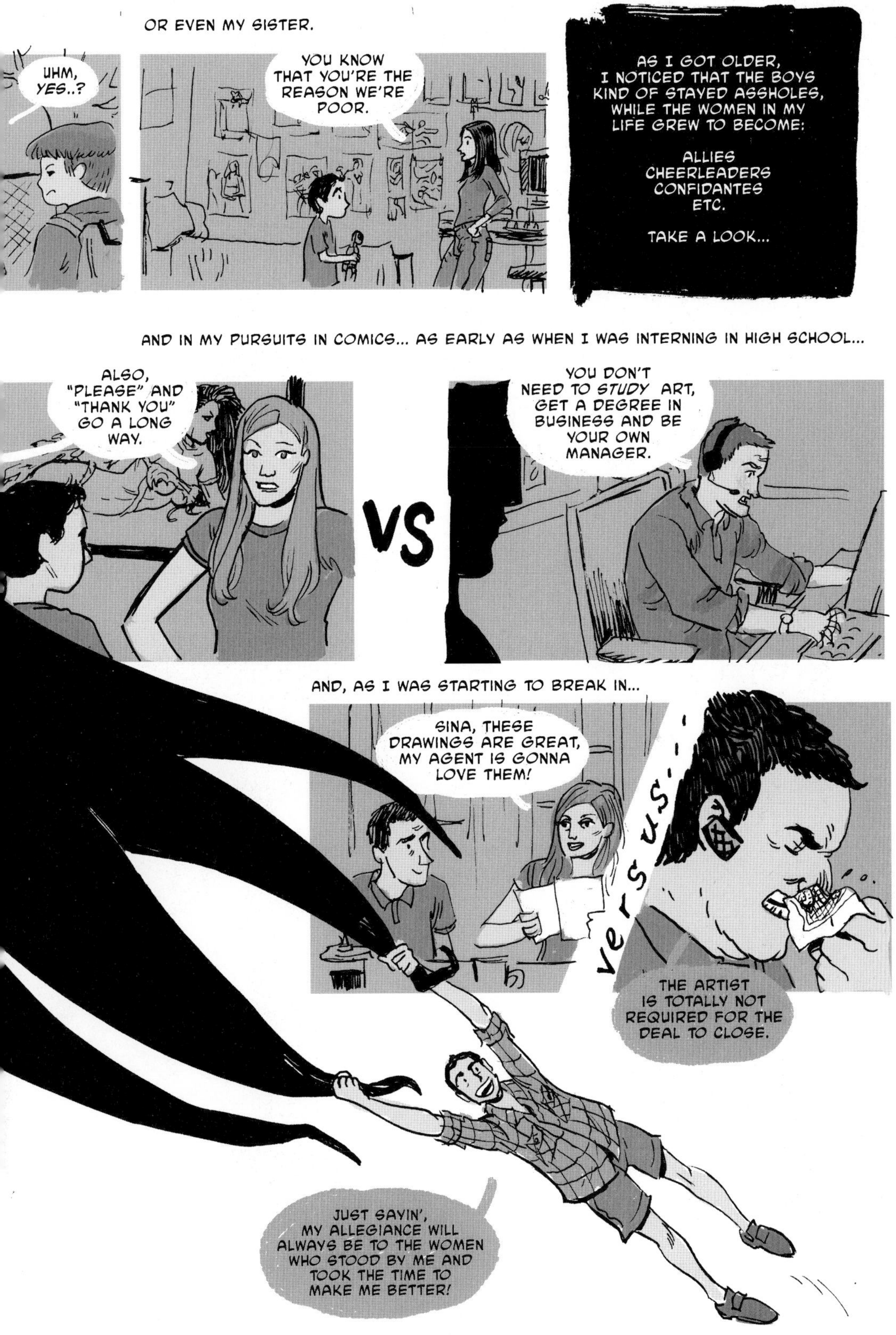
OR EVEN MY SISTER.
UHM, YES..?
YOU KNOW THAT YOU'RE THE REASON WE'RE POOR.
AS I GOT OLDER, I NOTICED THAT THE BOYS KIND OF STAYED ASSHOLES, WHILE THE WOMEN IN MY LIFE GREW TO BECOME:
ALLIES
CHEERLEADERS
CONFIDANTES
ETC.
TAKE A LOOK...
AND IN MY PURSUITS IN COMICS... AS EARLY AS WHEN I WAS INTERNING IN HIGH SCHOOL...
ALSO, "PLEASE" AND "THANK YOU" GO A LONG WAY.
VS
YOU DON'T NEED TO *STUDY* ART, GET A DEGREE IN BUSINESS AND BE YOUR OWN MANAGER.
AND, AS I WAS STARTING TO BREAK IN...
SINA, THESE DRAWINGS ARE GREAT, MY AGENT IS GONNA LOVE THEM!
versus...
THE ARTIST IS TOTALLY NOT REQUIRED FOR THE DEAL TO CLOSE.
JUST SAYIN', MY ALLEGIANCE WILL ALWAYS BE TO THE WOMEN WHO STOOD BY ME AND TOOK THE TIME TO MAKE ME BETTER!

Sina Grace in... Passive Manipulation

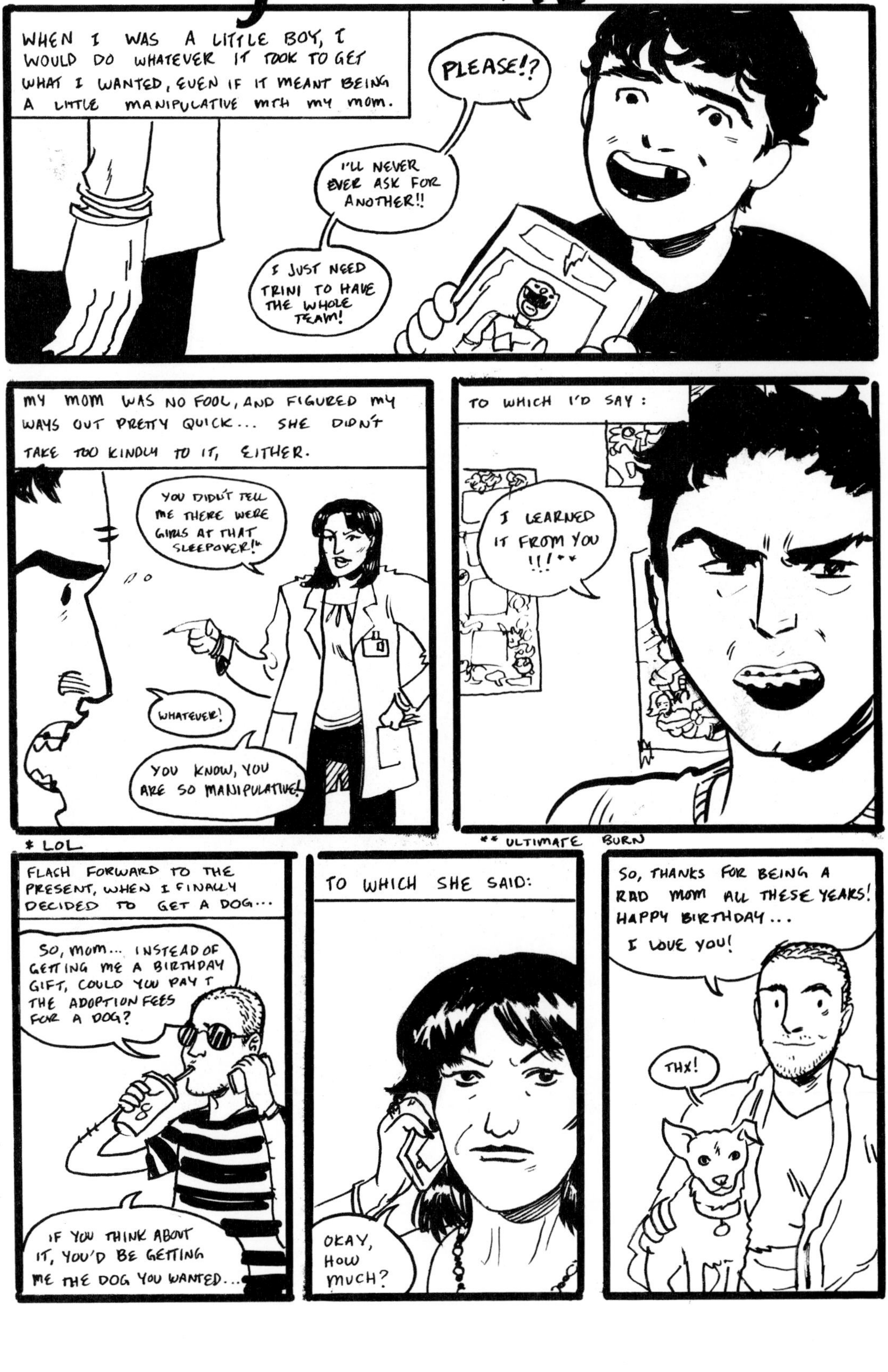

WHEN I WAS A LITTLE BOY, I WOULD DO WHATEVER IT TOOK TO GET WHAT I WANTED, EVEN IF IT MEANT BEING A LITTLE MANIPULATIVE WITH MY MOM.
PLEASE!?
I'LL NEVER EVER ASK FOR ANOTHER!!
I JUST NEED TRINI TO HAVE THE WHOLE TEAM!
MY MOM WAS NO FOOL, AND FIGURED MY WAYS OUT PRETTY QUICK... SHE DIDN'T TAKE TOO KINDLY TO IT, EITHER.
YOU DIDN'T TELL ME THERE WERE GIRLS AT THAT SLEEPOVER!*
WHATEVER!
YOU KNOW, YOU ARE SO MANIPULATIVE!
TO WHICH I'D SAY:
I LEARNED IT FROM YOU !!!**
* LOL
** ULTIMATE BURN
FLASH FORWARD TO THE PRESENT, WHEN I FINALLY DECIDED TO GET A DOG...
SO, MOM... INSTEAD OF GETTING ME A BIRTHDAY GIFT, COULD YOU PAY T THE ADOPTION FEES FOR A DOG?
IF YOU THINK ABOUT IT, YOU'D BE GETTING ME THE DOG YOU WANTED...
TO WHICH SHE SAID:
OKAY, HOW MUCH?
SO, THANKS FOR BEING A RAD MOM ALL THESE YEARS! HAPPY BIRTHDAY... I LOVE YOU!
THX!

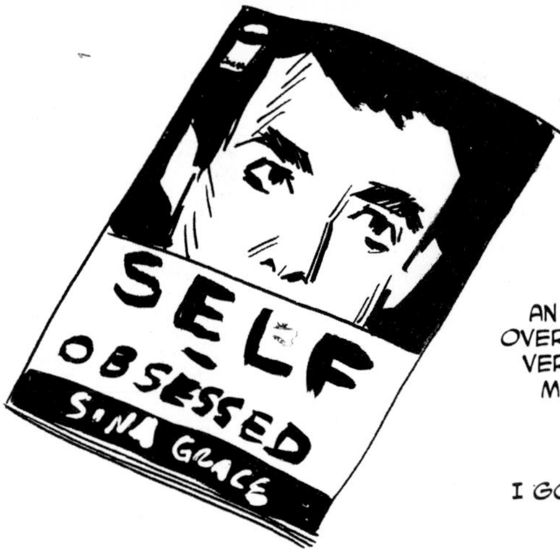
SELF OBSESSED
SINA GRACE

BACK IN APRIL, I RELEASED A ONE-SHOT THAT COLLECTED A LOAD OF AUTOBIO STRIPS, GOING AS FAR BACK AS MY DAYS IN HIGH SCHOOL.

AN EXPERIMENT IN SHOWING THE GROWTH OF AN ARTIST OVER A DECADE OF SELF-QUESTIONING, I THOUGHT AT THE VERY LEAST PEOPLE WOULD GET A KICK OUT OF SEEING MATERIAL THAT HAS PRETTY MUCH BEEN UNAVAILABLE FOR YEARS.

WHILE I CAN SAY THAT I'M PROUD OF THE BOOK, I GOT A SLEW OF DIFFERENT RESPONSES FROM FRIENDS, FAMILY, AND COMPLETE STRANGERS!

So, how did people react ??

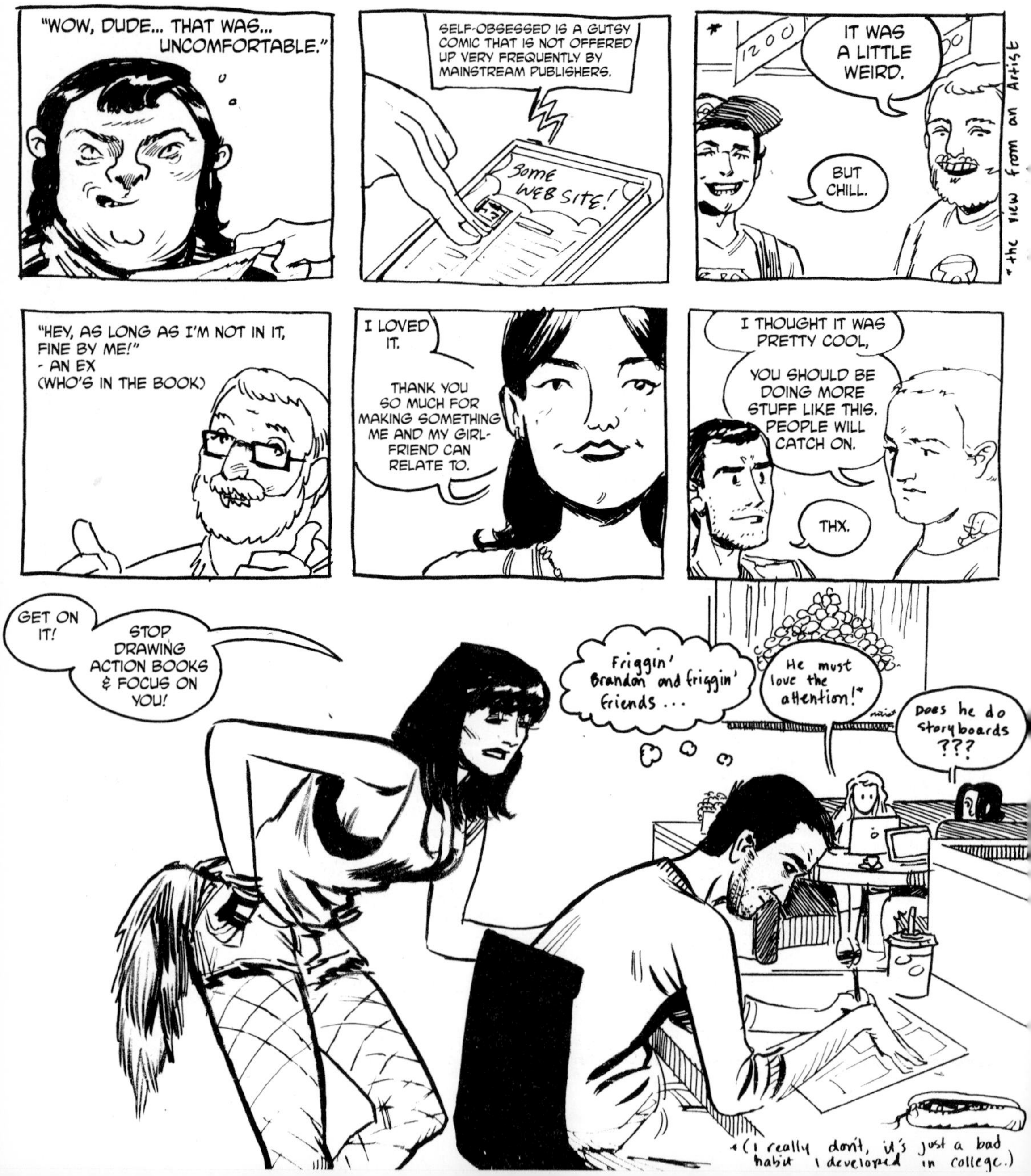
"WOW, DUDE... THAT WAS... UNCOMFORTABLE."
SELF-OBSESSED IS A GUTSY COMIC THAT IS NOT OFFERED UP VERY FREQUENTLY BY MAINSTREAM PUBLISHERS.
SOME WEB SITE!
IT WAS A LITTLE WEIRD.
BUT CHILL.
* the view from an Artist
"HEY, AS LONG AS I'M NOT IN IT, FINE BY ME!" - AN EX (WHO'S IN THE BOOK)
I LOVED IT.
THANK YOU SO MUCH FOR MAKING SOMETHING ME AND MY GIRL-FRIEND CAN RELATE TO.
I THOUGHT IT WAS PRETTY COOL,
YOU SHOULD BE DOING MORE STUFF LIKE THIS. PEOPLE WILL CATCH ON.
THX.
GET ON IT!
STOP DRAWING ACTION BOOKS & FOCUS ON YOU!
Friggin' Brandon and friggin' friends...
He must love the attention!*
Does he do storyboards ???
*(I really don't, it's just a bad habit I developed in college.)

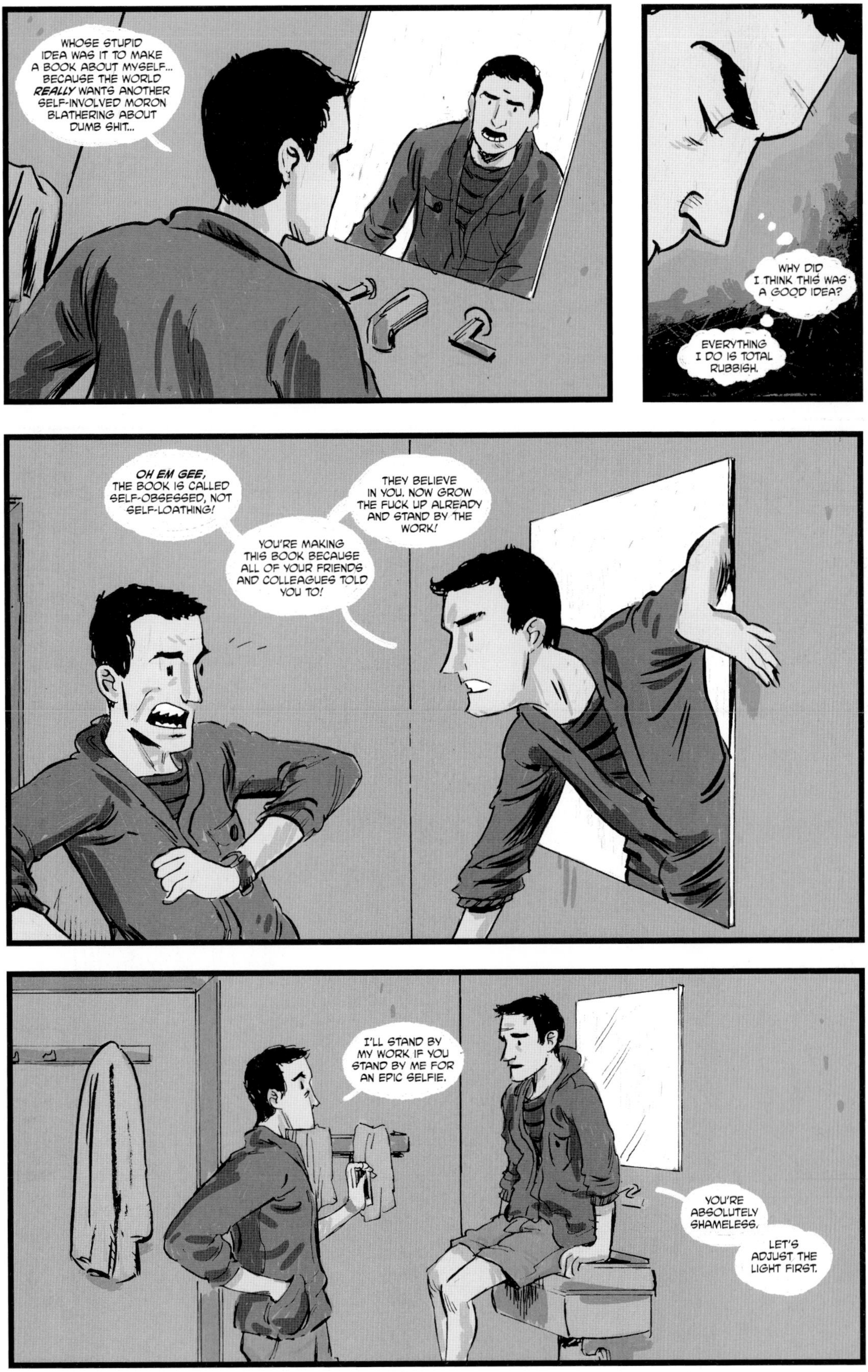
WHOSE STUPID IDEA WAS IT TO MAKE A BOOK ABOUT MYSELF... BECAUSE THE WORLD REALLY WANTS ANOTHER SELF-INVOLVED MORON BLATHERING ABOUT DUMB SHIT...
WHY DID I THINK THIS WAS A GOOD IDEA?
EVERYTHING I DO IS TOTAL RUBBISH.
OH EM GEE, THE BOOK IS CALLED SELF-OBSESSED, NOT SELF-LOATHING!
YOU'RE MAKING THIS BOOK BECAUSE ALL OF YOUR FRIENDS AND COLLEAGUES TOLD YOU TO!
THEY BELIEVE IN YOU. NOW GROW THE FUCK UP ALREADY AND STAND BY THE WORK!
I'LL STAND BY MY WORK IF YOU STAND BY ME FOR AN EPIC SELFIE.
YOU'RE ABSOLUTELY SHAMELESS.
LET'S ADJUST THE LIGHT FIRST.

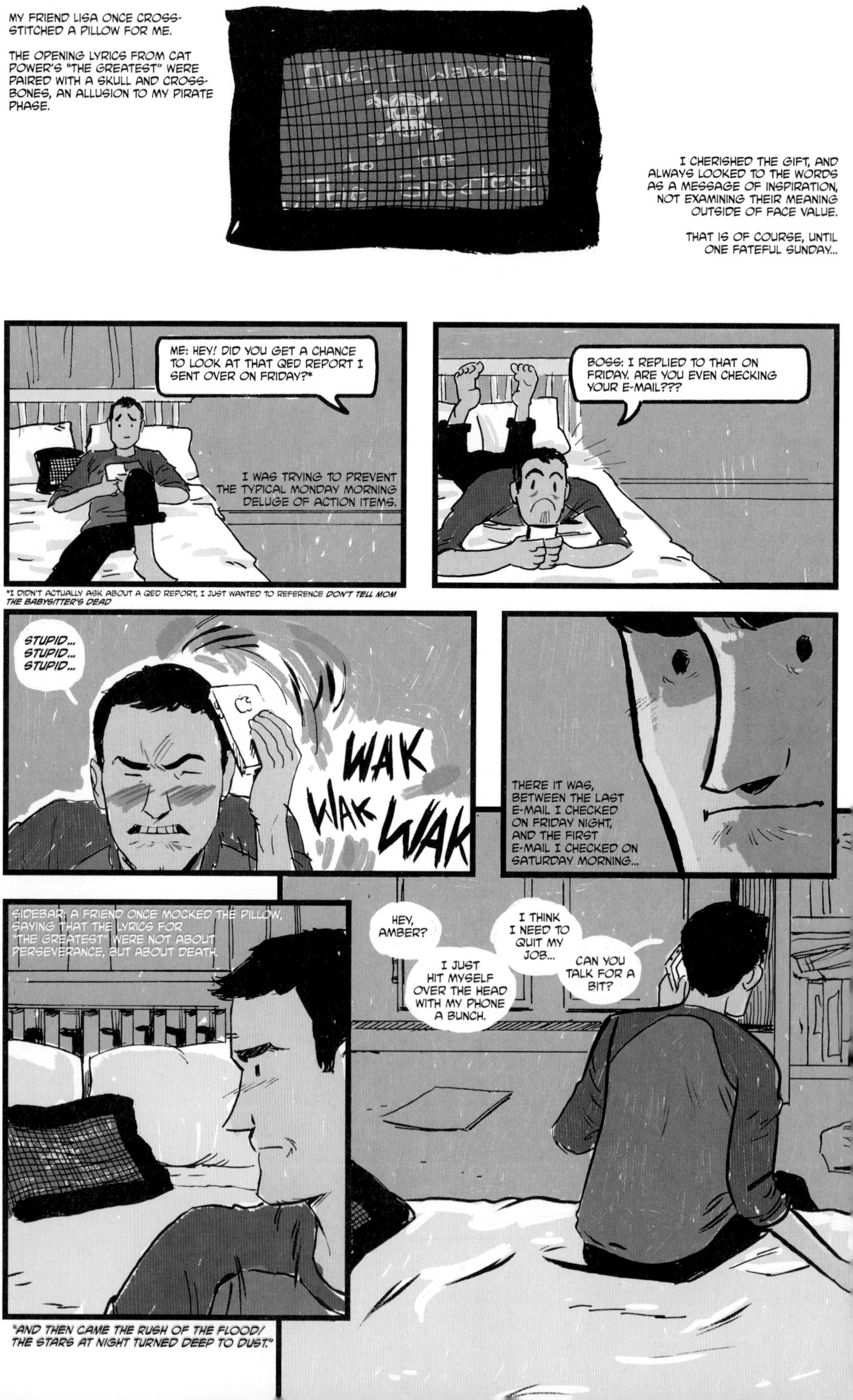
MY FRIEND LISA ONCE CROSS-STITCHED A PILLOW FOR ME.
THE OPENING LYRICS FROM CAT POWER'S "THE GREATEST" WERE PAIRED WITH A SKULL AND CROSS-BONES, AN ALLUSION TO MY PIRATE PHASE.
I CHERISHED THE GIFT, AND ALWAYS LOOKED TO THE WORDS AS A MESSAGE OF INSPIRATION, NOT EXAMINING THEIR MEANING OUTSIDE OF FACE VALUE.
THAT IS OF COURSE, UNTIL ONE FATEFUL SUNDAY...
ME: HEY! DID YOU GET A CHANCE TO LOOK AT THAT QED REPORT I SENT OVER ON FRIDAY?*
I WAS TRYING TO PREVENT THE TYPICAL MONDAY MORNING DELUGE OF ACTION ITEMS.
*I DIDN'T ACTUALLY ASK ABOUT A QED REPORT, I JUST WANTED TO REFERENCE DON'T TELL MOM THE BABYSITTER'S DEAD
BOSS: I REPLIED TO THAT ON FRIDAY. ARE YOU EVEN CHECKING YOUR E-MAIL???
STUPID... STUPID... STUPID...
WAK
WAK
WAK
THERE IT WAS, BETWEEN THE LAST E-MAIL I CHECKED ON FRIDAY NIGHT, AND THE FIRST E-MAIL I CHECKED ON SATURDAY MORNING...
SIDEBAR: A FRIEND ONCE MOCKED THE PILLOW, SAYING THAT THE LYRICS FOR "THE GREATEST" WERE NOT ABOUT PERSEVERANCE, BUT ABOUT DEATH.
"AND THEN CAME THE RUSH OF THE FLOOD/ THE STARS AT NIGHT TURNED DEEP TO DUST."
HEY, AMBER?
I JUST HIT MYSELF OVER THE HEAD WITH MY PHONE A BUNCH.
I THINK I NEED TO QUIT MY JOB...
CAN YOU TALK FOR A BIT?

Advice For People Who Want To Quit Their Jobs

ne craziest and most rational decision I made in the past year was to leave my incredibly challenging job as a mic book editor. The reason: to pursue my dreams of making my own graphic novels full-time. The decision me from inspecting a few variables and making sure I had the resources to last at least six months before any nd of freelance money could cover my bills. Here's what I did:

t Expenses: I'm sure there are adorable apps that help you manage your money, but I'm too much of a mess do the work for that... I wrote a list of my monthly expenses (rent, utilities, groceries, therapy, gas, EATING ND DRINKING OUT, etc), and I tried to cut it down by half. You'd be surprised how much "necessary" shit ou can drop if you want your day-to-day freedom. I remember once listening to a friend complain about how had no money to pay down a credit card, but like six or seven TV add-ons (premium cable! HBO! DVR! etflix!), and if someone's truly struggling, they could just Hulu Plus it for a while. Worse comes to worse, I uld move back in with my mom... we all know that's akin to suicide, but it would also be hundreds of dollars ed up and the convenience of a fully-stocked fridge... but: suicide.

fety Net #1- Mom: At the beginning of 2012, I told my mom that I wanted to save up and move to New York d try to make connections there in the publishing and fashion industry. She asked me how much I was trying save, and offered to "loan" me the amount so I could jump on the dream bandwagon sooner rather than later. hile an amazingly generous offer, I did not take her up on it. I DID — however — ask if an iteration of that fer stood for my current endeavor. She's there if things get bad, but so far I have not needed the net.

robably Download That Money-Managing App: Let's be real, we're not as good with our money as we'd like to lieve we are. Watching exactly where your money goes month in and month out will help you curb any haviors that you may not have even noticed (yeah, you didn't really need to buy a croissant with your coffee vice this week... you also didn't need to buy coffee when your roommate has a coffee maker at home). These ps include color codes, charts, and could be the actual wake-up call that you need to cut things out. You're aking a huge change, and you should change how you handle and look at money.

e Smart and Stop with the Frivolous: This doesn't mean avoiding a silly day at your mall or whatever, this eans coming up with smart ways around instances where you would want to buy something... I LOVE buying fts, I LOATHE coming to a party empty handed. Be smart — learn to make something cheap and by hand, buy your booze in bulk (and cheap) at Costco and have it ready. One of the best gifts I got this Christmas was necklace made from a chain door lock... it probably cost my friend all of ten dollars for parts, but it was neat d thoughtful (and yes, I'm aware not all of you can pull this accessory off, but that's for another essay). Every ty has so many free events — art openings, free concerts, museum days — you can still participate in your ty's nightlife on the cheap-cheap. Also, test yourself... shop down, too. If you do need a new jacket for hatever reason, challenge yourself to find it at the lower-end shops.

et Rid of Stuff: I am one of those guys with small collections of thises and thats. I have a brick of vinyl, some VDs, some books... nothing insane, but I have enough of these things that I have been systematically selling em for grocery money. There was some stuff I got from work that proved — err — lucrative on eBay, but I've so had to sell my guitar (giving up that dream of being in an indie band to pursue my aspirations... put THAT a mug). There's no need to be precious about items that are objectively "stuff."

afety Net #2- ??? : For most people, this would be an actual savings... sadly, I saved zero dollars while I was nployed. At my old job, there was a merit-based bonus that dropped in my bank account right around month vo of being jobless. Let's pretend that was me saving money. I know some people are smart and are able to earn "unemployment" while they take time to do some Me Time... that could be your safety net. Sadly, it's not mine.

e Prepared to Work: This isn't the first time I've been without a job and have had the luxury of free time to raw. Right after I graduated college, I would work a few hours a day on my art, take classes, and work ligently to grow as an artist and storyteller. Even during the busiest times of my editorial career, I could be und drawing in the middle of the night. I had an understanding of how to do the work, and how to build a gimented schedule so I wasn't just re-watching Gossip Girl on Netflix, or catching up with friends who had milar schedules.

Advice For People Who Want To Quit Their Jobs

Have a Business Plan: The DAY after I quit my job, I drove up to the Bay Area to promote my own comic bo The week after I quit my job, I worked tirelessly to meet a deadline for the book I'm promoting now... I did just sit at home, get a gym membership, and work my core. I only have money enough to last me about two m months... I don't intend to get a day job in the next few weeks. I want to be racking up enough freelance we that I can continue this lifestyle. There are several projects I have going on, and the hope is that ultimately c or all of them will be yielding me legit cash.

> *"I've also had to sell my guitar (giving up that dream of being in an indie band to pursue my aspirations... put THAT on a mug)."*

This isn't a fool-proof plan. You shouldn't even look at this as a proper blueprint for how to live the unemploy life of pursuing your dream... read this as an example of someone who needed to devote time to his person pursuits, and did it responsibly. If you want a better life, it will not be handed to you. It's hard work, and so days it will suck, but a friend once told me: nothing is more important than your personal health. This decis is the best yet, and I'm glad that I have no one to answer to except myself... and my editors. And my landlo

And my mom.

Sina Gra

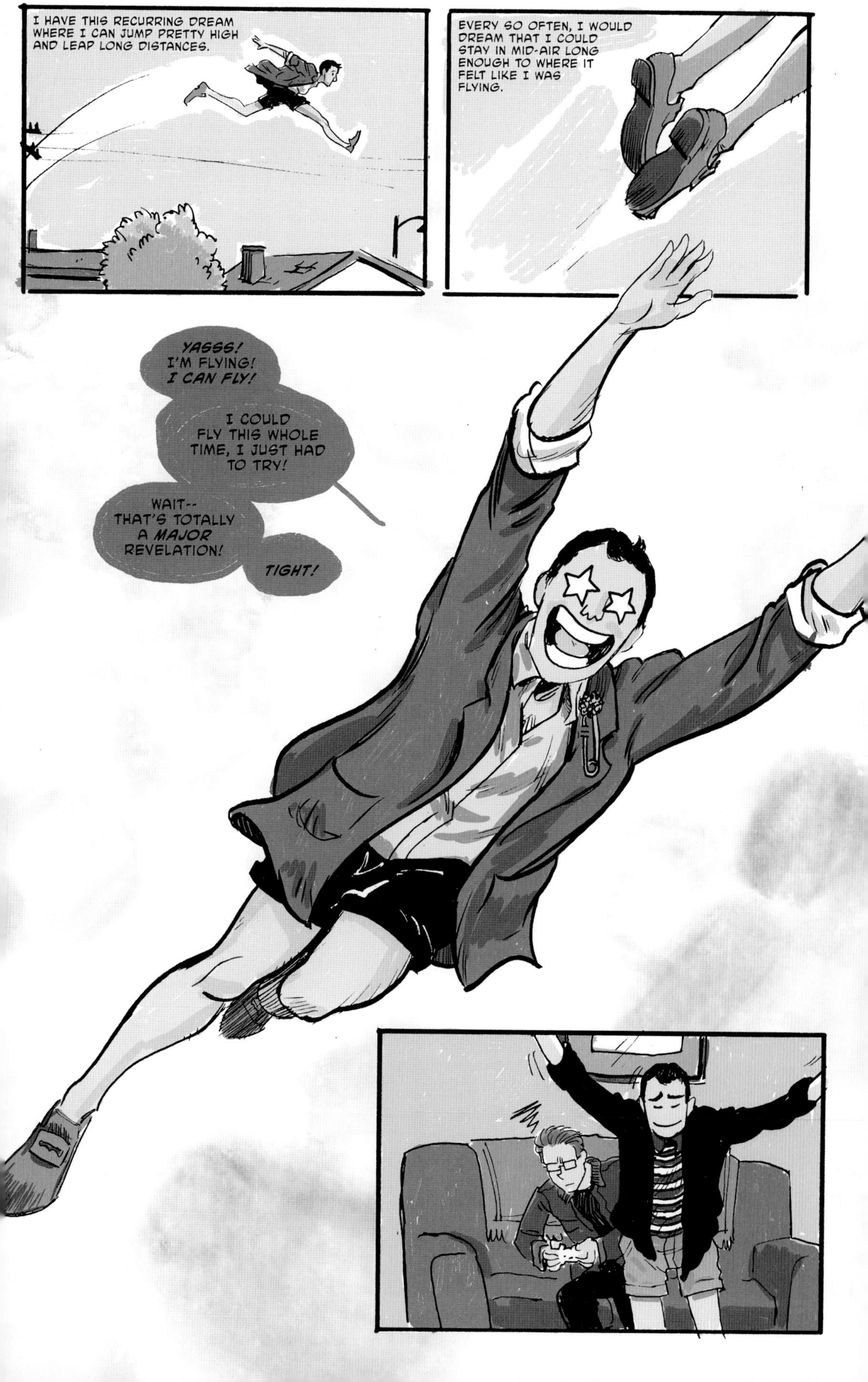
I HAVE THIS RECURRING DREAM WHERE I CAN JUMP PRETTY HIGH AND LEAP LONG DISTANCES.
EVERY SO OFTEN, I WOULD DREAM THAT I COULD STAY IN MID-AIR LONG ENOUGH TO WHERE IT FELT LIKE I WAS FLYING.
YASSS! I'M FLYING! I CAN FLY!
I COULD FLY THIS WHOLE TIME, I JUST HAD TO TRY!
WAIT-- THAT'S TOTALLY A MAJOR REVELATION!
TIGHT!

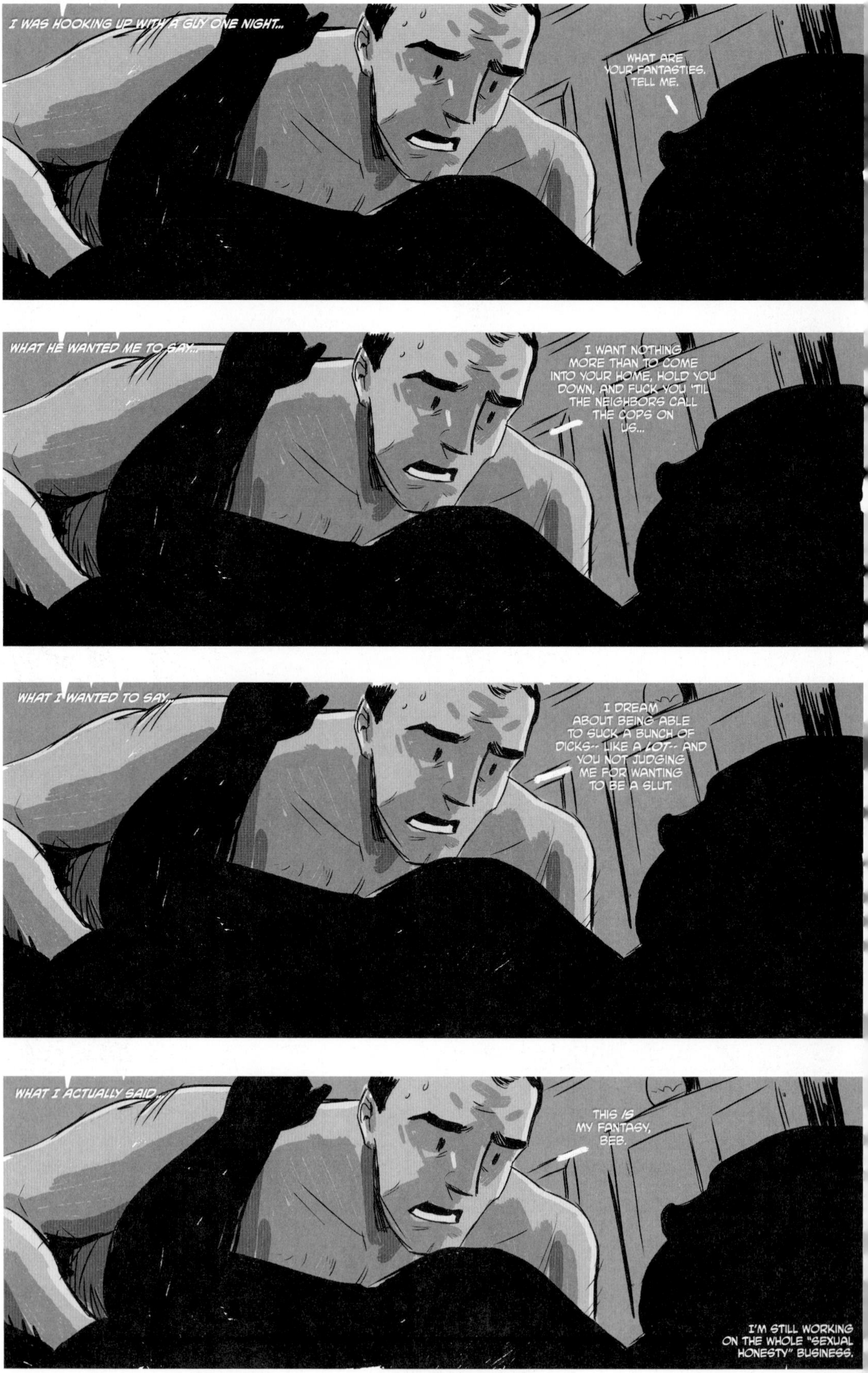
I WAS HOOKING UP WITH A GUY ONE NIGHT...
WHAT ARE YOUR FANTASTIES. TELL ME.
WHAT HE WANTED ME TO SAY...
I WANT NOTHING MORE THAN TO COME INTO YOUR HOME, HOLD YOU DOWN, AND FUCK YOU 'TIL THE NEIGHBORS CALL THE COPS ON US...
WHAT I WANTED TO SAY...
I DREAM ABOUT BEING ABLE TO SUCK A BUNCH OF DICKS-- LIKE A *LOT*-- AND YOU NOT JUDGING ME FOR WANTING TO BE A SLUT.
WHAT I ACTUALLY SAID...
THIS *IS* MY FANTASY, BEB.
I'M STILL WORKING ON THE WHOLE "SEXUAL HONESTY" BUSINESS.

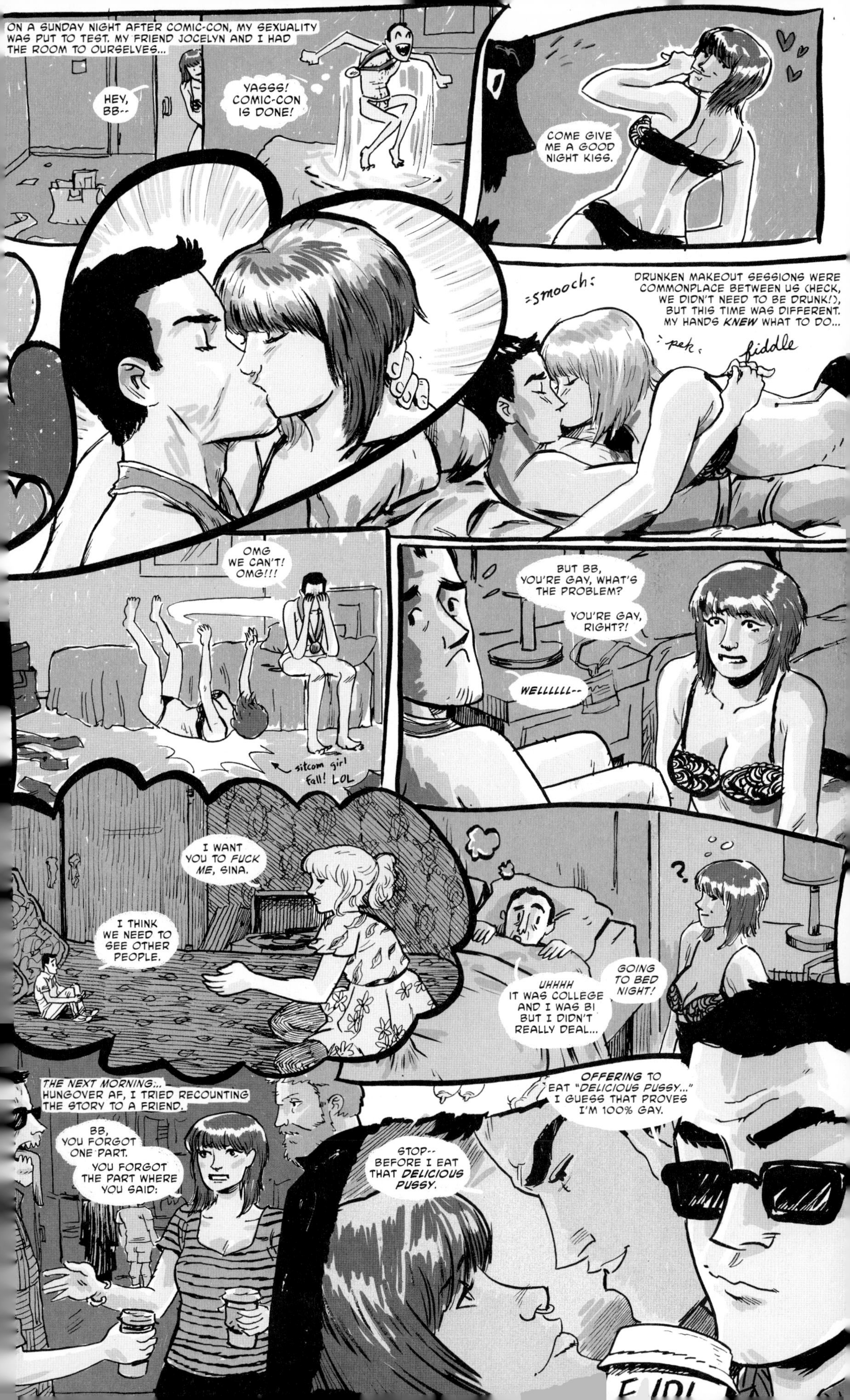
ON A SUNDAY NIGHT AFTER COMIC-CON, MY SEXUALITY WAS PUT TO TEST. MY FRIEND JOCELYN AND I HAD THE ROOM TO OURSELVES...
HEY, BB--
YASSS! COMIC-CON IS DONE!
COME GIVE ME A GOOD NIGHT KISS.
=smooch=
DRUNKEN MAKEOUT SESSIONS WERE COMMONPLACE BETWEEN US (HECK, WE DIDN'T NEED TO BE DRUNK!), BUT THIS TIME WAS DIFFERENT. MY HANDS KNEW WHAT TO DO...
:pek:
fiddle
OMG WE CAN'T! OMG!!!
sitcom girl fall! LOL
BUT BB, YOU'RE GAY, WHAT'S THE PROBLEM?
YOU'RE GAY, RIGHT?!
WELLLLLLL--
I WANT YOU TO FUCK ME, SINA.
I THINK WE NEED TO SEE OTHER PEOPLE.
?
UHHHH IT WAS COLLEGE AND I WAS BI BUT I DIDN'T REALLY DEAL...
GOING TO BED NIGHT!
THE NEXT MORNING... HUNGOVER AF, I TRIED RECOUNTING THE STORY TO A FRIEND.
BB, YOU FORGOT ONE PART.
YOU FORGOT THE PART WHERE YOU SAID:
STOP-- BEFORE I EAT THAT DELICIOUS PUSSY.
OFFERING TO EAT "DELICIOUS PUSSY..." I GUESS THAT PROVES I'M 100% GAY.

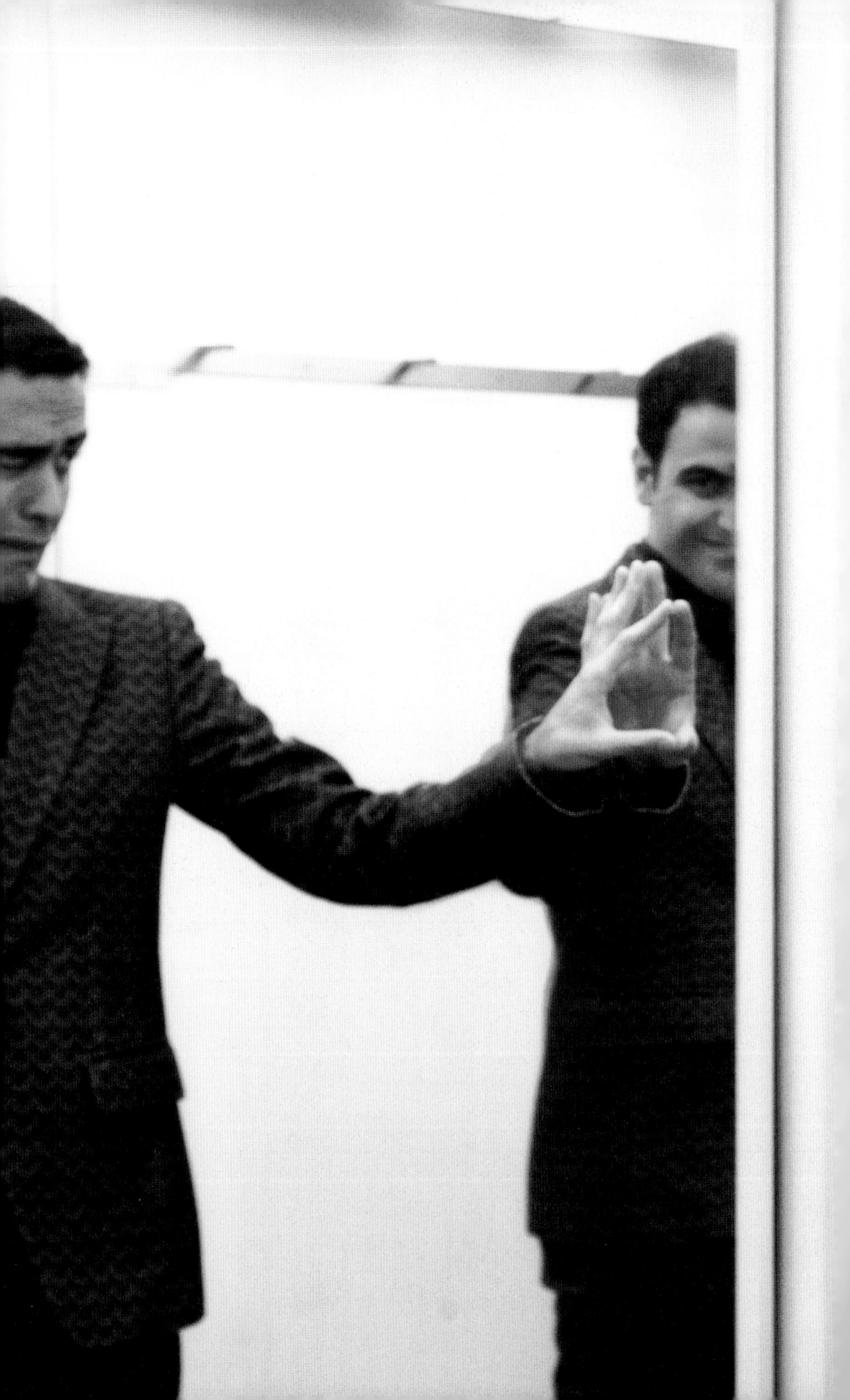

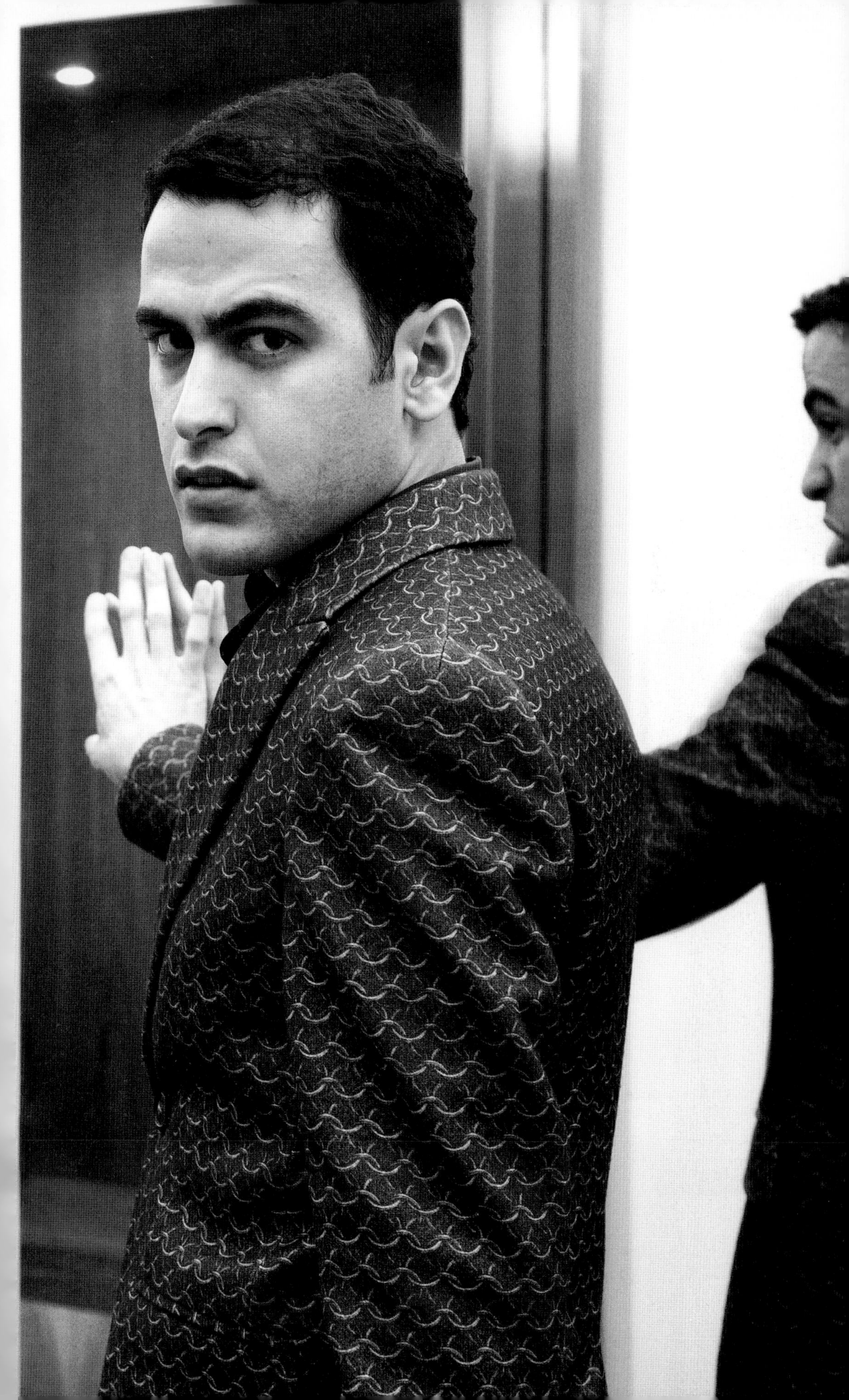

My Sarah Jessica Problem

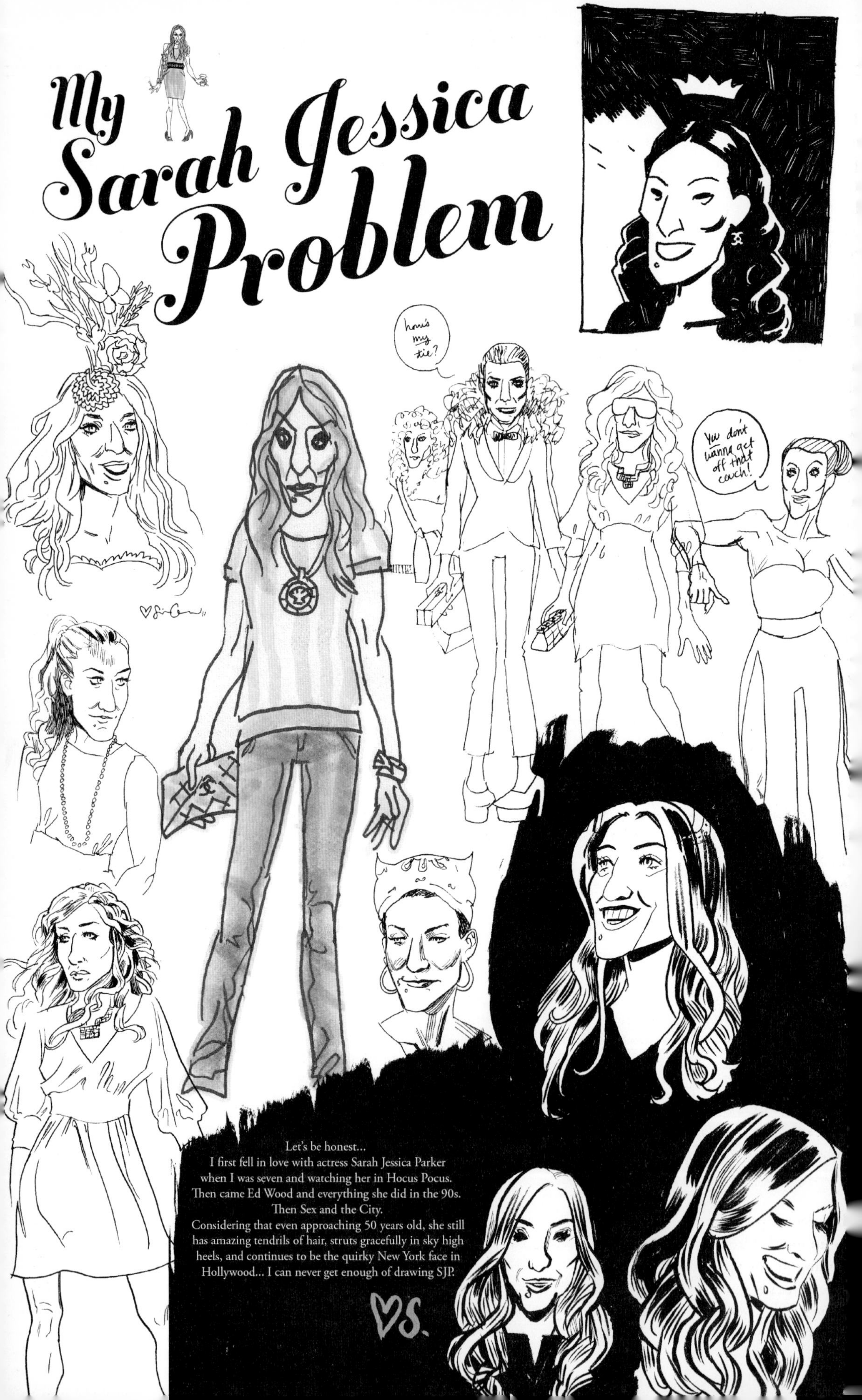

how's my tie?
You don't wanna get off that couch!

Let's be honest...
I first fell in love with actress Sarah Jessica Parker when I was seven and watching her in Hocus Pocus.
Then came Ed Wood and everything she did in the 90s.
Then Sex and the City.
Considering that even approaching 50 years old, she still has amazing tendrils of hair, struts gracefully in sky high heels, and continues to be the quirky New York face in Hollywood... I can never get enough of drawing SJP.

♡S.

That Time I Didn't Buy SJPs

just put a new comic book to bed this month. It's a one-shot called Self-Obsessed. It takes all the
tobiographical strips I've produced here and there over the past ten years, and is presented to the reader as the
urney yours truly takes to become a comic artist. It's like reading a less-funny, much younger David Sedaris
lk about boys and comic books. In combing through dozens of sketchbooks, art boards, and binders, I had to
ugh at the frantic entries revolving around my dating life when I could have taken the time to meditate on
reer choices, dreams, or doing anything more than just complaining. While I'm proud of this little confection
a book, I am also happy that I can look at the person these pages represent and happily say there's a much
lmer, smarter version of himself now.

ere's something else you need to know about me: I really dug Sex and the City. The clothes, the low-hanging
uit we call puns, the drama, and most importantly: Carrie Bradshaw. Sarah Jessica Parker made the world of
flawed and narcissistic New Yorker look charming, and believable to boot. I love Sarah Jessica Parker so much,
e even gets her own page of doodles in Self-Obsessed. For a time, I was one of millions of women and queer
en who thought that if I concentrated hard enough on writing about love, and stared hard enough out a
indow, I would be the Optimus Prime of love: a fierce warrior whose abrasive compassion saves the day. There's
value to that notion, I'm sure, but there's just as much value in seeking professional help for when you're
eating the same problems over and over and over again. The quixotic ramblings of Carrie Bradshaw still amuse
d touch me, but I recognize that in real life, accountability is not as easy as writing my version of the truth
d putting it online for everyone to read, judge, and disseminate.

ow, here's something else you need to know about Sex and the City: I may be getting the exact details of this
rong, but Carrie mentions buying a pair of shoes after finishing every article (never mind the myriad essays
ritten about how implausible it is for a Manhattanite to buy Manolo Blahniks weekly off cruddy freelance
aychecks). It's her reward for a job well done. I like that. I do stuff like that, too. There's a Missoni cardigan I
ught myself after landing a gig providing illustrations for a kids' book. When I finished my action comic,
urn the Orphanage, I went and got myself a pretty bad-ass leather jacket, man. My charitable side is exercised
gularly with monetary and "prize" donations (i.e. original art), so when I have the opportunity to be
nabashedly selfish, I take it. Carrie and I had this in common: no matter how ridiculous the ritual, we had them
d honored them. Selfishly.

ack to the events of this week. I was uploading all the files to my publisher. I had been up all night working,
d I still hadn't figured out my selfish, selfish reward. At one point, I was so exhausted and emotionally empty
at I almost convinced myself to buy a pair of the Nordstrom collaboration pair of Sarah Jessica Parker shoes
he SJP, if you will). My thinking was, "What better way to honor this part of my past than to do exactly what
rrie would do, buy a pair of shoes?" The SJPs represented the perfect way to close the book on the
lf-obsessed chapter of my life where wondering why so-and-so was an asshole and why He didn't love me were
ore important topics than, say, World News? Politics? History? I truly did think to myself, "Buying these
JPs is gonna be so ****ing poignant."

here's two problems with that line of thinking—and I'm not even going to get into the fact that I am a MAN
anting to buy a pair of women's shoes to display on my bookshelf as some kind of objet d'art. The first
oblem would be that these shoes are expensive. For several hundred dollars, I can participate in the Sarah
ssica Parker brand, which is a far more classy (read: subdued) and understated look than the oft-times
tlandish Carrie Bradshaw styles. These are not the Alexander McQueen armadillo shoes, my friends. I'm
pfront about how I will gladly throw down a month's rent on a statement coat, but that's only if it is truly
markable and/or made of gold. The range of prices on the SJPs go from $195 to $495, and you can imagine
here the more noteworthy pieces lie on that scale. You can also imagine that I wouldn't settle for an espadrille
ith some grosgrain sewn on it, either.

he second problem with wanting to reward myself with a pair of shoes is that—if you really think about
—an exorbitant purchase actually goes against everything that should be good about finishing Self-Obsessed.
ooking at the stories I wanted to tell, and the person I was from my late teens through my early 20s, I feel a
nse of pride knowing that the comic book representation of "Sina" was the best version of himself he could
, but I also saw some aspects of myself I was happy to put to bed. It's cool to have wanderlust, it's cool to
ake fun of your parents in a comic book... for a time. I have been able to move past a lot of the issues that

plagued me for years, and I find I've been happier and more productive without them. I'm not the kind of persc who could make a frivolous purchase anymore. Credit debt is not chic. After ten years, I should be able to fe rewarded by the work I've done, and the growth shown in the pages. Wasting money on a collector's item wou be a pretty disappointing way to end Self-Obsessed.

While coming to this conclusion totally happened on my own (big props!), I have to credit my friend Sydney fi the words I'm typing now. As I was joking with her about the big if of buying a pair of "Bobbie" sandals in mir (my favorite color), I mused that I would just draw the shoe and call it a day. This whole time, I knew n defenses were weak and I just wanted to buy something for the sake of buying something. When Sydne encouraged me doing the drawing, the real reward presented itself: More. Work!

> **"I have been able to move past a lot of the issues that plagued me for years, and I find I've been happier and more productive without them."**

That's all life is, right? We work, we sleep, we work some more, all in the hopes that we'll get better at it, so can be easier the next day. The glib conversation with Sydney was more potent than the rush of frivolous spending $300 on a pair of shoes, and I was able to re-focus my energies, and treat myself to a coffee while doodled shoes. Yes, I sat in a cafe and drew women's shoes, which turned out to be more like a pleasant diversic than something you'd imagine a creeper doing. After the stress of a deadline, I was able to enjoy my work agai and felt more energized for the next chapter than I would have been after an expensive walk to Nordstrom. I' utterly aware that these sentiments may not put an end to consumerism, or motivate thousands of individua to take charge and be more creative…but they did save me $294.50 (coffee is expensive in Los Angeles, and I lik to tip).

Sina Gra

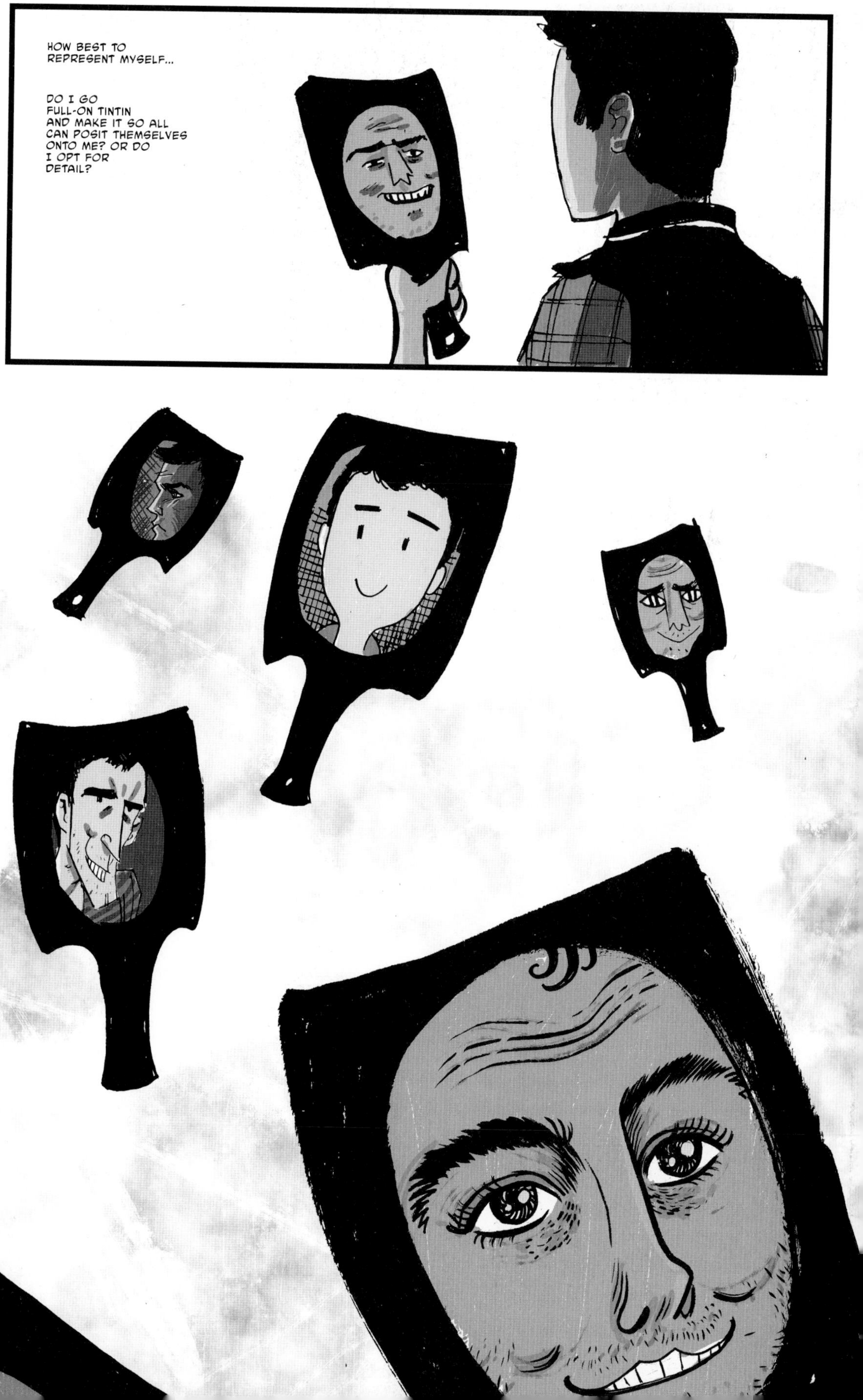
HOW BEST TO REPRESENT MYSELF...
DO I GO FULL-ON TINTIN AND MAKE IT SO ALL CAN POSIT THEMSELVES ONTO ME? OR DO I OPT FOR DETAIL?

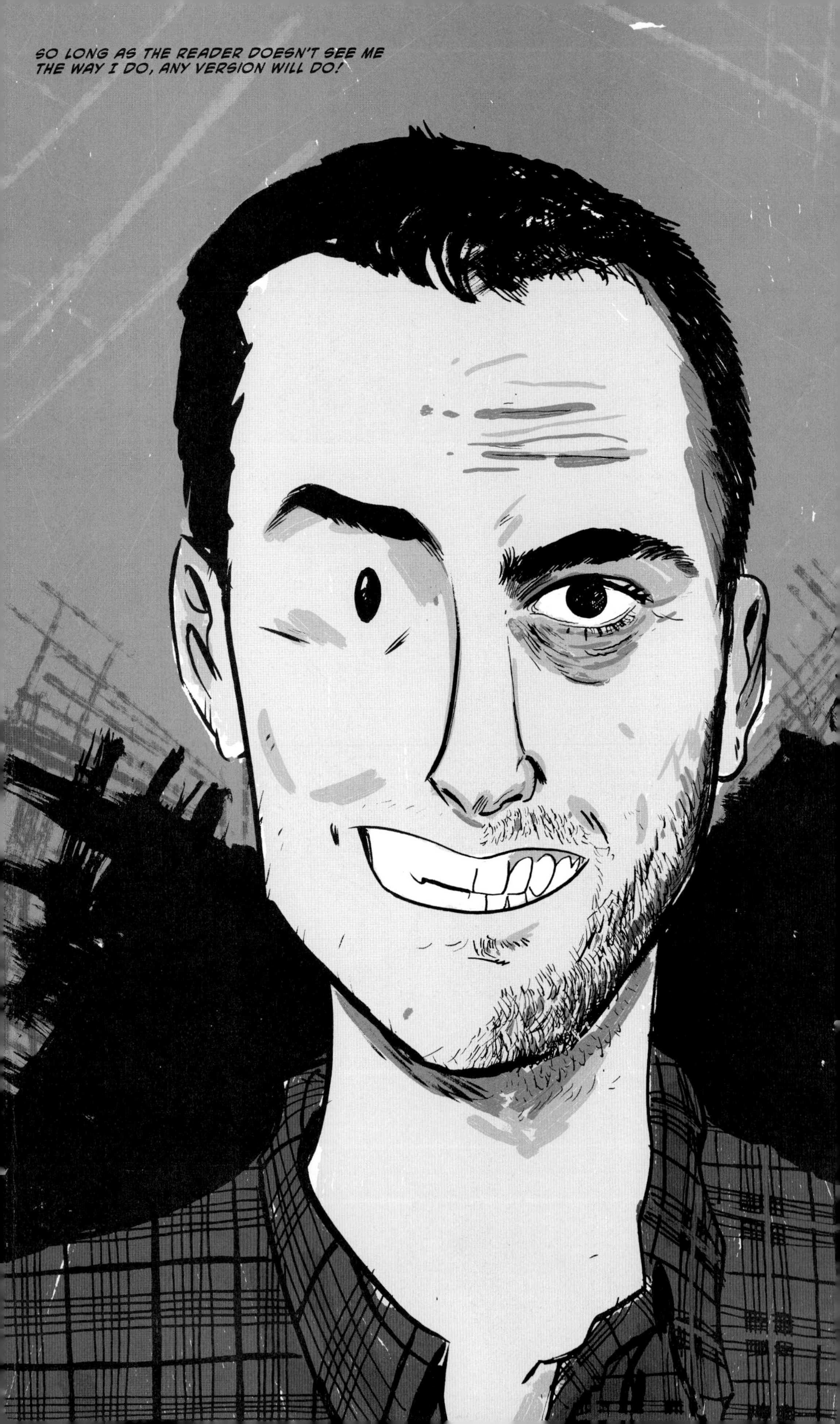
SO LONG AS THE READER DOESN'T SEE ME THE WAY I DO, ANY VERSION WILL DO!

WHEN I DECIDED I NEEDED TO MOVE ON FROM EDITING COMIC BOOKS TO PURSUE THE MORE FULFILLING PROSPECT OF WRITING AND DRAWING MY OWN COMICS, MY FRIEND AMBER SAID THIS TO ME:

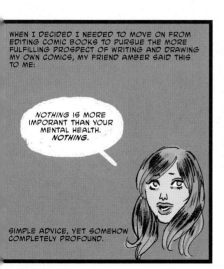

NOTHING IS MORE IMPORANT THAN YOUR MENTAL HEALTH. NOTHING.

SIMPLE ADVICE, YET SOMEHOW COMPLETELY PROFOUND.

WHEN THINGS WERE STARTING TO GET ROUGH FOR ME LAST YEAR, I TURNED TO AMBER AGAIN. A LOT OF BAD NEWS WAS HITTING ME ALL AT ONCE, INCLUDING THE CANCELLATION OF MY COMIC BOOK, *BURN THE ORPHANAGE.*

WE MET BY ECHO PARK LAKE TO ABSORB SOME FRESH AIR...

OH, SJP-- WHAT WOULD YOU DO IF YOU WERE IN MY SHOES?

"I'M SORRY, SINA! IM JUST YOUR TYPICAL OHIO GIRL WITH A PENCHANT FOR FASHION-FORWARD SHOES WITH A SENSIBLE HEEL. I CAN'T RELATE."

SO KIND, SO USELESS. *SIGH*

LUCKILY AMBER'S ADVICE WAS A LITTLE MORE USEFUL. SHE TOLD ME TO CLEAR MY HEAD, AND FIND MY HAPPY PLACE... THAT MY BEST WORK COMES FROM THAT ELUSIVE SPOT.

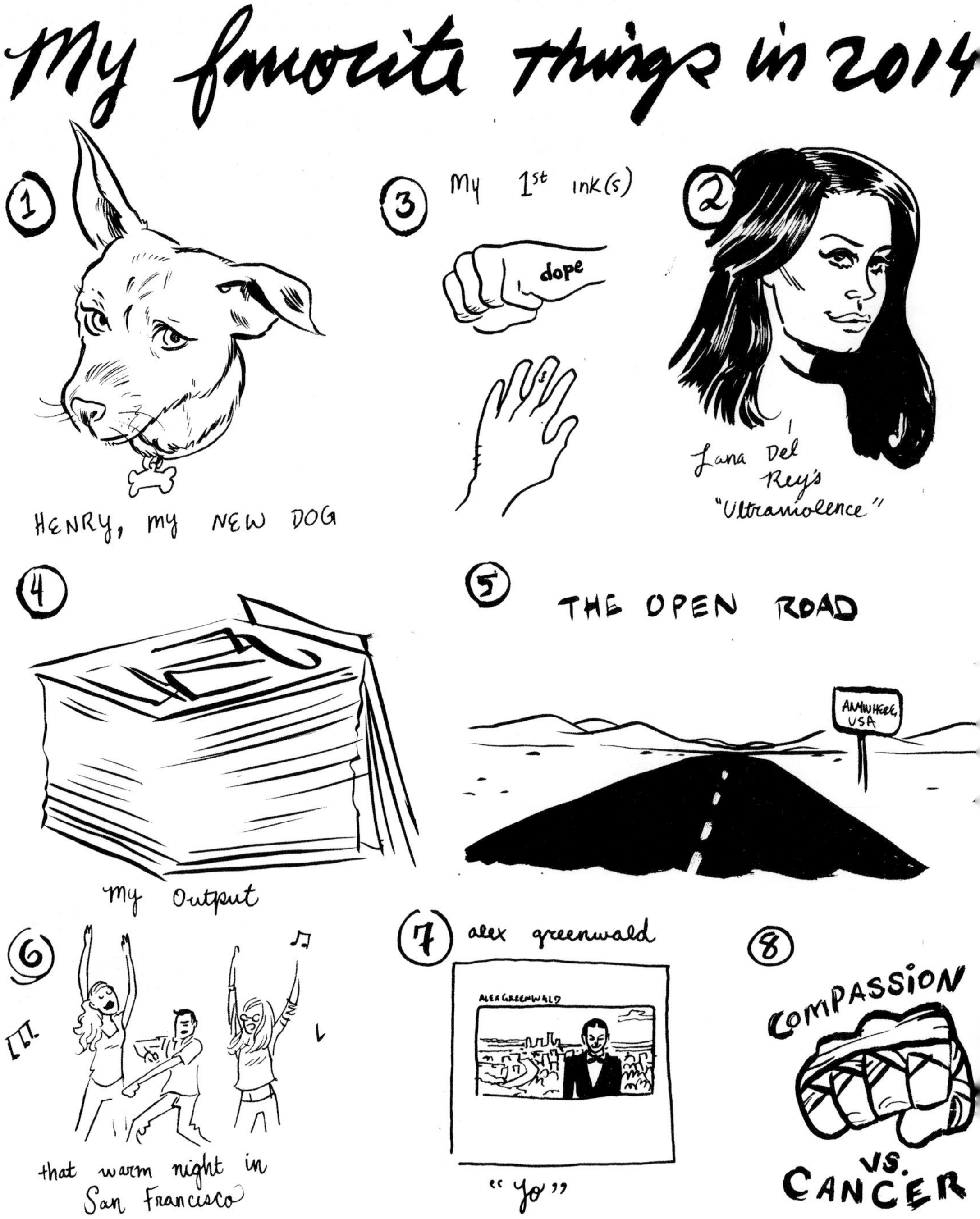
My favorite things in 2014
1
HENRY, MY NEW DOG
3
My 1st ink(s)
dope
2
Lana Del Rey's "Ultraviolence"
4
My Output
5
THE OPEN ROAD
ANYWHERE, USA
6
that warm night in San Francisco
7
alex greenwald
ALEX GREENWALD
"Yo"
8
COMPASSION VS. CANCER

NOTE: THIS LIST WAS SUPPOSED TO GO UP TO 14, BUT I COULDN'T THINK OF ANY OTHER HIGHLIGHTS IN THE YEAR.

بابا اب داد

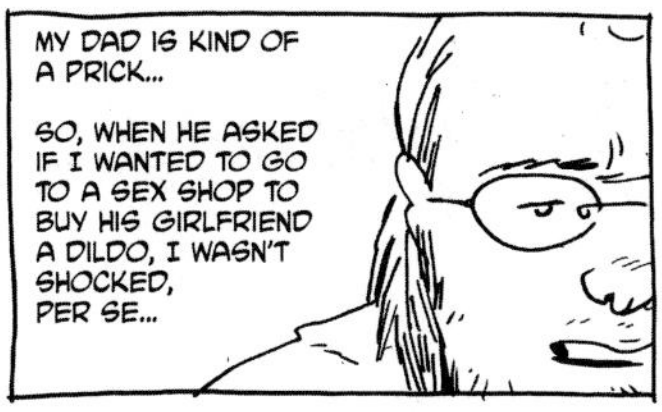
MY DAD IS KIND OF A PRICK...
SO, WHEN HE ASKED IF I WANTED TO GO TO A SEX SHOP TO BUY HIS GIRLFRIEND A DILDO, I WASN'T SHOCKED, PER SE...

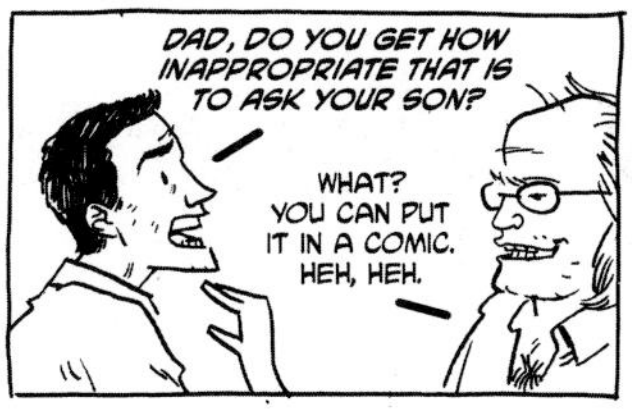
DAD, DO YOU GET HOW INAPPROPRIATE THAT IS TO ASK YOUR SON?
WHAT? YOU CAN PUT IT IN A COMIC. HEH, HEH.

WELL, OKAY.

YOU WANT ME TO PUT YOUR STORIES IN MY COMICS, PAPA?

LET'S START WITH WHAT I CAN REMEMBER FROM MY CHILDHOOD...

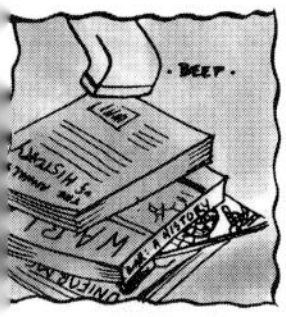
BEEP.

I REMEMBER HIDING A COMIC THAT I ACTUALLY WANTED IN A PILE OF BOOKS YOU WANTED ME TO HAVE, SO THAT WAY YOU COULDN'T TOSS IT AT THE REGISTER.

I REMEMBER YOU ALWAYS TAKING US TO GET YOURSELF THAI FOOD.

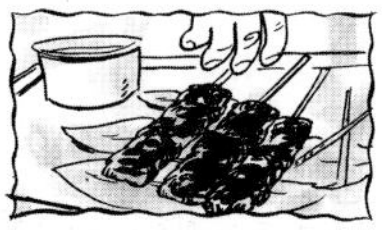

I REMEMBER WHEN YOU SLAPPED YOUR CIGARETTE OUT OF MY MOUTH AFTER A TRIP TO TOYS 'R' US.

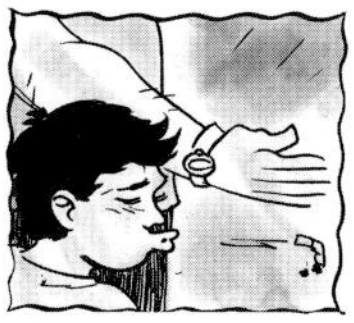

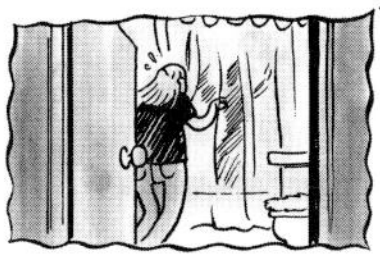

I REMEMBER WHEN YOU TRIED TO DO MOM THROUGH THE SHOWER CURTAIN AFTER YOU TWO HAD DIVORCED.

THANKS FOR THE MEMORIES, DAD. WE CAN ADD THIS PRICK TO THE LIST!

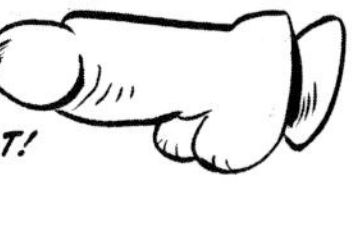

STAR WARS

as a metaphor for relationships

BY SINA GRACE
(idea came from the lovely Kevin Sonnichsen)

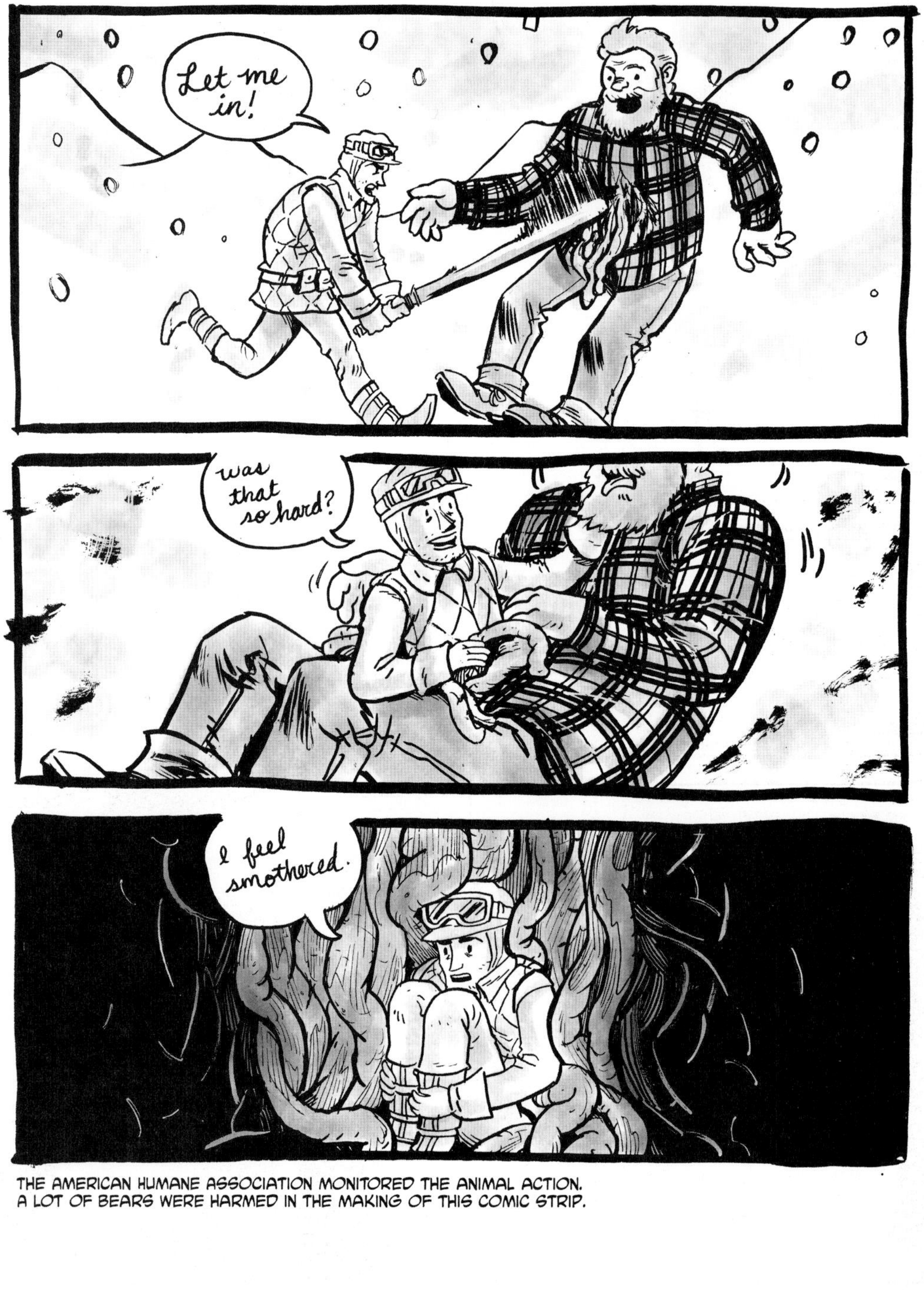

Let me in!
was that so hard?
I feel smothered.

THE AMERICAN HUMANE ASSOCIATION MONITORED THE ANIMAL ACTION.
A LOT OF BEARS WERE HARMED IN THE MAKING OF THIS COMIC STRIP.

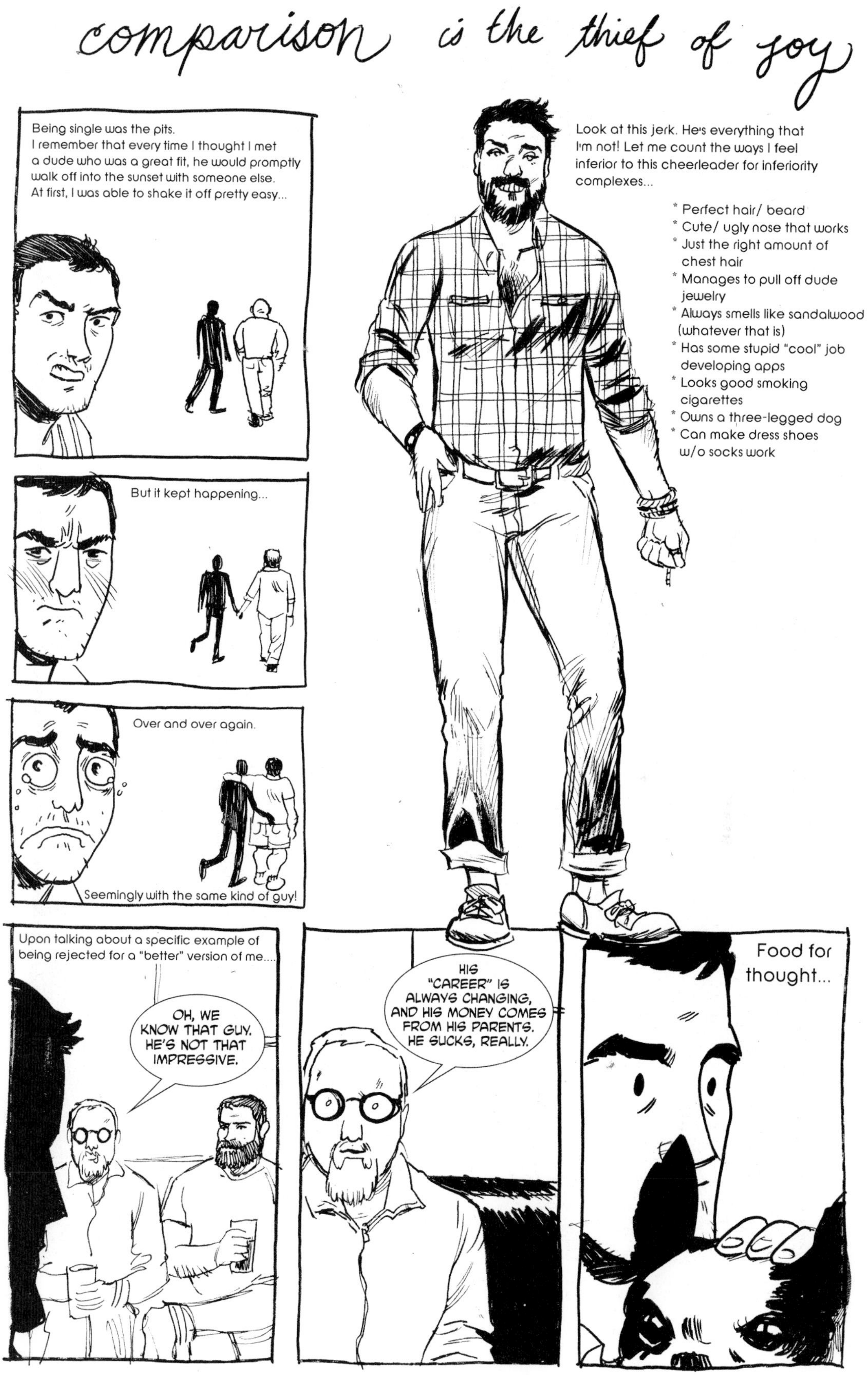
comparison is the thief of joy
Being single was the pits.
I remember that every time I thought I met a dude who was a great fit, he would promptly walk off into the sunset with someone else.
At first, I was able to shake it off pretty easy...
Look at this jerk. He's everything that I'm not! Let me count the ways I feel inferior to this cheerleader for inferiority complexes...
* Perfect hair/ beard
* Cute/ ugly nose that works
* Just the right amount of chest hair
* Manages to pull off dude jewelry
* Always smells like sandalwood (whatever that is)
* Has some stupid "cool" job developing apps
* Looks good smoking cigarettes
* Owns a three-legged dog
* Can make dress shoes w/o socks work
But it kept happening...
Over and over again.
Seemingly with the same kind of guy!
Upon talking about a specific example of being rejected for a "better" version of me....
OH, WE KNOW THAT GUY. HE'S NOT THAT IMPRESSIVE.
HIS "CAREER" IS ALWAYS CHANGING, AND HIS MONEY COMES FROM HIS PARENTS. HE SUCKS, REALLY.
Food for thought...

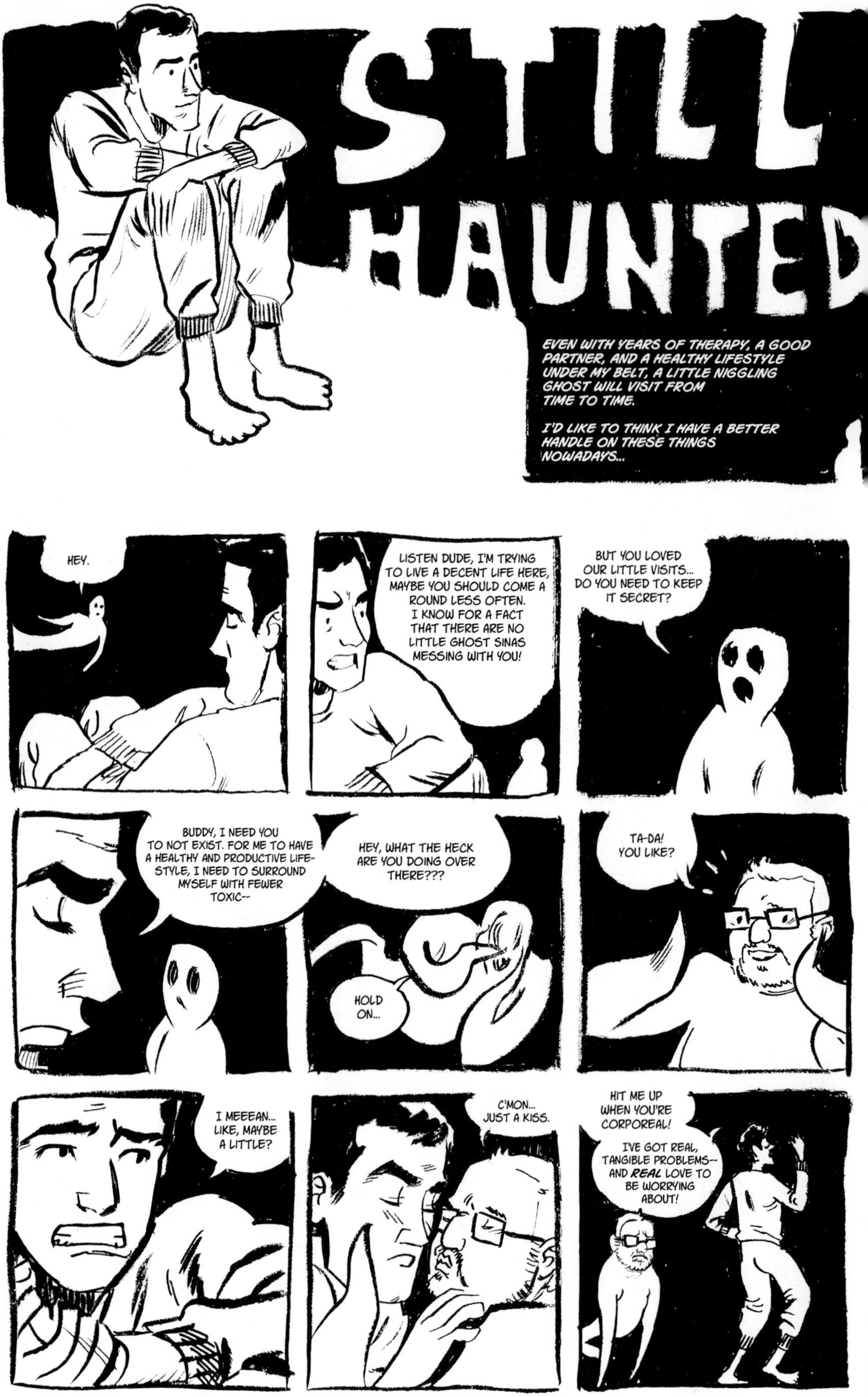
STILL HAUNTED
EVEN WITH YEARS OF THERAPY, A GOOD PARTNER, AND A HEALTHY LIFESTYLE UNDER MY BELT, A LITTLE NIGGLING GHOST WILL VISIT FROM TIME TO TIME.
I'D LIKE TO THINK I HAVE A BETTER HANDLE ON THESE THINGS NOWADAYS...
HEY.
LISTEN DUDE, I'M TRYING TO LIVE A DECENT LIFE HERE, MAYBE YOU SHOULD COME A ROUND LESS OFTEN. I KNOW FOR A FACT THAT THERE ARE NO LITTLE GHOST SINAS MESSING WITH YOU!
BUT YOU LOVED OUR LITTLE VISITS... DO YOU NEED TO KEEP IT SECRET?
BUDDY, I NEED YOU TO NOT EXIST. FOR ME TO HAVE A HEALTHY AND PRODUCTIVE LIFE-STYLE, I NEED TO SURROUND MYSELF WITH FEWER TOXIC--
HEY, WHAT THE HECK ARE YOU DOING OVER THERE???
HOLD ON...
TA-DA! YOU LIKE?
I MEEEAN... LIKE, MAYBE A LITTLE?
C'MON... JUST A KISS.
HIT ME UP WHEN YOU'RE CORPOREAL!
I'VE GOT REAL, TANGIBLE PROBLEMS-- AND REAL LOVE TO BE WORRYING ABOUT!

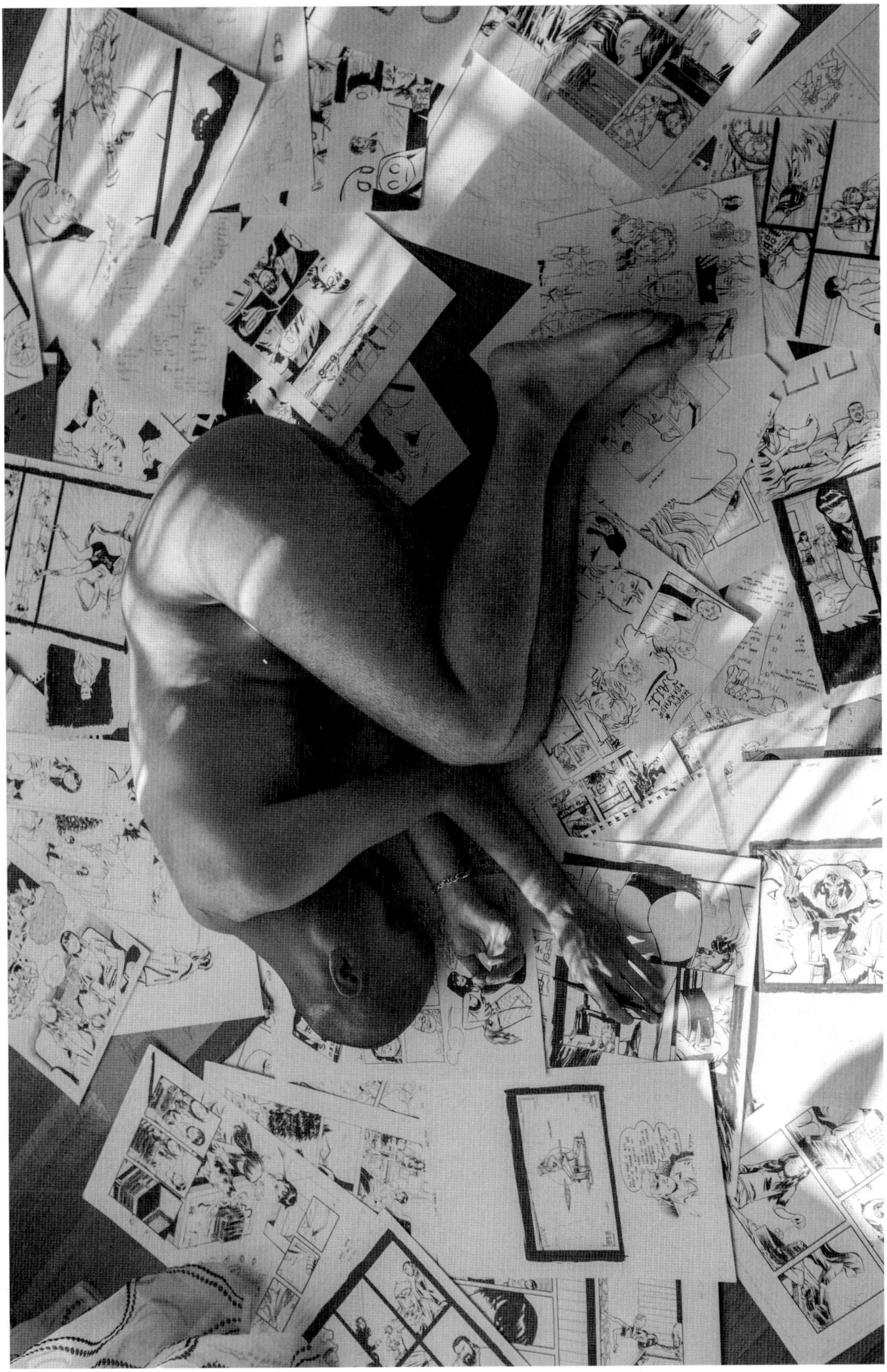

Shokat Jamehborzorg- or "Maman Shokat" as she went by
more regularly- helped raise me and my sister through all of
grade school, and kept my mother company in the years we
both left the nest to pursue the adventures of college and
adulthood. She was tiny and round, and had a wonderfully
loud laugh. My sister and I would call her a Furby when she
got into her little fits of laughter, chatter, and prayer. She
was humble, giving, worldly, and tired. I never thought it
was a privilege to know her until she was gone.
The qualities I can instantly recall about her are as follows:
- She loved French Fries
- She thought Ross was the funniest Friend
- Golden Girls was her favorite, and she called them "The
Roommates"
- She was excellent at Tarafing (look it up)
- Anything that was hers, was ours
I didn't get to properly say good-bye to her. Fluid was build-
ing up around her heart through the year, and every time
she had a close call, she came right back to her home in
Iran... a little weaker but still alive. She had been let out of
the hospital the week before she died, with plans made to
have full-time help watching her, preserving her. I thought I
had time to give her a legitimate phone call, and not a quick,
vacant greeting. I didn't get that chance. She passed away
last Sunday, in the middle of the night.
And now she's not here. I miss her soft hands. She had
short, thin hair that never succumbed to any styling beyond
the Ramona Quimby bob (sans the blunt bangs). I can still
see her glassy eyes, getting cloudier and cloudier every
visit.

Be kind to your elders. Ask them a question that is real, and
listen when they answer.
Eating a french fry in grandma's honor,
Sina

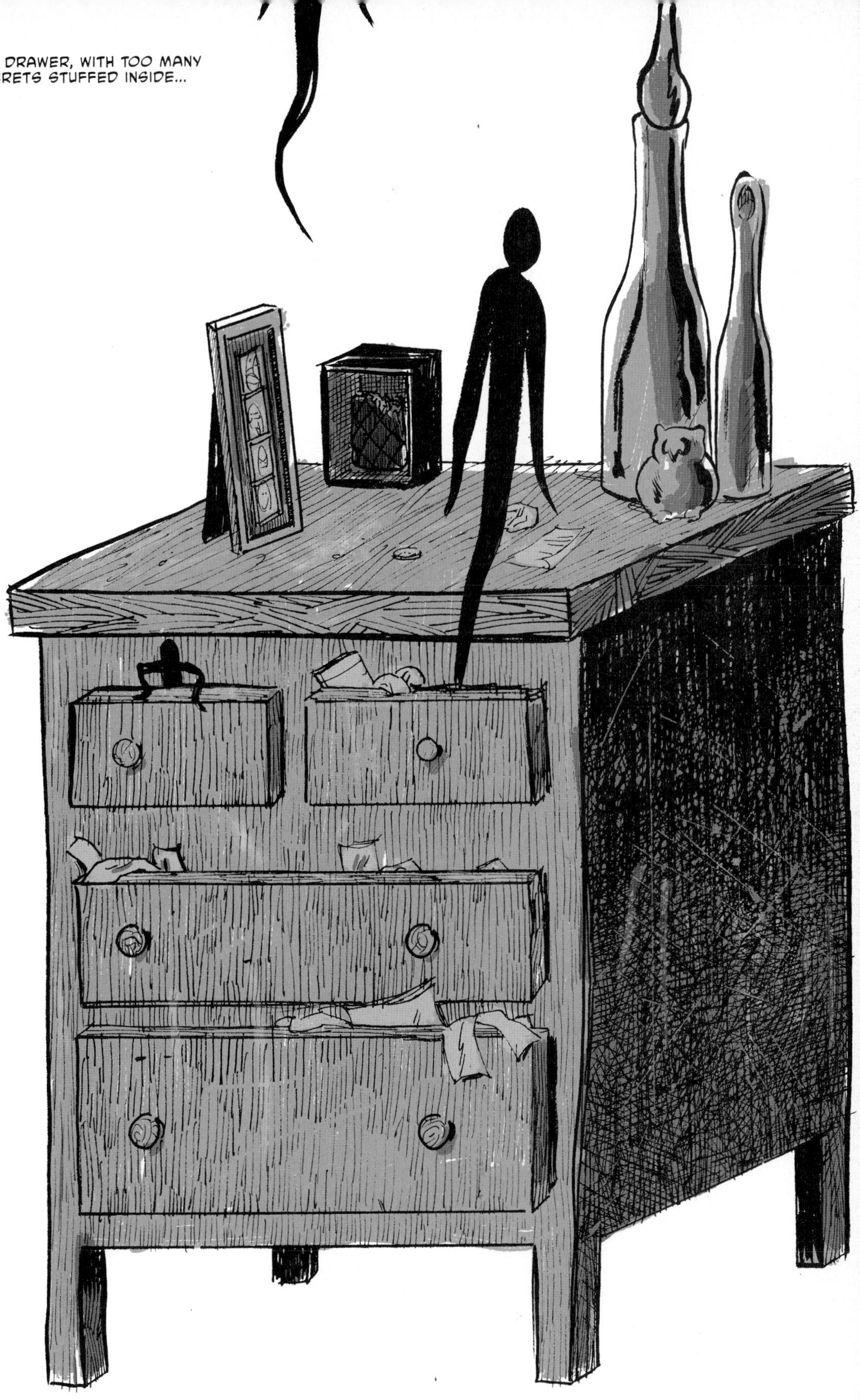
THE DRAWER, WITH TOO MANY SECRETS STUFFED INSIDE...

A Tale of Two Sinas

illustrations by Jason Fischer

Picture It: San Diego Comic-Con, circa 2006. A young Sina Grace runs into a longtime friend, only to be introduced to a smiling bohemian brit named... SINA. At first, I felt like I had lost a significant part of my identity: being the only gay comic artist named Sina. How was there another person who could claim to have the same journey and struggle that I thought was unique to me?

Pretty self-involved thinking. It's now many years later, with a fake feud and true kinship under our collective "Sina" belt, I'm honored to know another Sina out there who gets it.

Sina Grace: Readers at this point know enough about me... but what they DON'T know is about my doppelganger across the pond- Sina Sparrow! In a sentence or two, how would you describe yourself and your work?

Sina Sparrow: Hi! I would describe myself as a queer, British comics artist/ writer of Iranian descent who does weird gay comics and illustrations. My work is mainly about my life and my feeeeeelings, sex, identity, sex, emotions, relationships, sex... People say my work is kind of dirty and that always surprises me but I don't really always think of it like that I just write and draw about what I'm interested in.

SG: Tell me what it was like for you to grow up with our name in the UK. Over here, I was about 10 years old when Xena was a major pop culture phenomenon, so I went through a lot of grade school trying to overcome the "Warrior Princess" moniker. Of course now I'd love to own that title, but I didn't have that a proper sense of courage and pride back then.

SS: Growing up with the name Sina was hard over here too. "I'm a few years older than you," as Stevie Nicks once said, so Xena didn't hit till I was in my late teens or early twenties, but just generally when I was younger till about the age of 17 or 18 I was teased for having - quote, unquote - a "girl's name." It was actually just part of a broader background of being bullied for being seen as not masculine enough, gay, and also a foreigner. I wonder if you had similar problems in primary or secondary school... I mean, not just about your name, but in terms of both being seen as an outsider because of your heritage and maybe cause of the gay stuff too?

As a side note, queer cartoonist Nick Leon first made me aware of Xena and sent me adjusted postcard of her that said "Sina, War Princess" when she first appeared in the Sta so I always liked her 'cause of that... But t said, it is vaguely irritating when you m someone for the first time and that's the f thing they say. Cmon, popular culture has mo on ;-)

What kind of reactions do you get to talk gayness, sex or relationships in your work? you ever do erotic art and if and when you ha what has the reaction been?

> **"People say my work is kind of dirty and that always surprises me...I just write and draw about what I'm interested in."**
> **Sina Sparrow**

SG: It seems like we took the school shaming a went two different directions with it! I feel lik may have closed-up once I realized the thi that made me unique also made me an outsi All my drawings from grade school seem to be shit that people would think is cool (South P and Batman etc). I drew for other kids' approv it seems. It's been hard to shake the anticipat of reaction when I work. To answer yo question in a roundabout fashion: I've been n only with support when I do more queer-then work. I have a tendency to assume that no o wants me to be myself, like I have to trick reader towards subversion. One of these days do more erotic work, but I've never be compelled to make my gaze more sexual. Also feel like whatever I do would be so pedestrian a just come off as sexist or something.

This book is sort of my first attempt at sayi "Y'know what, fuck what anyone thinks. I've g a good head and a heart and I'm gonna tell yo brilliant story." If I end up sucking, at least have proof of it, rather than hypotheticals.

Nice Stevie quote... tell me a bit about yo relationship with art and music. I feel like I constantly trying to bridge the two because don't have the skill to ever be a musician myse

: I'm sure I did a little bit of that drawing to please e other kids too. But more than that I think drawing d comics were my escape from the bullying (along ith music) and when I discovered zines and ternative comics it was a way of finding a voice and ing drawing to express myself and say what I really anted to say. Like you I think when I am honest and en in my comics the response has been erwhelmingly positive. I guess I do sometimes worry out how the sexual aspects of my work are taken t they do seem to overall be taken well and it courages me to keep being open and honest!

rt and music - I DJ at a club night in London and I the artwork for it, as well as doing comics, so yeah I ess my main creative outlets are related to these and ey were both ways of expressing myself when I was kid. Or... I mean it's kind of different because I don't ake music myself, it I do DJ which is sort of more e curating and choosing songs that express a certain eling together.

I wish I had better words to describe the relationship between music and comics, because there is a link there. Both forms of media allow consumers to feel bonded to the artist in a way... There's a culture that comes with being a fan, y'know? From the production standpoint, I think comic artists and musicians have the same goal: to use their medium to make listeners/ readers feel something palpable. Of course I'm looking at this from a storyteller perspective and not the corporate "how do we make millions" mentality... But I don't know I feel like there's a lot of creative agency in both: you have a handful of tools and a handful of people working with you- and there doesn't need to be a larger production, just a group of creatives trying to entertain.

I know that for me, I've turned the focus on "what's entertaining for me?" While making Self-Obsessed.

Sina Grace

Sina Sparrow

ut yeah when I discovered indie music when I was bout 16 it coincided with coming out and with tarting to do more personal gay-themed comics so hey are quite strongly-linked in my mind, and I oticed a lot of people in bands seem to be into comics r have links with comics artists. How do you feel the onnection works for you? And tell me a bit more bout your new book?

G: Oh, music, music, music!

I'm only considering the reader in that I hope they don't feel ripped off by the material or that my point is getting across. I'm no longer making a point FOR them.

Last question: how do you think you'd be different if you had a more traditional name? I always wonder if I would be more subdued if I was Kevin from Santa Monica! Maybe I'd feel like I don't have to defend myself or anticipate being called "exotic" upon meeting people..

SS: I think pleasing yourself and thinking about what's entertaining or meaningful or exciting for you is the best way to make comics and not censor yourself. Obviously you still want the work to communicate and be clear (unless you're deliberately trying to confuse people) but I think focusing on "what's entertaining for me" or "what kind of comic would *I* want to read?" is the best route to making good, individual, original comics.

“I know that for me, I've turned the focus on "what's entertaining for me?" While making Self-Obsessed.”

Sina Grace

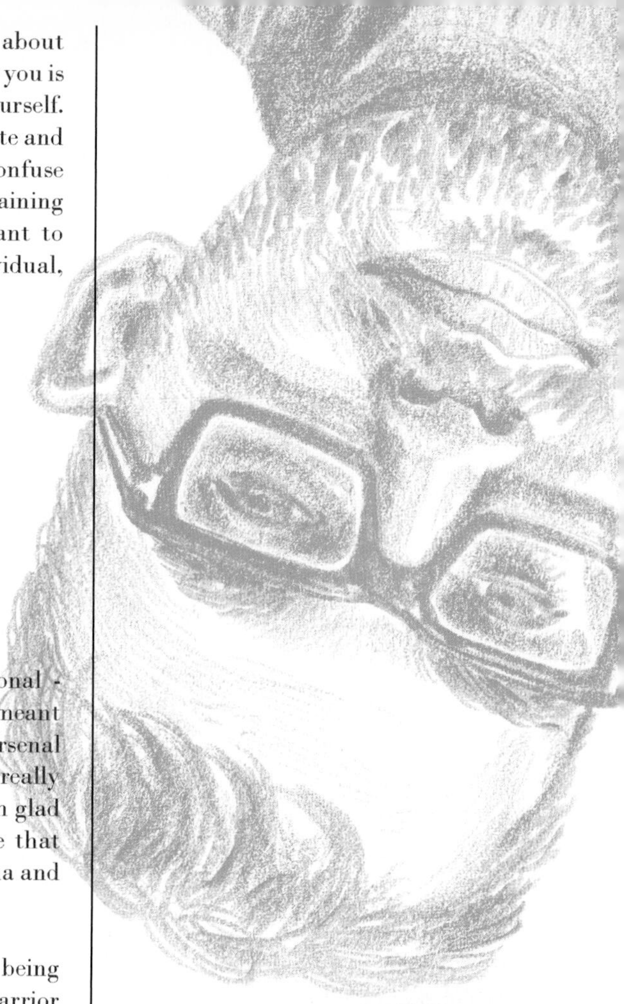

Yeah I definitely think having a more traditional - that is, a more Western first name - would have meant that there wasn't yet another weapon in the arsenal with which to attack a faggy brown boy. But I really like our name! NOW - I'm glad I have it and I'm glad we both have it! It sort of feels magical to me that there's another gay Iranian cartoonist named Sina and I know him :-)

SG: I agree wholeheartedly! Thank you, Sina, for being a friend and an inspiration. You make a warrior princess proud of his namesake.

For more information about Sina Sparrow's work, please visit www.boycazyboy.com

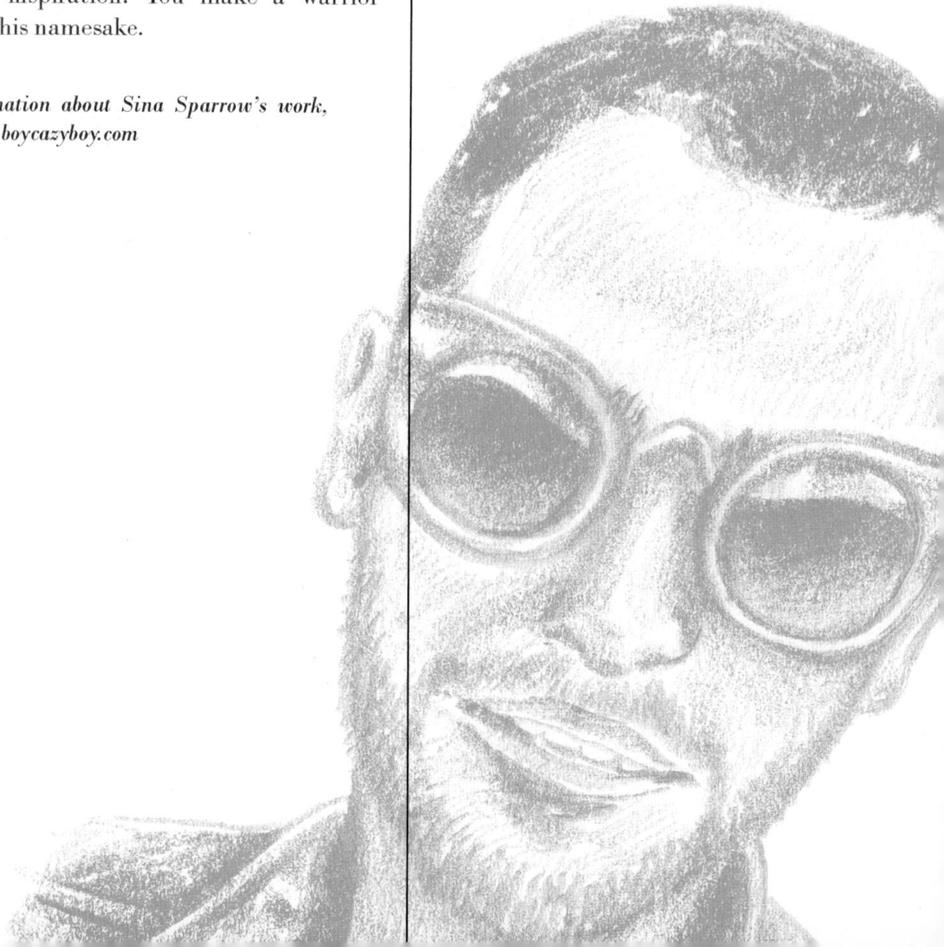

"I'd rather be poor and happy than Rich & Alone."

Lady Gaga
"Dope"

I CAN'T BE THE ONLY ONE WITH TINKERBELL COMPLEX.

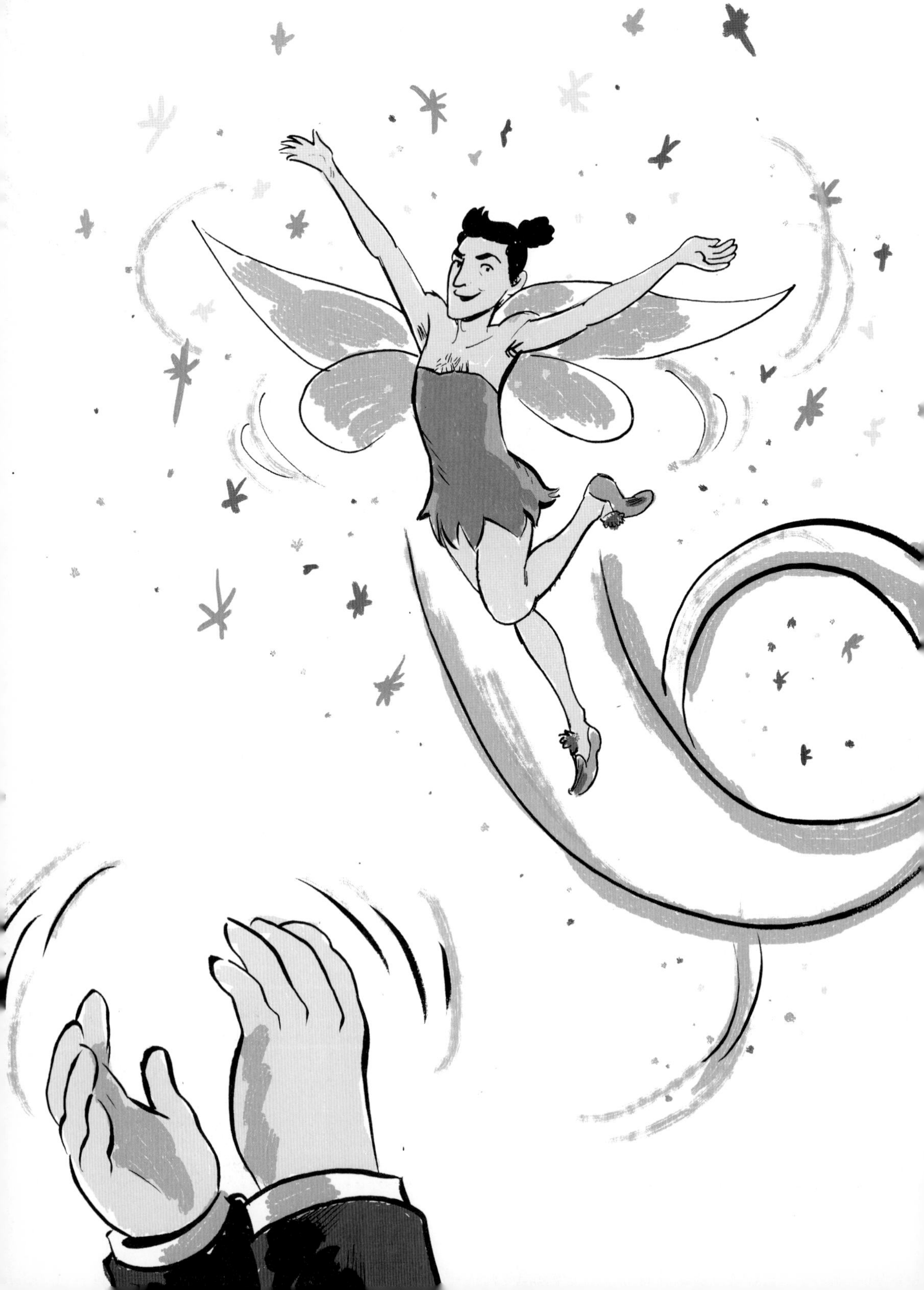

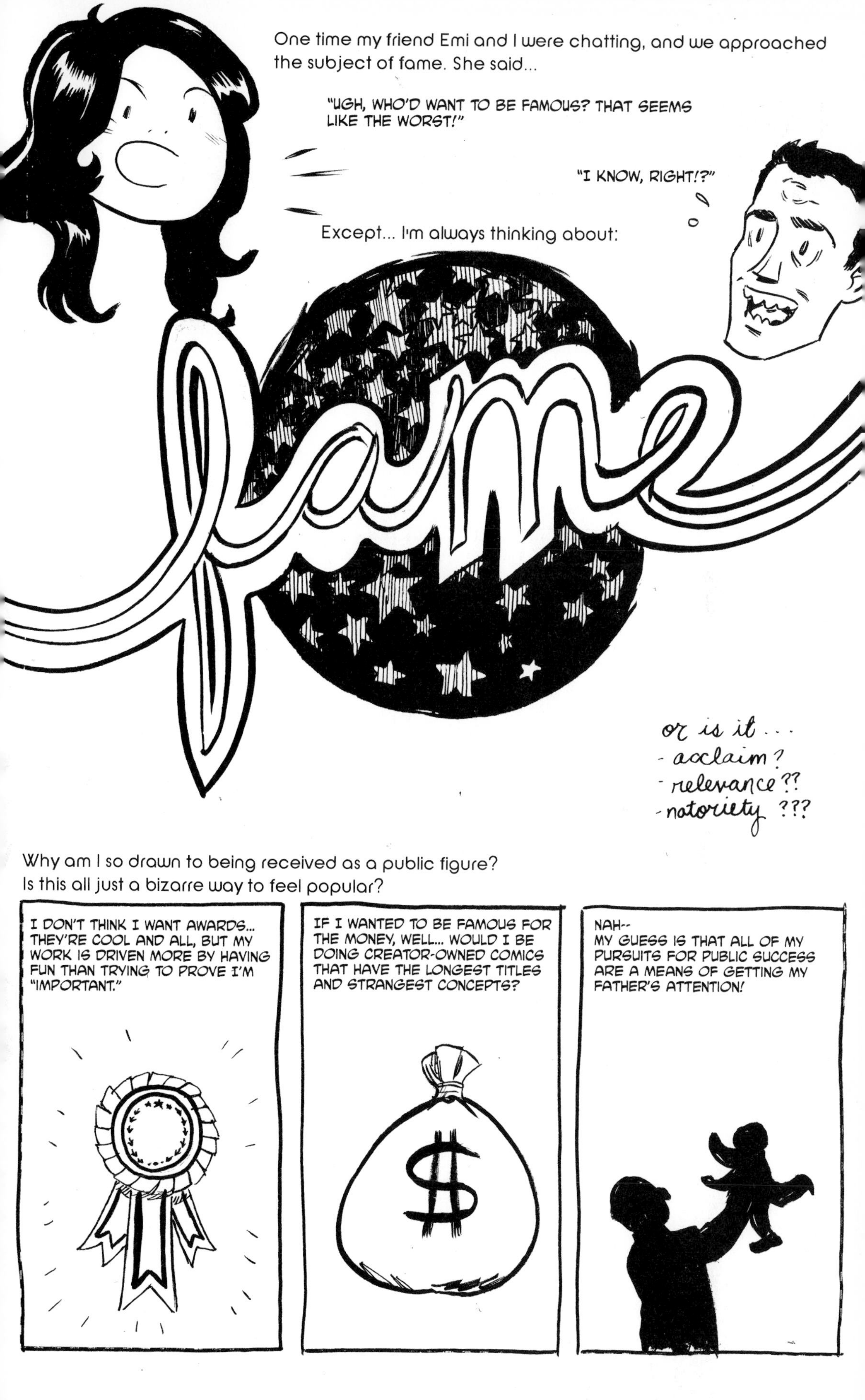
One time my friend Emi and I were chatting, and we approached the subject of fame. She said...
"UGH, WHO'D WANT TO BE FAMOUS? THAT SEEMS LIKE THE WORST!"
"I KNOW, RIGHT!?"
Except... I'm always thinking about:
fame
or is it...
- acclaim?
- relevance??
- notoriety???
Why am I so drawn to being received as a public figure?
Is this all just a bizarre way to feel popular?
I DON'T THINK I WANT AWARDS... THEY'RE COOL AND ALL, BUT MY WORK IS DRIVEN MORE BY HAVING FUN THAN TRYING TO PROVE I'M "IMPORTANT."
IF I WANTED TO BE FAMOUS FOR THE MONEY, WELL... WOULD I BE DOING CREATOR-OWNED COMICS THAT HAVE THE LONGEST TITLES AND STRANGEST CONCEPTS?
$
NAH--
MY GUESS IS THAT ALL OF MY PURSUITS FOR PUBLIC SUCCESS ARE A MEANS OF GETTING MY FATHER'S ATTENTION!

I SAW AN ACTOR FRIEND OF MINE LEAVE A COMIC-CON PARTY...

I WAS AMAZED (BUT NOT?) BY THE LENGTHS PEOPLE WENT TO FOR WHAT SEEMED LIKE AN UNSATISFACTORY SELFIE.

I BET THAT'S WHY CELEBRITIES CRAVE THE VIP SECTIONS... TO BE PROTECTED IN A SMALL BOX.

THE "PERKS" OF FAME SEEM TO BE ACCESS TO SMALLER AND SMALLER BOXES. DRESS THEM UP, CALL THEM "CHIC," BUT THEY'RE STILL BOXES.

WHY IS A BOX MY IDEA OF PARADISE?

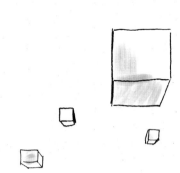

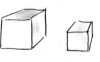

WHY IS IT ANYBODY'S?

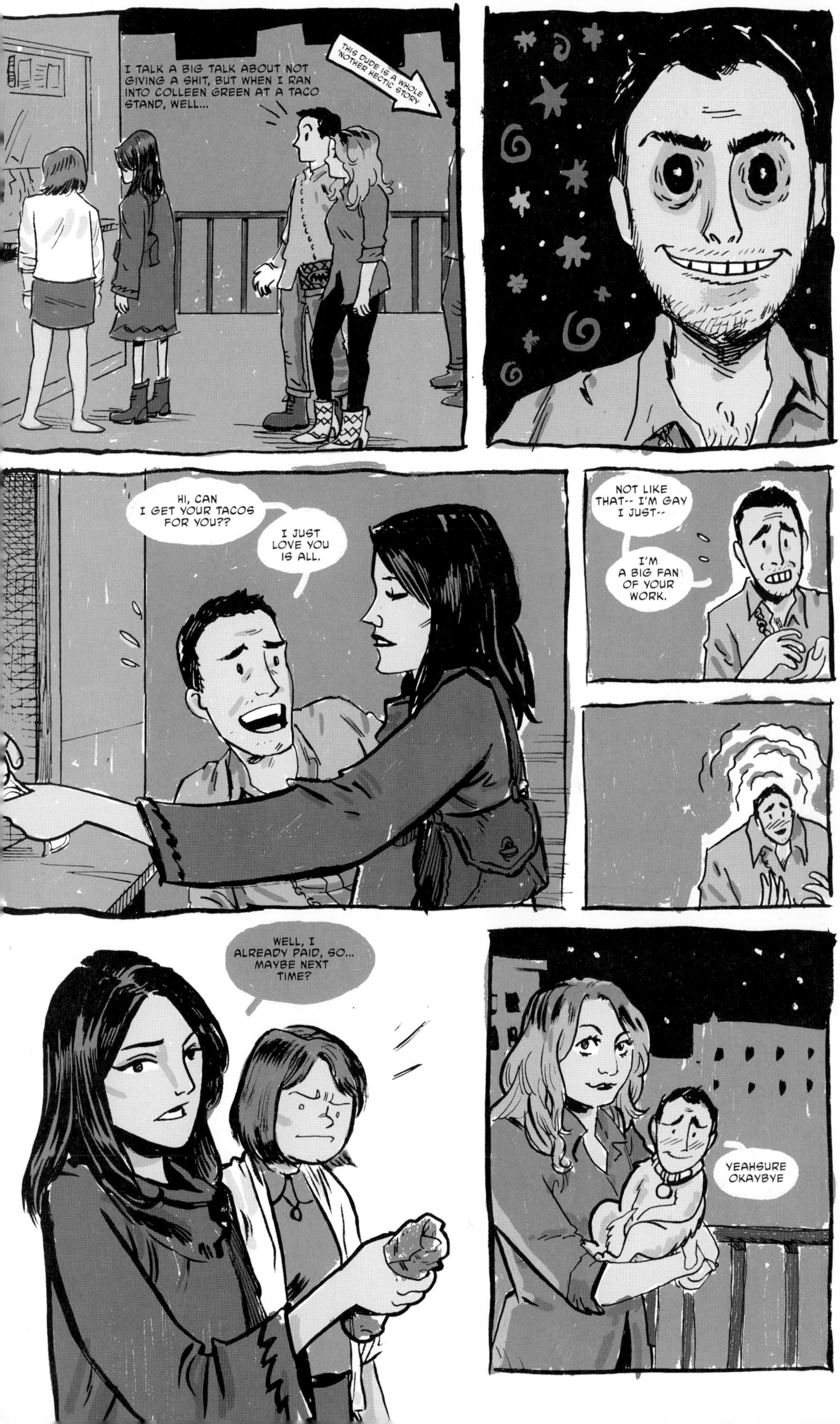

I TALK A BIG TALK ABOUT NOT GIVING A SHIT, BUT WHEN I RAN INTO COLLEEN GREEN AT A TACO STAND, WELL...
THIS DUDE IS A WHOLE 'NOTHER HECTIC STORY
HI, CAN I GET YOUR TACOS FOR YOU??
I JUST LOVE YOU IS ALL.
NOT LIKE THAT-- I'M GAY I JUST--
I'M A BIG FAN OF YOUR WORK.
WELL, I ALREADY PAID, SO... MAYBE NEXT TIME?
YEAHSURE OKAYBYE

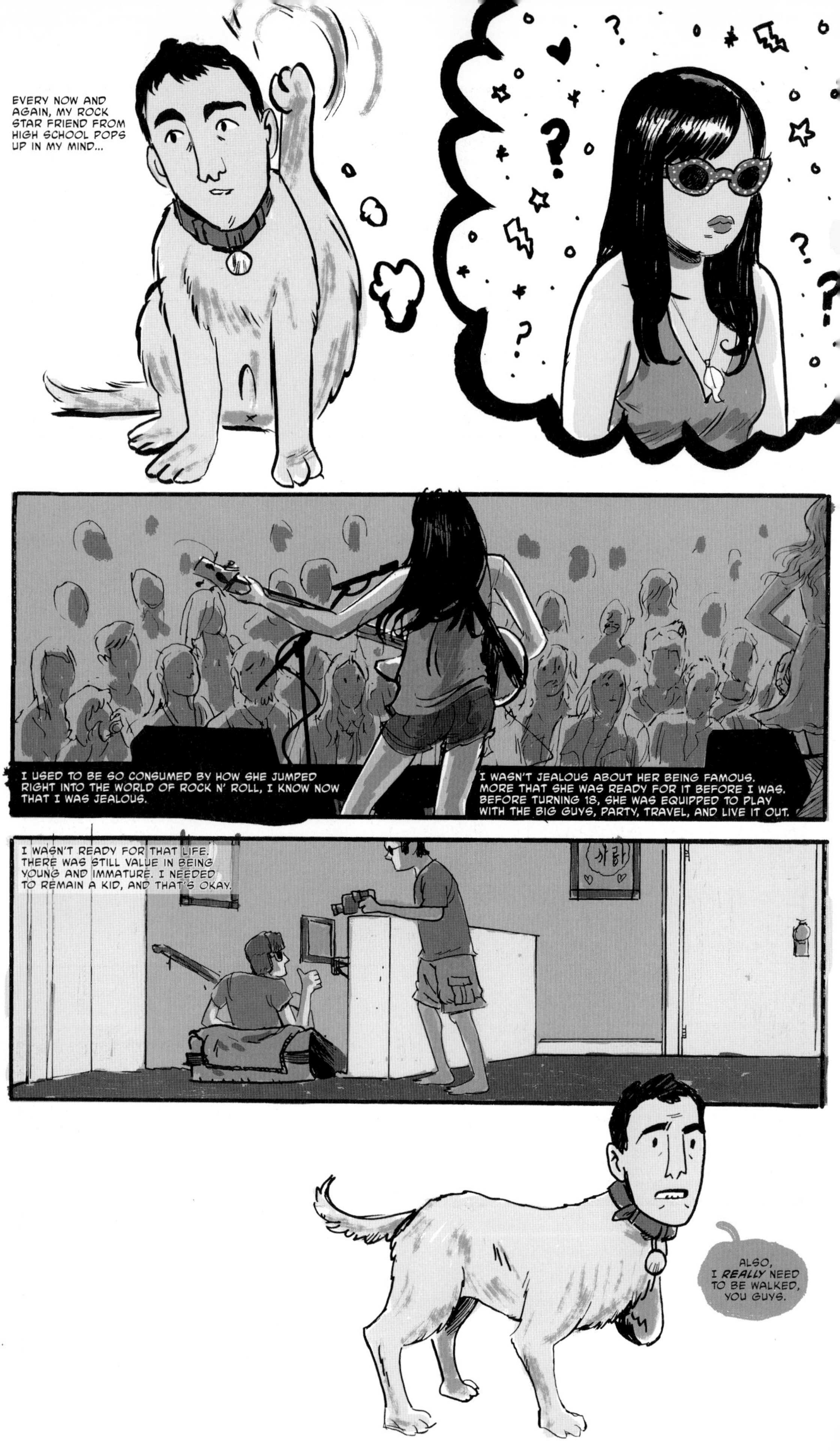
EVERY NOW AND AGAIN, MY ROCK STAR FRIEND FROM HIGH SCHOOL POPS UP IN MY MIND...
I USED TO BE SO CONSUMED BY HOW SHE JUMPED RIGHT INTO THE WORLD OF ROCK N' ROLL, I KNOW NOW THAT I WAS JEALOUS.
I WASN'T JEALOUS ABOUT HER BEING FAMOUS. MORE THAT SHE WAS READY FOR IT BEFORE I WAS. BEFORE TURNING 18, SHE WAS EQUIPPED TO PLAY WITH THE BIG GUYS, PARTY, TRAVEL, AND LIVE IT OUT.
I WASN'T READY FOR THAT LIFE. THERE WAS STILL VALUE IN BEING YOUNG AND IMMATURE. I NEEDED TO REMAIN A KID, AND THAT'S OKAY.
ALSO, I *REALLY* NEED TO BE WALKED, YOU GUYS.

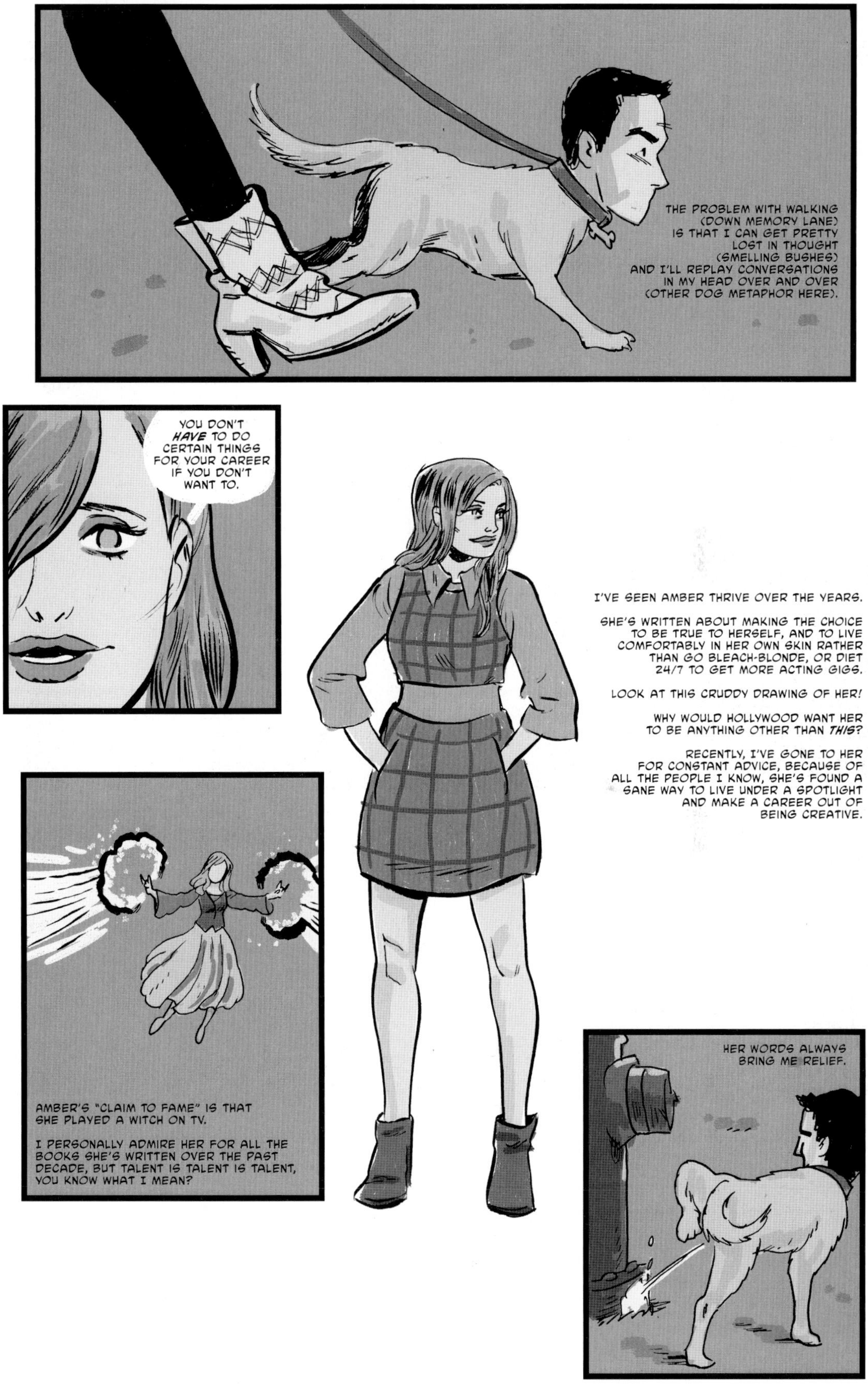
THE PROBLEM WITH WALKING (DOWN MEMORY LANE) IS THAT I CAN GET PRETTY LOST IN THOUGHT (SMELLING BUSHES) AND I'LL REPLAY CONVERSATIONS IN MY HEAD OVER AND OVER (OTHER DOG METAPHOR HERE).
YOU DON'T *HAVE* TO DO CERTAIN THINGS FOR YOUR CAREER IF YOU DON'T WANT TO.
I'VE SEEN AMBER THRIVE OVER THE YEARS.
SHE'S WRITTEN ABOUT MAKING THE CHOICE TO BE TRUE TO HERSELF, AND TO LIVE COMFORTABLY IN HER OWN SKIN RATHER THAN GO BLEACH-BLONDE, OR DIET 24/7 TO GET MORE ACTING GIGS.
LOOK AT THIS CRUDDY DRAWING OF HER!
WHY WOULD HOLLYWOOD WANT HER TO BE ANYTHING OTHER THAN *THIS*?
RECENTLY, I'VE GONE TO HER FOR CONSTANT ADVICE, BECAUSE OF ALL THE PEOPLE I KNOW, SHE'S FOUND A SANE WAY TO LIVE UNDER A SPOTLIGHT AND MAKE A CAREER OUT OF BEING CREATIVE.
AMBER'S "CLAIM TO FAME" IS THAT SHE PLAYED A WITCH ON TV.
I PERSONALLY ADMIRE HER FOR ALL THE BOOKS SHE'S WRITTEN OVER THE PAST DECADE, BUT TALENT IS TALENT IS TALENT, YOU KNOW WHAT I MEAN?
HER WORDS ALWAYS BRING ME RELIEF.

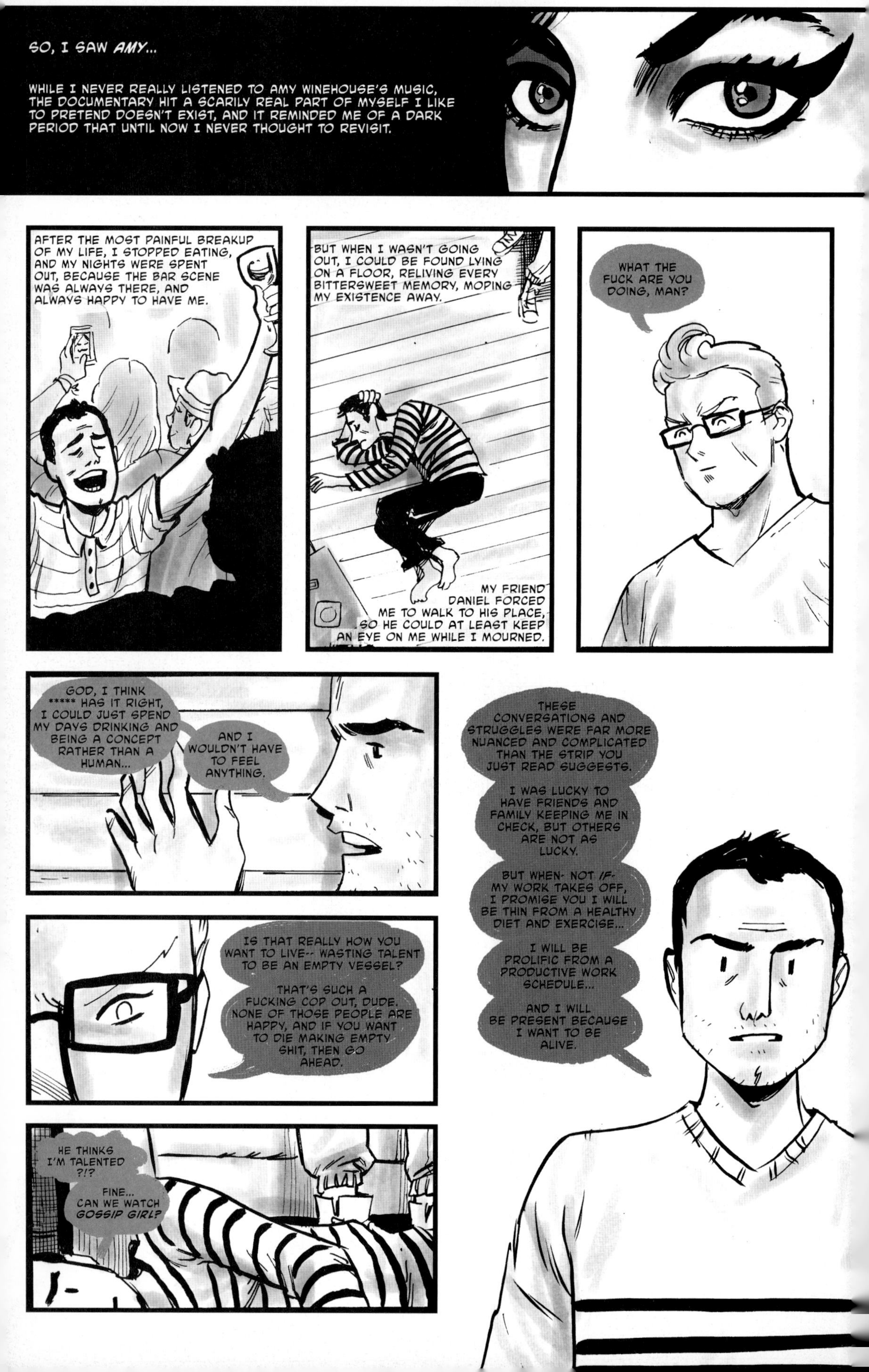
SO, I SAW *AMY*...
WHILE I NEVER REALLY LISTENED TO AMY WINEHOUSE'S MUSIC, THE DOCUMENTARY HIT A SCARILY REAL PART OF MYSELF I LIKE TO PRETEND DOESN'T EXIST, AND IT REMINDED ME OF A DARK PERIOD THAT UNTIL NOW I NEVER THOUGHT TO REVISIT.
AFTER THE MOST PAINFUL BREAKUP OF MY LIFE, I STOPPED EATING, AND MY NIGHTS WERE SPENT OUT, BECAUSE THE BAR SCENE WAS ALWAYS THERE, AND ALWAYS HAPPY TO HAVE ME.
BUT WHEN I WASN'T GOING OUT, I COULD BE FOUND LYING ON A FLOOR, RELIVING EVERY BITTERSWEET MEMORY, MOPING MY EXISTENCE AWAY.
MY FRIEND DANIEL FORCED ME TO WALK TO HIS PLACE, SO HE COULD AT LEAST KEEP AN EYE ON ME WHILE I MOURNED.
WHAT THE FUCK ARE YOU DOING, MAN?
GOD, I THINK ***** HAS IT RIGHT, I COULD JUST SPEND MY DAYS DRINKING AND BEING A CONCEPT RATHER THAN A HUMAN...
AND I WOULDN'T HAVE TO FEEL ANYTHING.
IS THAT REALLY HOW YOU WANT TO LIVE-- WASTING TALENT TO BE AN EMPTY VESSEL?
THAT'S SUCH A FUCKING COP OUT, DUDE. NONE OF THOSE PEOPLE ARE HAPPY, AND IF YOU WANT TO DIE MAKING EMPTY SHIT, THEN GO AHEAD.
HE THINKS I'M TALENTED ?!?
FINE... CAN WE WATCH *GOSSIP GIRL*?
THESE CONVERSATIONS AND STRUGGLES WERE FAR MORE NUANCED AND COMPLICATED THAN THE STRIP YOU JUST READ SUGGESTS.
I WAS LUCKY TO HAVE FRIENDS AND FAMILY KEEPING ME IN CHECK, BUT OTHERS ARE NOT AS LUCKY.
BUT WHEN- NOT *IF*- MY WORK TAKES OFF, I PROMISE YOU I WILL BE THIN FROM A HEALTHY DIET AND EXERCISE...
I WILL BE PROLIFIC FROM A PRODUCTIVE WORK SCHEDULE...
AND I WILL BE PRESENT BECAUSE I WANT TO BE ALIVE.

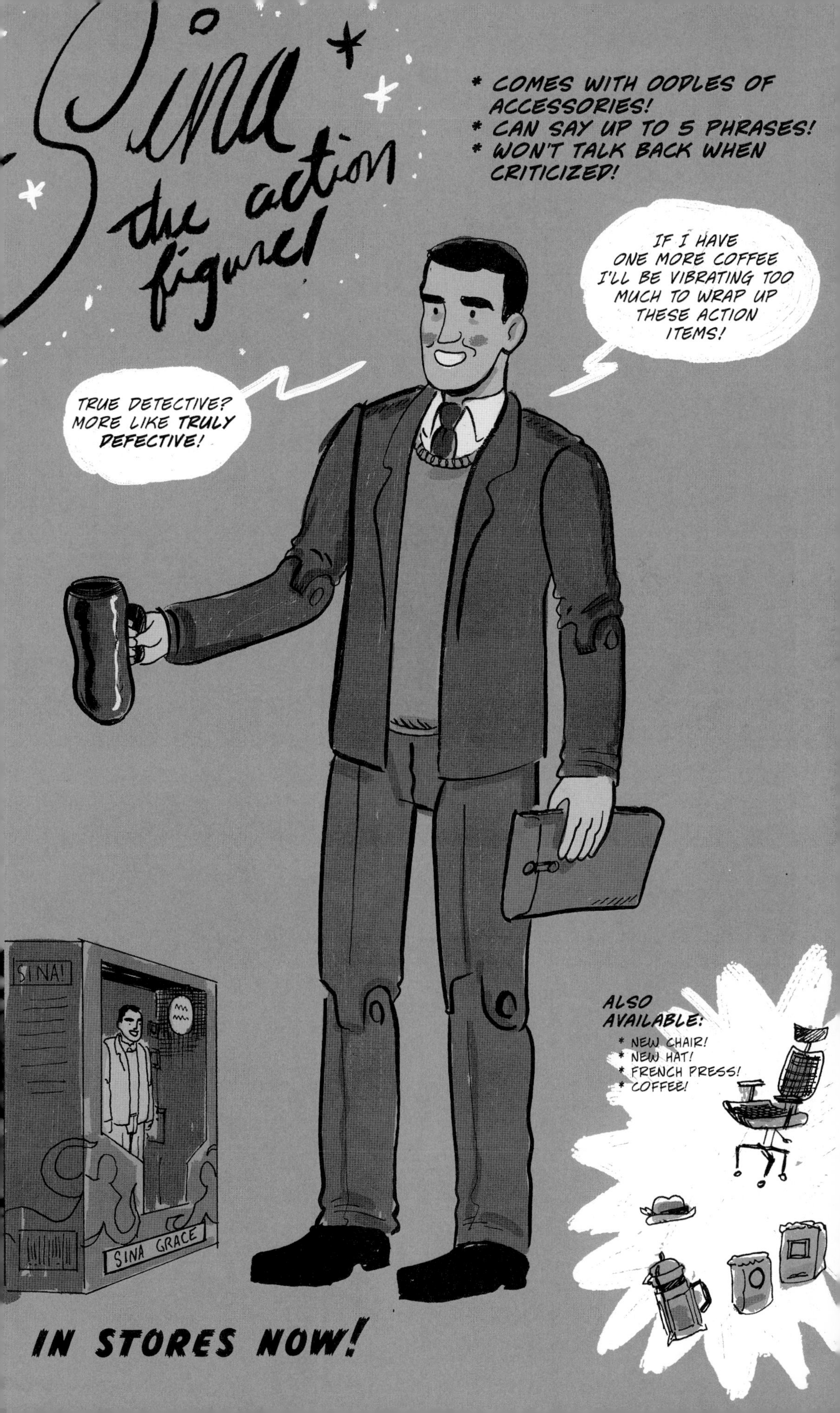
Sina the action figure!
* COMES WITH OODLES OF ACCESSORIES!
* CAN SAY UP TO 5 PHRASES!
* WON'T TALK BACK WHEN CRITICIZED!
IF I HAVE ONE MORE COFFEE I'LL BE VIBRATING TOO MUCH TO WRAP UP THESE ACTION ITEMS!
TRUE DETECTIVE? MORE LIKE TRULY DEFECTIVE!
SINA!
SINA GRACE
ALSO AVAILABLE:
* NEW CHAIR!
* NEW HAT!
* FRENCH PRESS!
* COFFEE!
IN STORES NOW!

THERAPY IS A GREAT SPACE TO LEARN MORE ABOUT YOURSELF, AND WHAT ISN'T ACCEPTABLE BEHAVIOR FROM OTHERS.

FOR EXAMPLE: THE SOLICITATION OF INTIMATE TOUCHING FROM A HIGH SCHOOL TEACHER.

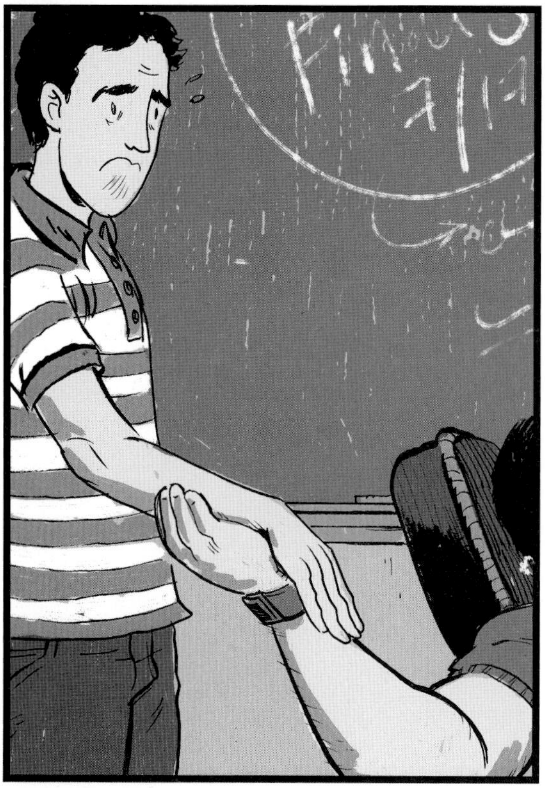

EXAMPLE: BEING ENDLESSLY RIDICULED BY A DATE BECAUSE "HE'S A COMEDIAN!"

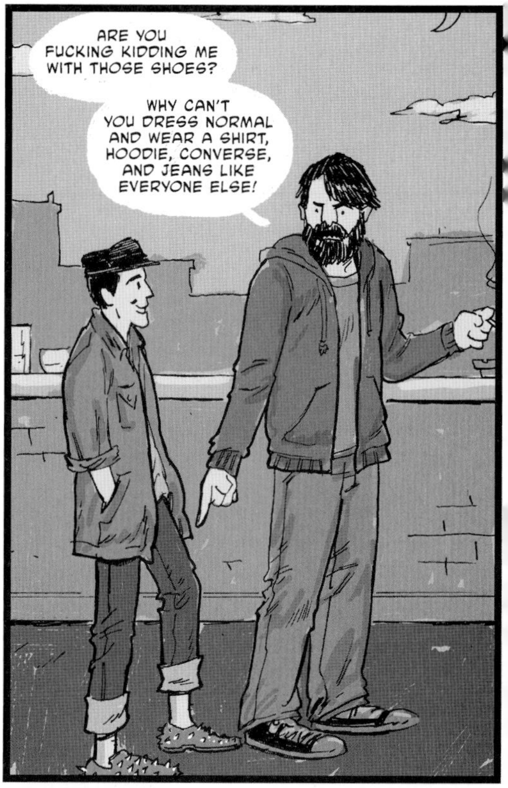
ARE YOU FUCKING KIDDING ME WITH THOSE SHOES?
WHY CAN'T YOU DRESS NORMAL AND WEAR A SHIRT, HOODIE, CONVERSE, AND JEANS LIKE EVERYONE ELSE!

EXAMPLE: PUTTING UP WITH A TOXIC DATE'S NEGATIVE COMMENTS... CONSTANTLY.

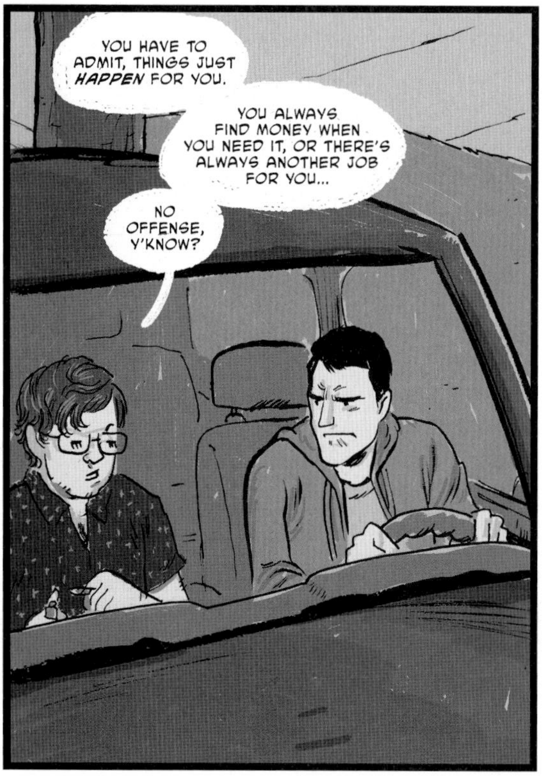
YOU HAVE TO ADMIT, THINGS JUST *HAPPEN* FOR YOU.
YOU ALWAYS FIND MONEY WHEN YOU NEED IT, OR THERE'S ALWAYS ANOTHER JOB FOR YOU...
NO OFFENSE, Y'KNOW?

EXAMPLE: BEING WITH SOMEONE WHO EXACERBATES YOUR BODY DYSMORPHIA.

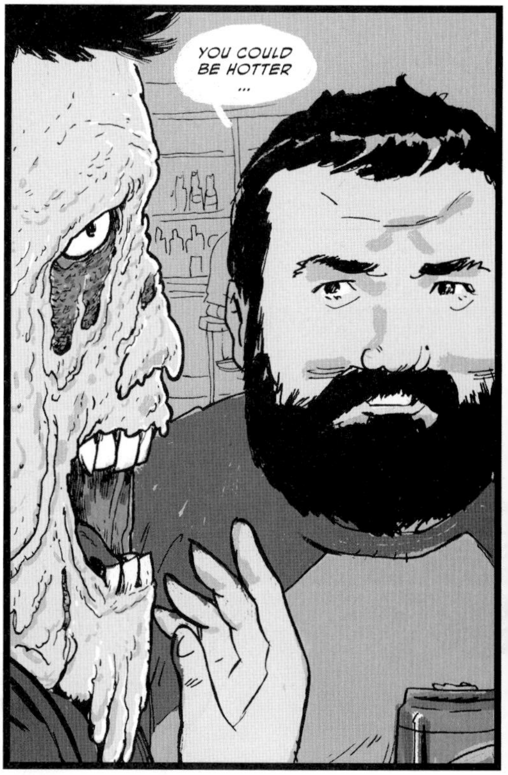
YOU COULD BE HOTTER ...

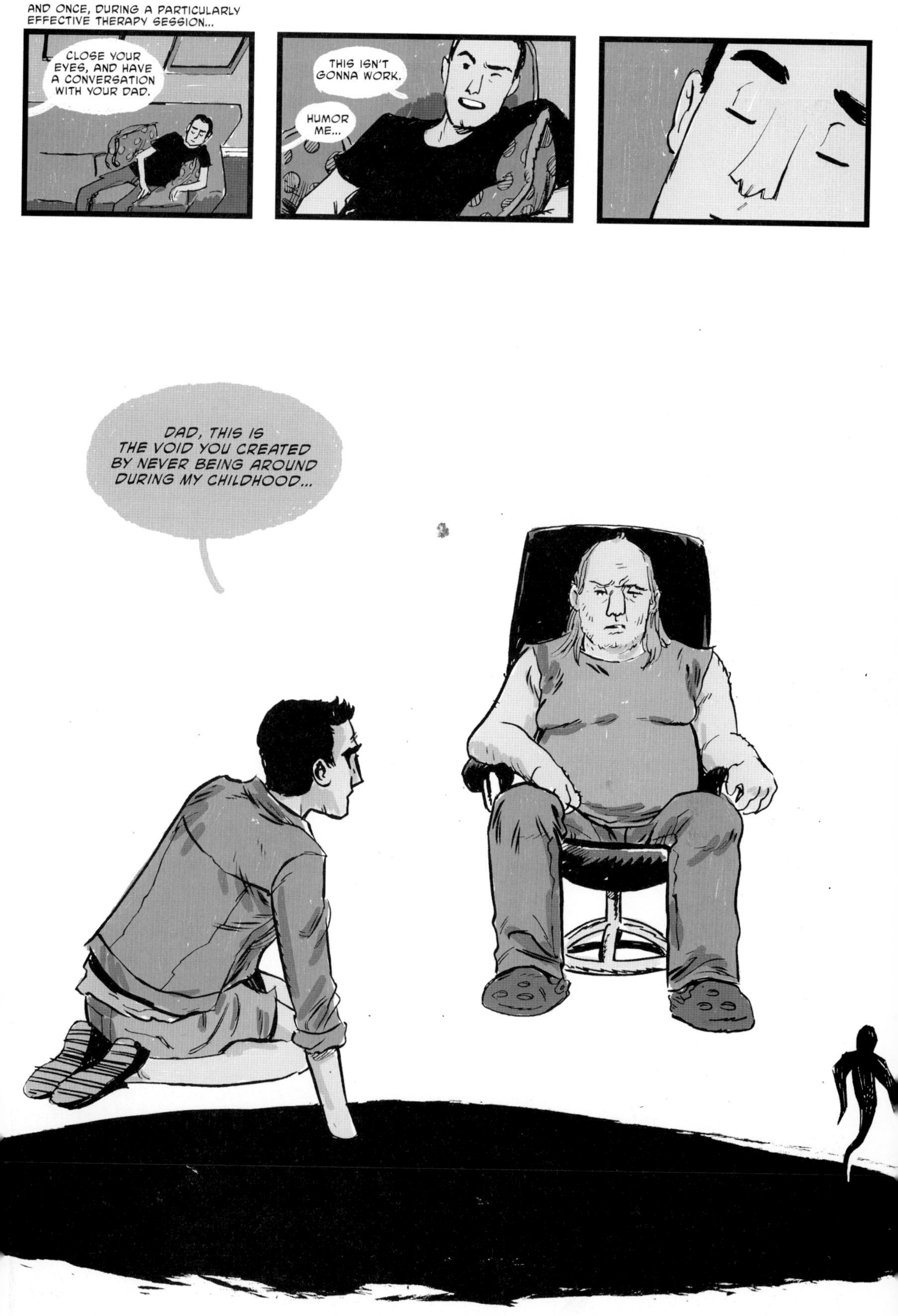
AND ONCE, DURING A PARTICULARLY EFFECTIVE THERAPY SESSION...
CLOSE YOUR EYES, AND HAVE A CONVERSATION WITH YOUR DAD.
THIS ISN'T GONNA WORK.
HUMOR ME...
DAD, THIS IS THE VOID YOU CREATED BY NEVER BEING AROUND DURING MY CHILDHOOD...

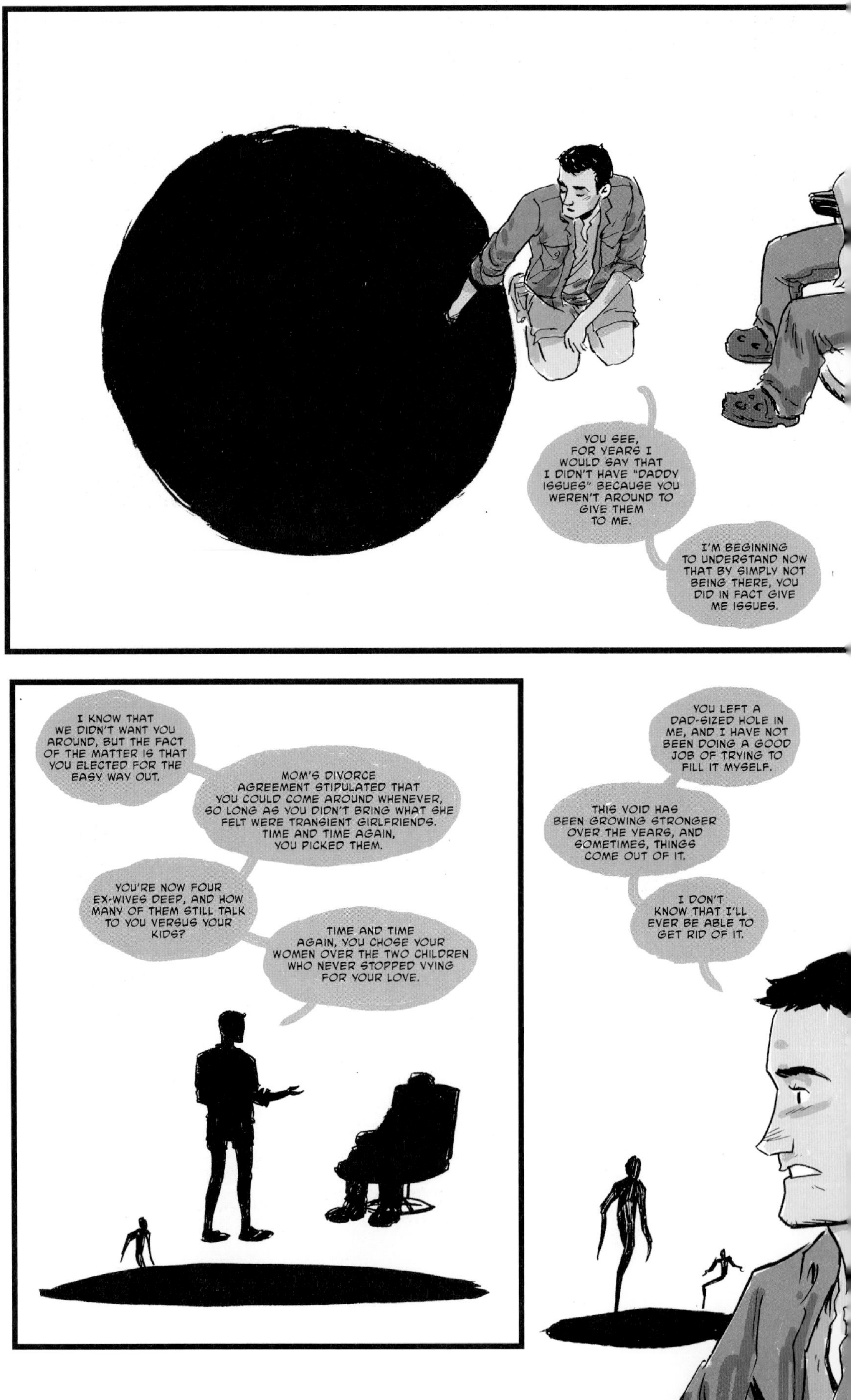
YOU SEE, FOR YEARS I WOULD SAY THAT I DIDN'T HAVE "DADDY ISSUES" BECAUSE YOU WEREN'T AROUND TO GIVE THEM TO ME.
I'M BEGINNING TO UNDERSTAND NOW THAT BY SIMPLY NOT BEING THERE, YOU DID IN FACT GIVE ME ISSUES.
I KNOW THAT WE DIDN'T WANT YOU AROUND, BUT THE FACT OF THE MATTER IS THAT YOU ELECTED FOR THE EASY WAY OUT.
MOM'S DIVORCE AGREEMENT STIPULATED THAT YOU COULD COME AROUND WHENEVER, SO LONG AS YOU DIDN'T BRING WHAT SHE FELT WERE TRANSIENT GIRLFRIENDS. TIME AND TIME AGAIN, YOU PICKED THEM.
YOU'RE NOW FOUR EX-WIVES DEEP, AND HOW MANY OF THEM STILL TALK TO YOU VERSUS YOUR KIDS?
TIME AND TIME AGAIN, YOU CHOSE YOUR WOMEN OVER THE TWO CHILDREN WHO NEVER STOPPED VYING FOR YOUR LOVE.
YOU LEFT A DAD-SIZED HOLE IN ME, AND I HAVE NOT BEEN DOING A GOOD JOB OF TRYING TO FILL IT MYSELF.
THIS VOID HAS BEEN GROWING STRONGER OVER THE YEARS, AND SOMETIMES, THINGS COME OUT OF IT.
I DON'T KNOW THAT I'LL EVER BE ABLE TO GET RID OF IT.

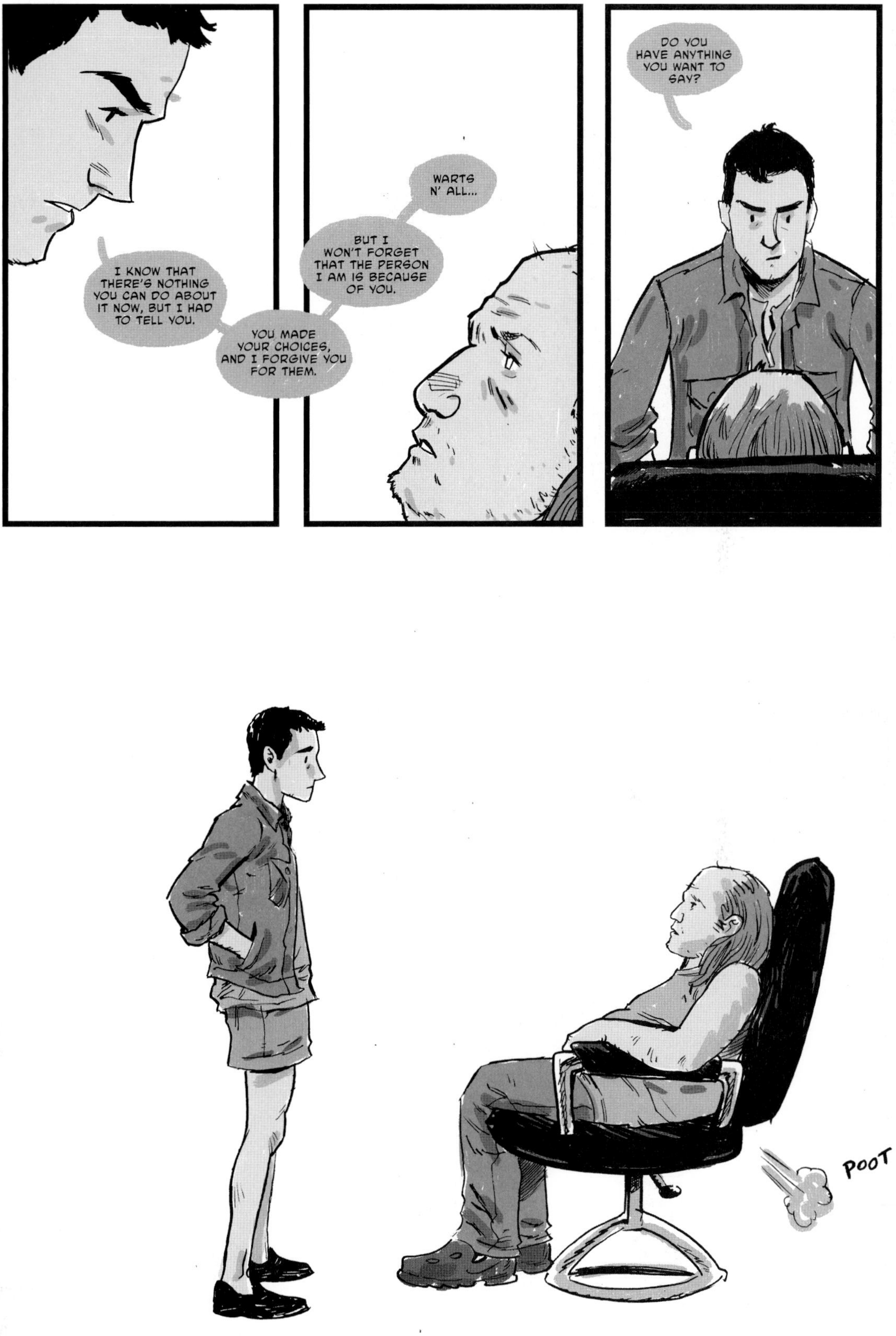
I KNOW THAT THERE'S NOTHING YOU CAN DO ABOUT IT NOW, BUT I HAD TO TELL YOU.
YOU MADE YOUR CHOICES, AND I FORGIVE YOU FOR THEM.
BUT I WON'T FORGET THAT THE PERSON I AM IS BECAUSE OF YOU.
WARTS N' ALL...
DO YOU HAVE ANYTHING YOU WANT TO SAY?
POOT

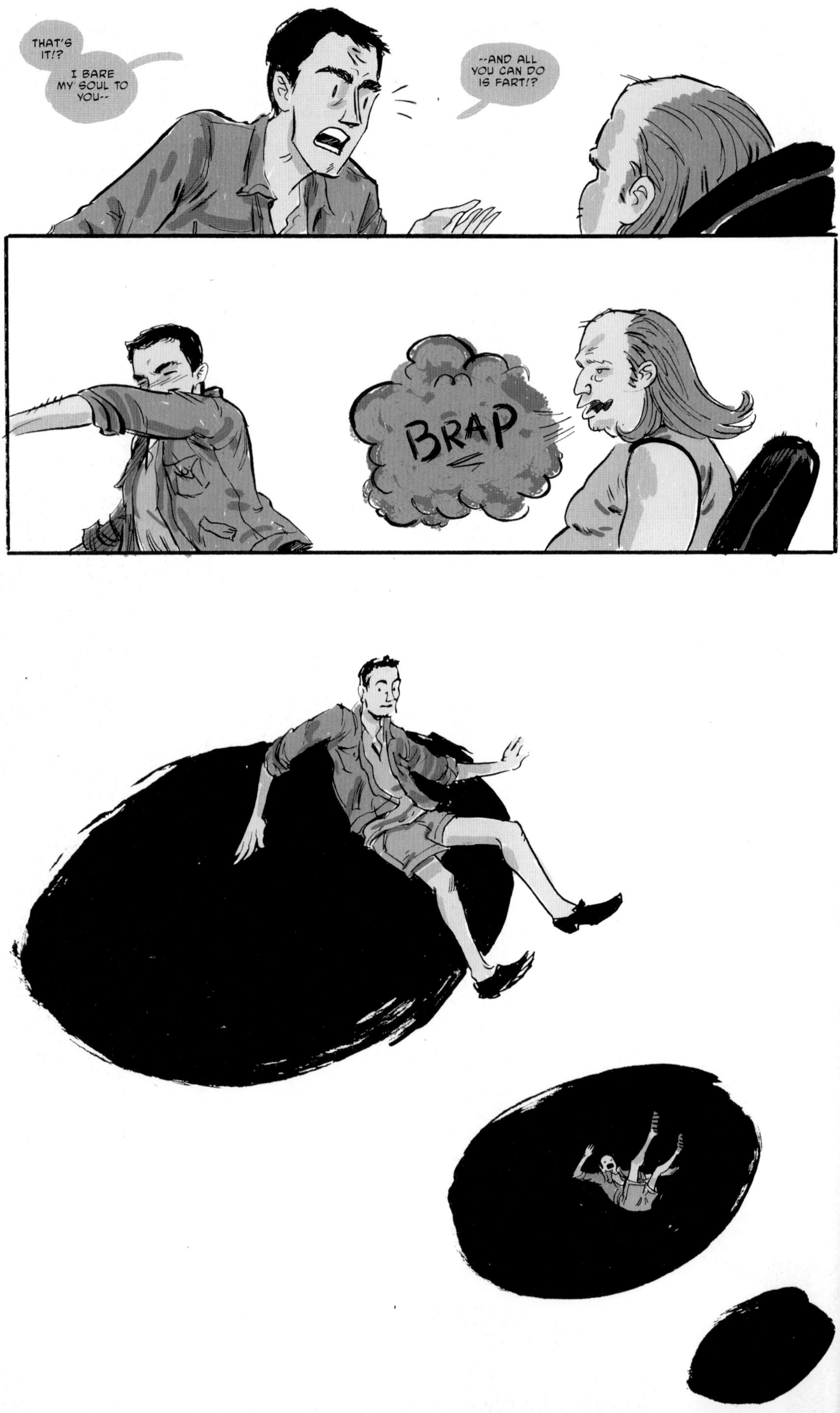
THAT'S IT!? I BARE MY SOUL TO YOU--
--AND ALL YOU CAN DO IS FART!?
BRAP

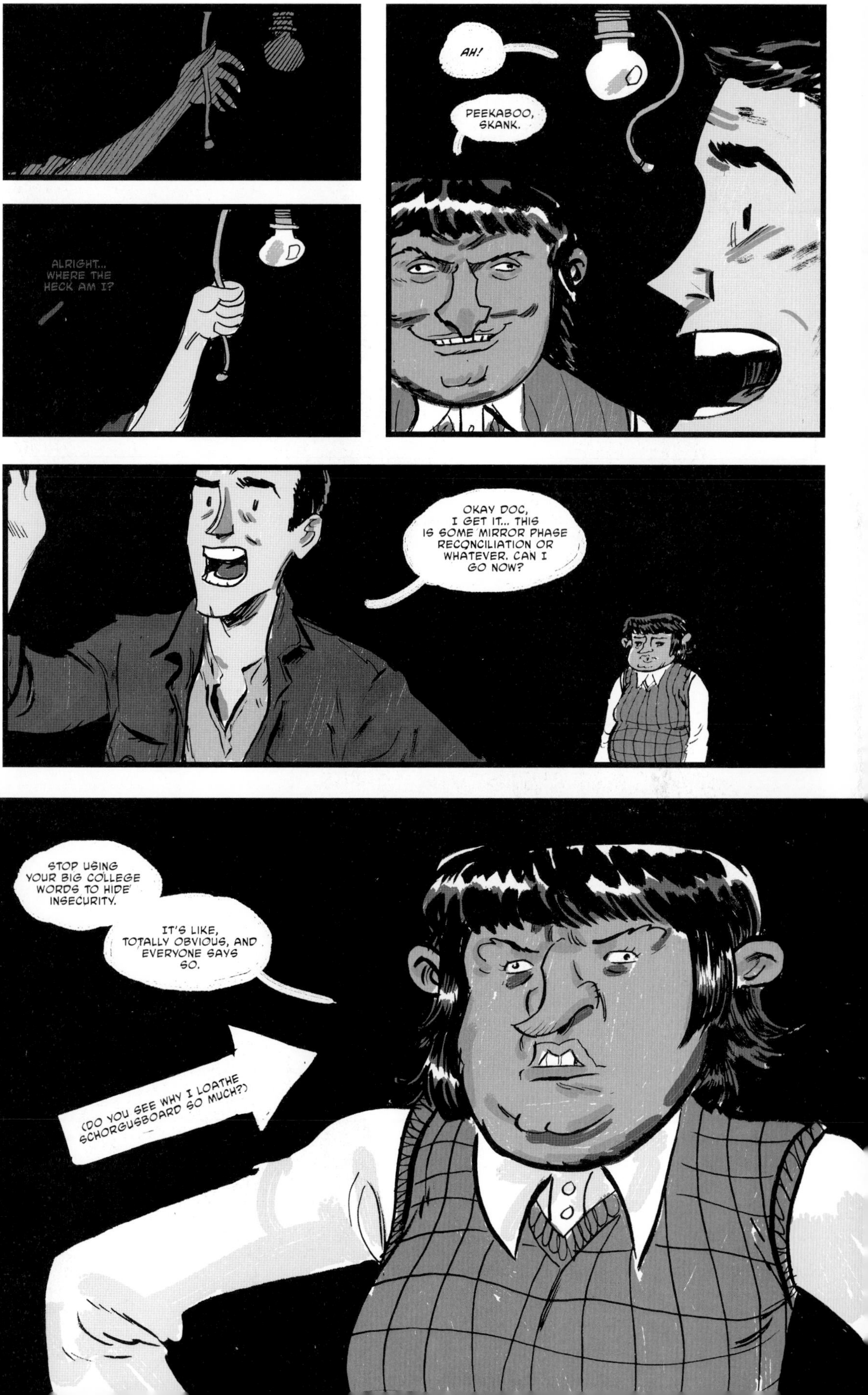
ALRIGHT... WHERE THE HECK AM I?
AH!
PEEKABOO, SKANK.
OKAY DOC, I GET IT... THIS IS SOME MIRROR PHASE RECONCILIATION OR WHATEVER. CAN I GO NOW?
STOP USING YOUR BIG COLLEGE WORDS TO HIDE INSECURITY.
IT'S LIKE, TOTALLY OBVIOUS, AND EVERYONE SAYS SO.
(DO YOU SEE WHY I LOATHE SCHORGUSBOARD SO MUCH?)

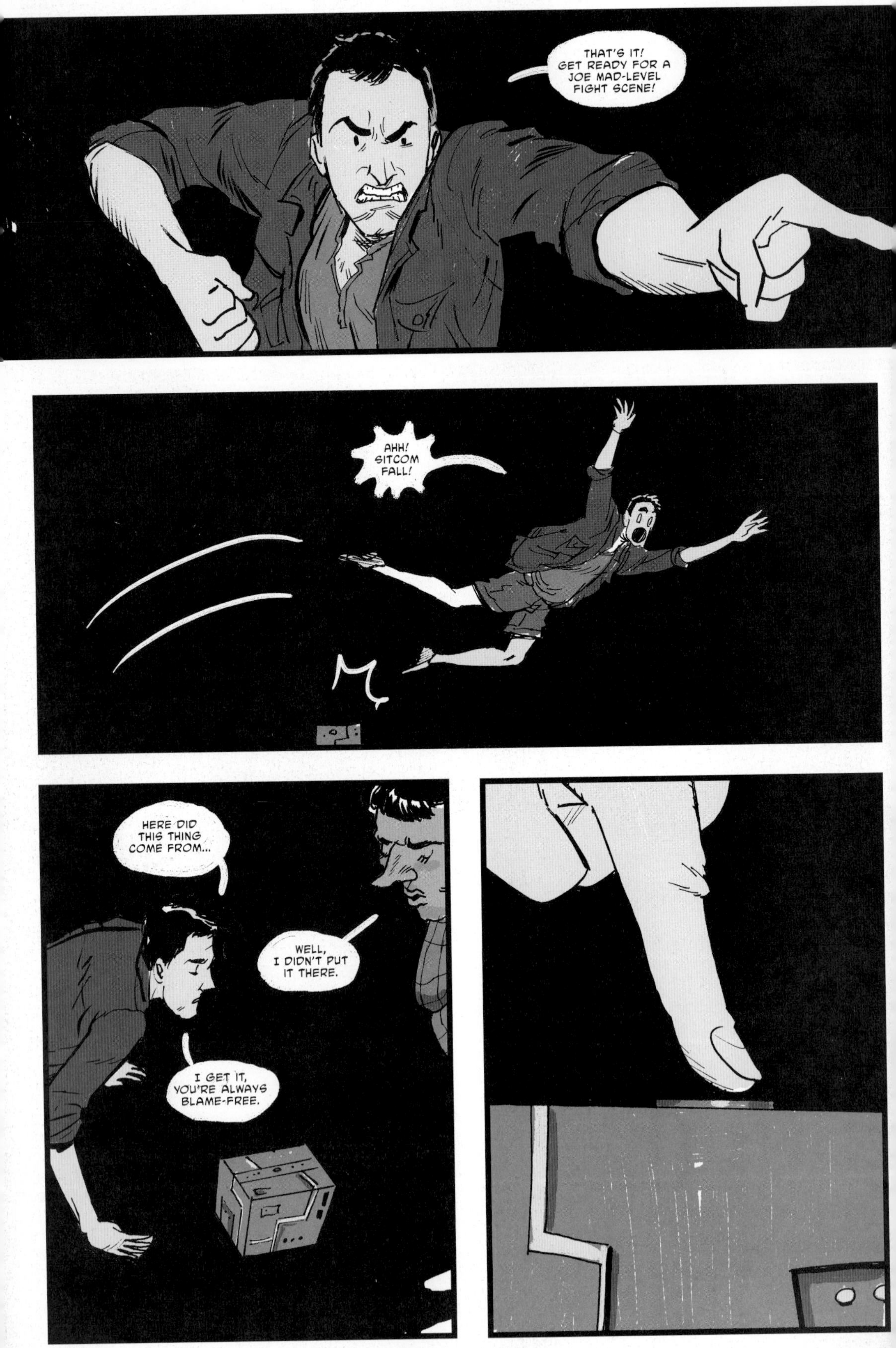
THAT'S IT! GET READY FOR A JOE MAD-LEVEL FIGHT SCENE!
AHH! SITCOM FALL!
HERE DID THIS THING COME FROM...
WELL, I DIDN'T PUT IT THERE.
I GET IT, YOU'RE ALWAYS BLAME-FREE.

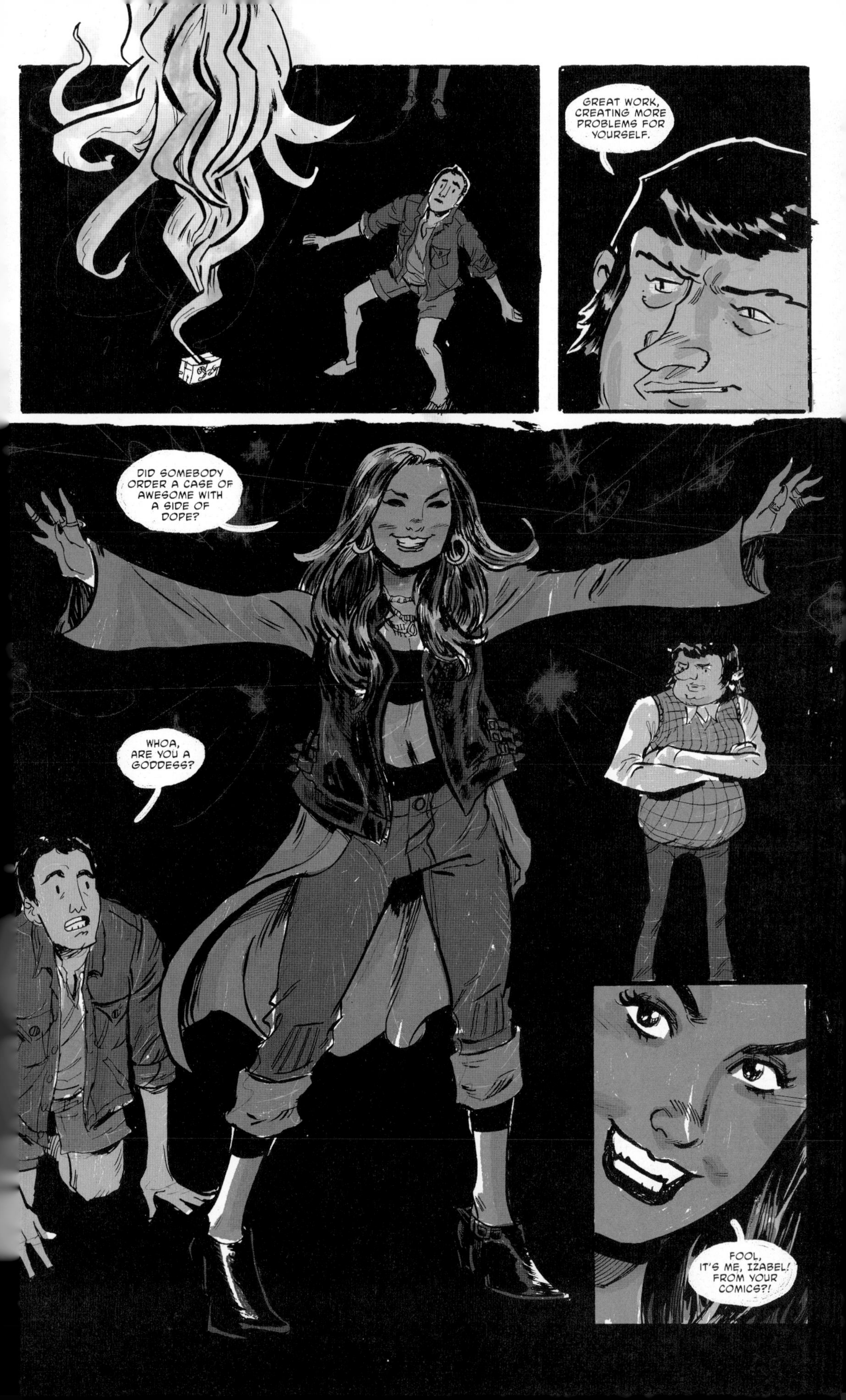
GREAT WORK, CREATING MORE PROBLEMS FOR YOURSELF.
DID SOMEBODY ORDER A CASE OF AWESOME WITH A SIDE OF DOPE?
WHOA, ARE YOU A GODDESS?
FOOL, IT'S ME, IZABEL! FROM YOUR COMICS?!

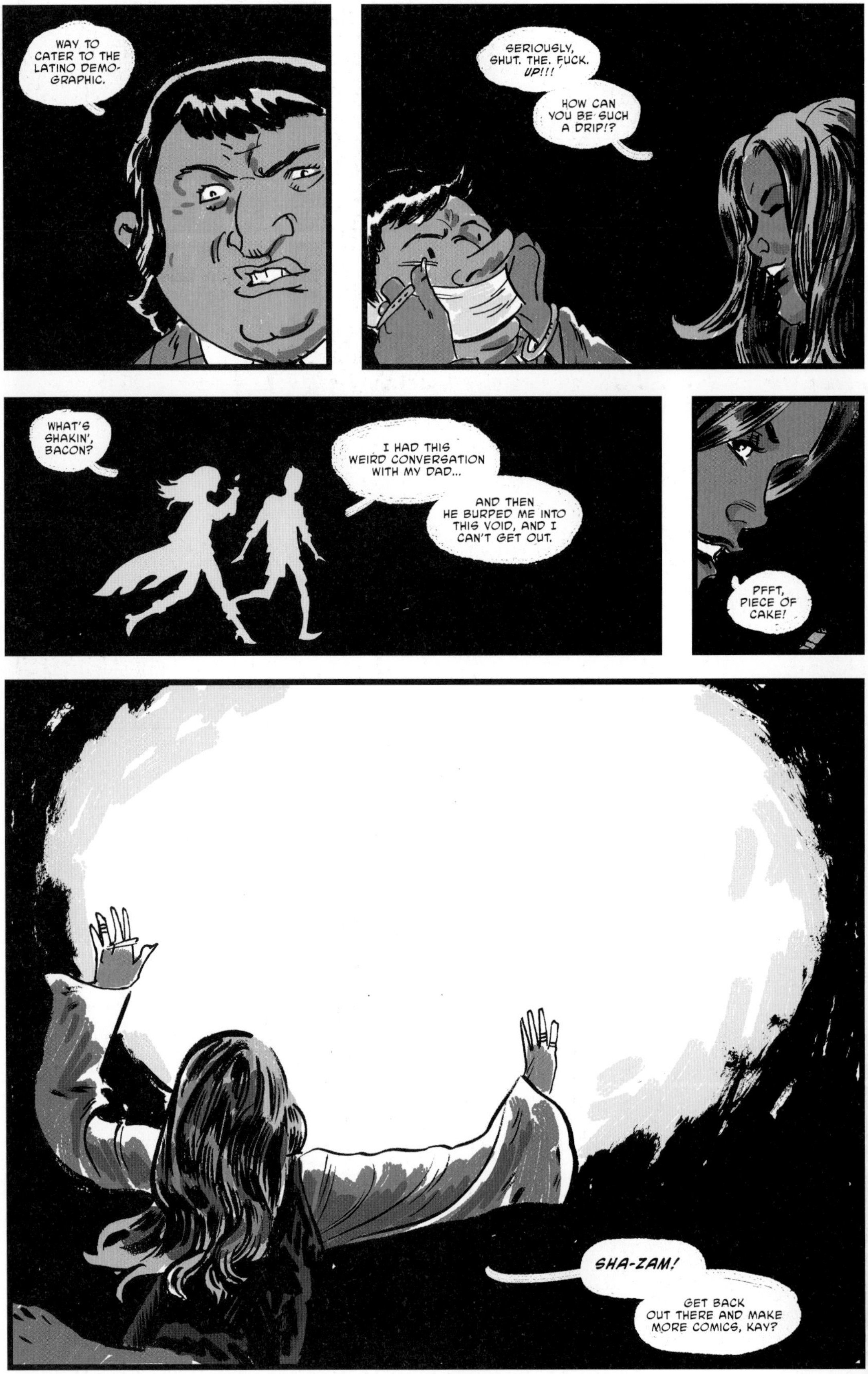
WAY TO CATER TO THE LATINO DEMO-GRAPHIC.
SERIOUSLY, SHUT. THE. FUCK. *UP!!!*
HOW CAN YOU BE SUCH A DRIP!?
WHAT'S SHAKIN', BACON?
I HAD THIS WEIRD CONVERSATION WITH MY DAD...
AND THEN HE BURPED ME INTO THIS VOID, AND I CAN'T GET OUT.
PFFT, PIECE OF CAKE!
SHA-ZAM!
GET BACK OUT THERE AND MAKE MORE COMICS, KAY?

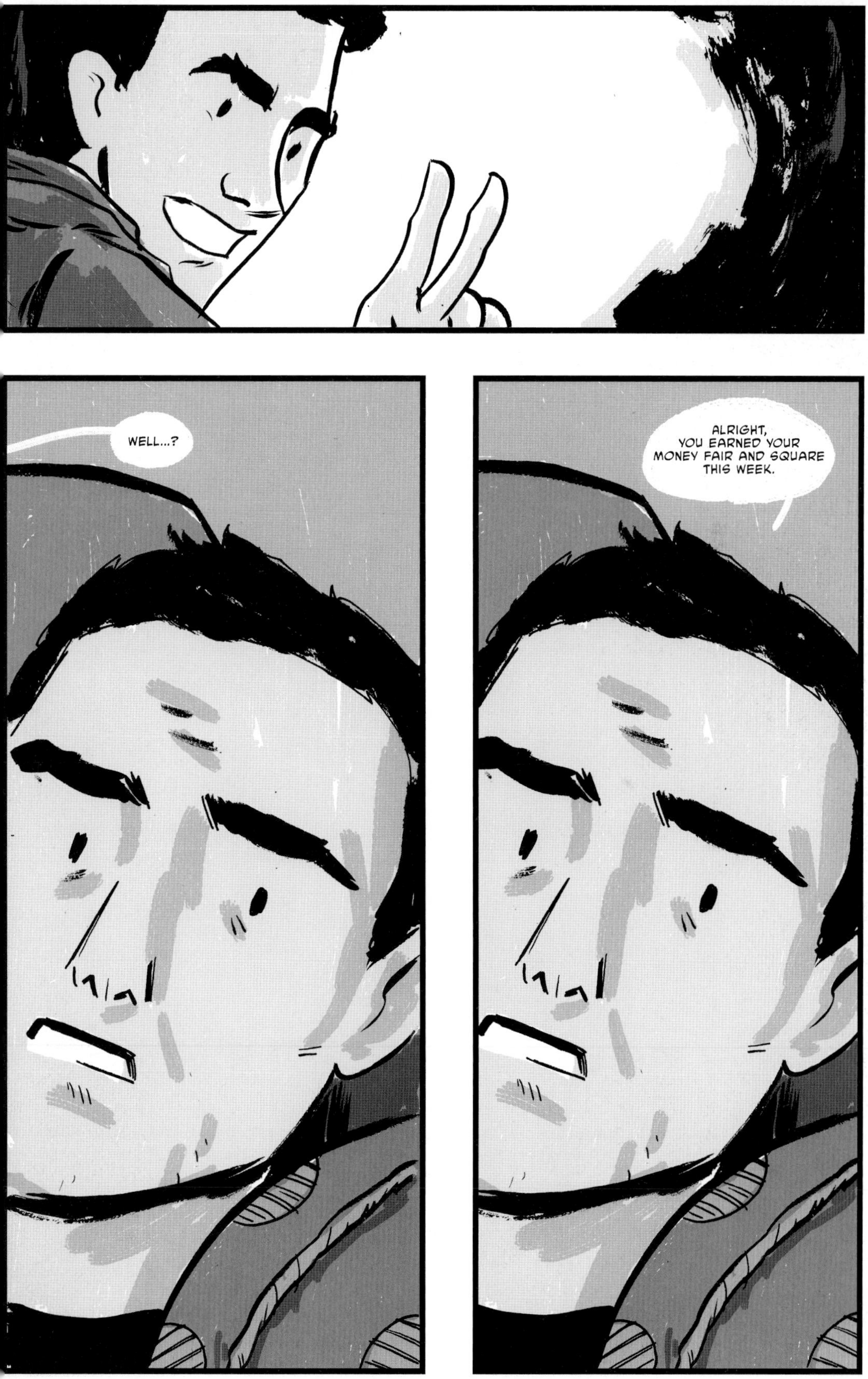
WELL...?
ALRIGHT, YOU EARNED YOUR MONEY FAIR AND SQUARE THIS WEEK.

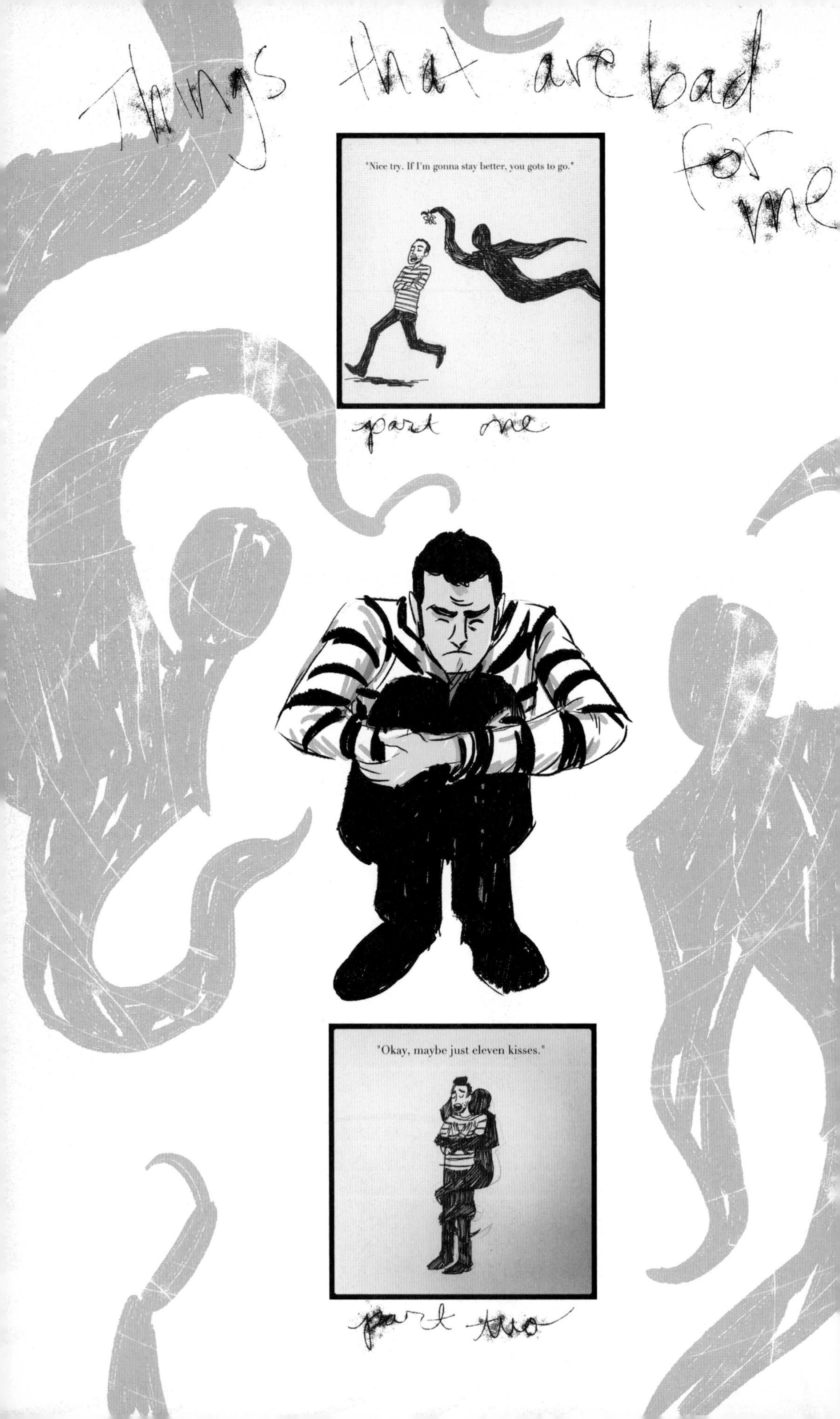
things that are bad for me
"Nice try. If I'm gonna stay better, you gots to go."
part one
"Okay, maybe just eleven kisses."
part two

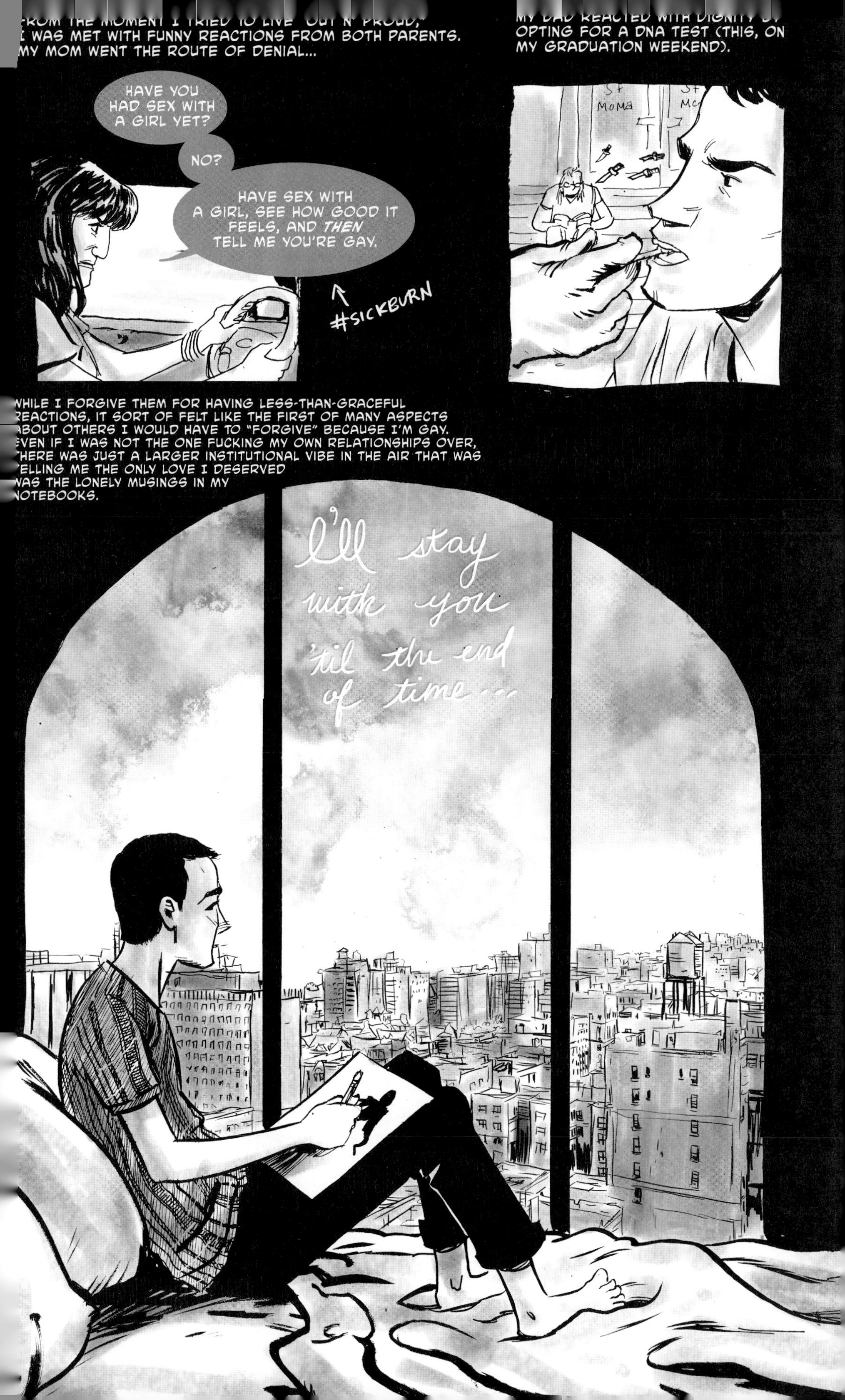
FROM THE MOMENT I TRIED TO LIVE "OUT N' PROUD," I WAS MET WITH FUNNY REACTIONS FROM BOTH PARENTS. MY MOM WENT THE ROUTE OF DENIAL...
HAVE YOU HAD SEX WITH A GIRL YET?
NO?
HAVE SEX WITH A GIRL, SEE HOW GOOD IT FEELS, AND *THEN* TELL ME YOU'RE GAY.
#SICKBURN
MY DAD REACTED WITH DIGNITY BY OPTING FOR A DNA TEST (THIS, ON MY GRADUATION WEEKEND).
SF MOMA
WHILE I FORGIVE THEM FOR HAVING LESS-THAN-GRACEFUL REACTIONS, IT SORT OF FELT LIKE THE FIRST OF MANY ASPECTS ABOUT OTHERS I WOULD HAVE TO "FORGIVE" BECAUSE I'M GAY. EVEN IF I WAS NOT THE ONE FUCKING MY OWN RELATIONSHIPS OVER, THERE WAS JUST A LARGER INSTITUTIONAL VIBE IN THE AIR THAT WAS TELLING ME THE ONLY LOVE I DESERVED WAS THE LONELY MUSINGS IN MY NOTEBOOKS.
I'll stay with you 'til the end of time...

BUT THEN--

OVER THE COURSE OF THE SUMMER, SOME MAJOR SHIT WENT DOWN IN THE UNITED STATES' HISTORY!

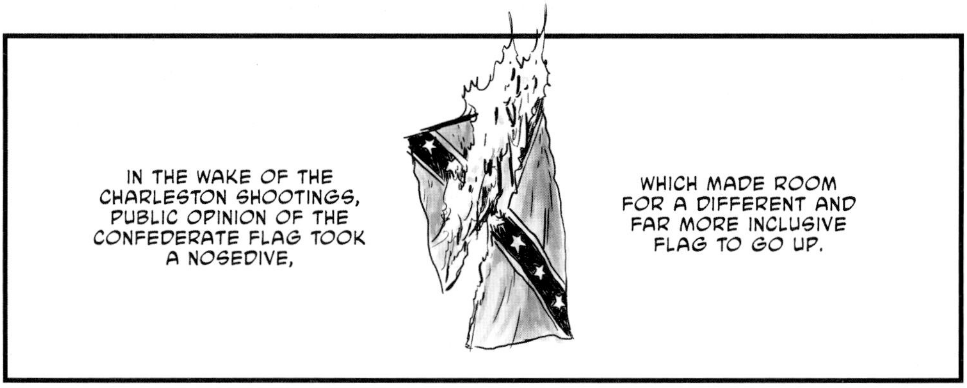
IN THE WAKE OF THE CHARLESTON SHOOTINGS, PUBLIC OPINION OF THE CONFEDERATE FLAG TOOK A NOSEDIVE,
WHICH MADE ROOM FOR A DIFFERENT AND FAR MORE INCLUSIVE FLAG TO GO UP.

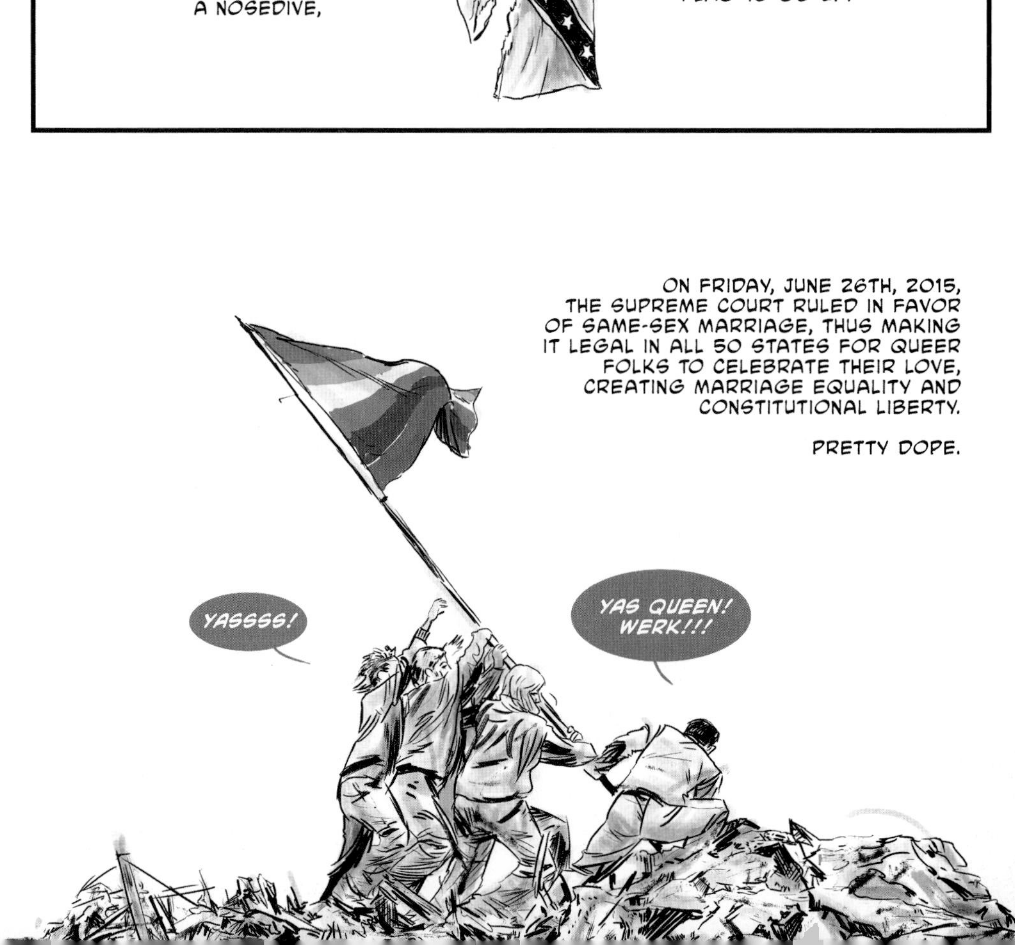
ON FRIDAY, JUNE 26TH, 2015, THE SUPREME COURT RULED IN FAVOR OF SAME-SEX MARRIAGE, THUS MAKING IT LEGAL IN ALL 50 STATES FOR QUEER FOLKS TO CELEBRATE THEIR LOVE, CREATING MARRIAGE EQUALITY AND CONSTITUTIONAL LIBERTY.
PRETTY DOPE.
YASSSS!
YAS QUEEN! WERK!!!

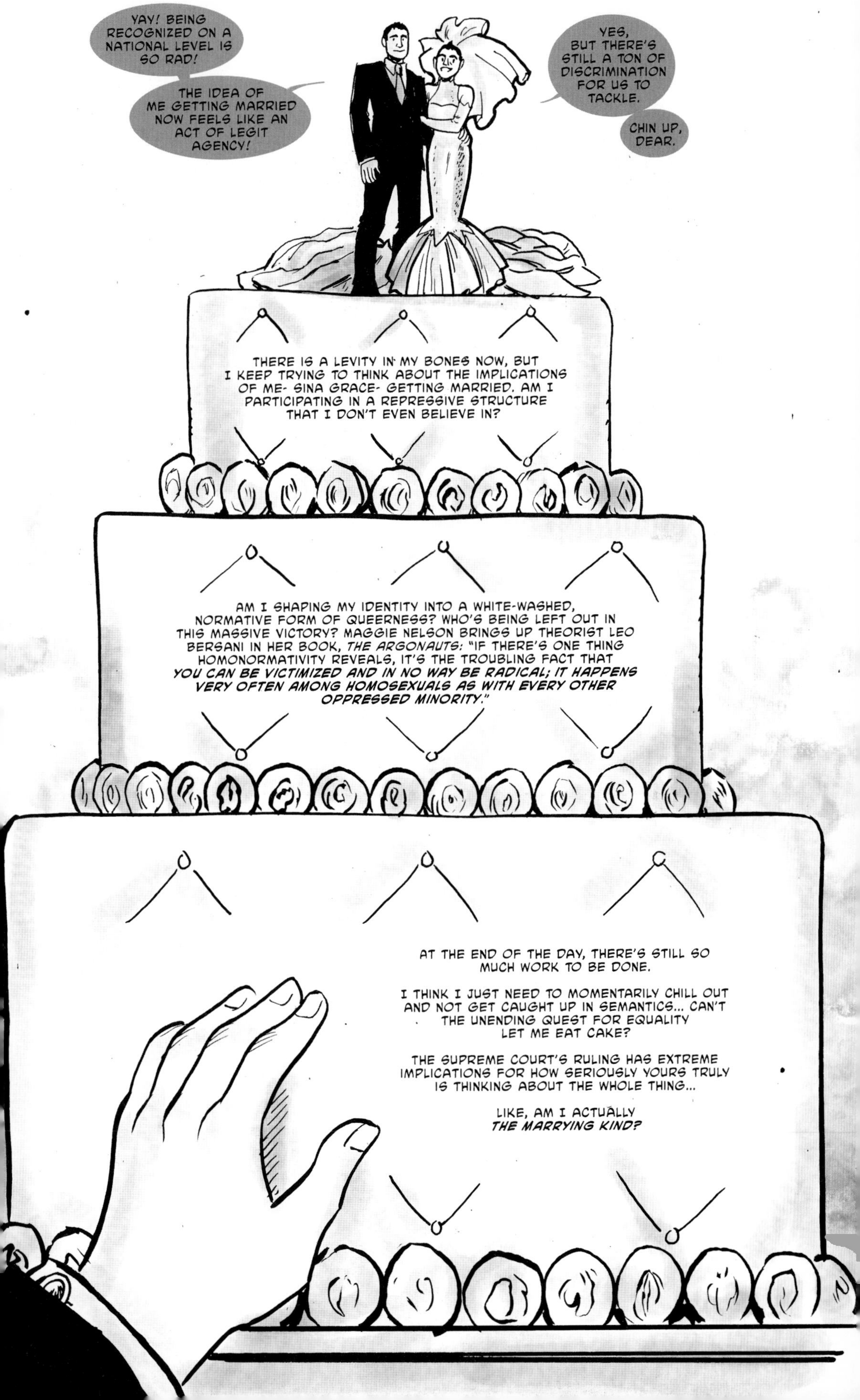

YAY! BEING RECOGNIZED ON A NATIONAL LEVEL IS SO RAD!
THE IDEA OF ME GETTING MARRIED NOW FEELS LIKE AN ACT OF LEGIT AGENCY!
YES, BUT THERE'S STILL A TON OF DISCRIMINATION FOR US TO TACKLE.
CHIN UP, DEAR.
THERE IS A LEVITY IN MY BONES NOW, BUT I KEEP TRYING TO THINK ABOUT THE IMPLICATIONS OF ME- SINA GRACE- GETTING MARRIED. AM I PARTICIPATING IN A REPRESSIVE STRUCTURE THAT I DON'T EVEN BELIEVE IN?
AM I SHAPING MY IDENTITY INTO A WHITE-WASHED, NORMATIVE FORM OF QUEERNESS? WHO'S BEING LEFT OUT IN THIS MASSIVE VICTORY? MAGGIE NELSON BRINGS UP THEORIST LEO BERSANI IN HER BOOK, *THE ARGONAUTS:* "IF THERE'S ONE THING HOMONORMATIVITY REVEALS, IT'S THE TROUBLING FACT THAT *YOU CAN BE VICTIMIZED AND IN NO WAY BE RADICAL; IT HAPPENS VERY OFTEN AMONG HOMOSEXUALS AS WITH EVERY OTHER OPPRESSED MINORITY.*"
AT THE END OF THE DAY, THERE'S STILL SO MUCH WORK TO BE DONE.
I THINK I JUST NEED TO MOMENTARILY CHILL OUT AND NOT GET CAUGHT UP IN SEMANTICS... CAN'T THE UNENDING QUEST FOR EQUALITY LET ME EAT CAKE?
THE SUPREME COURT'S RULING HAS EXTREME IMPLICATIONS FOR HOW SERIOUSLY YOURS TRULY IS THINKING ABOUT THE WHOLE THING...
LIKE, AM I ACTUALLY *THE MARRYING KIND?*

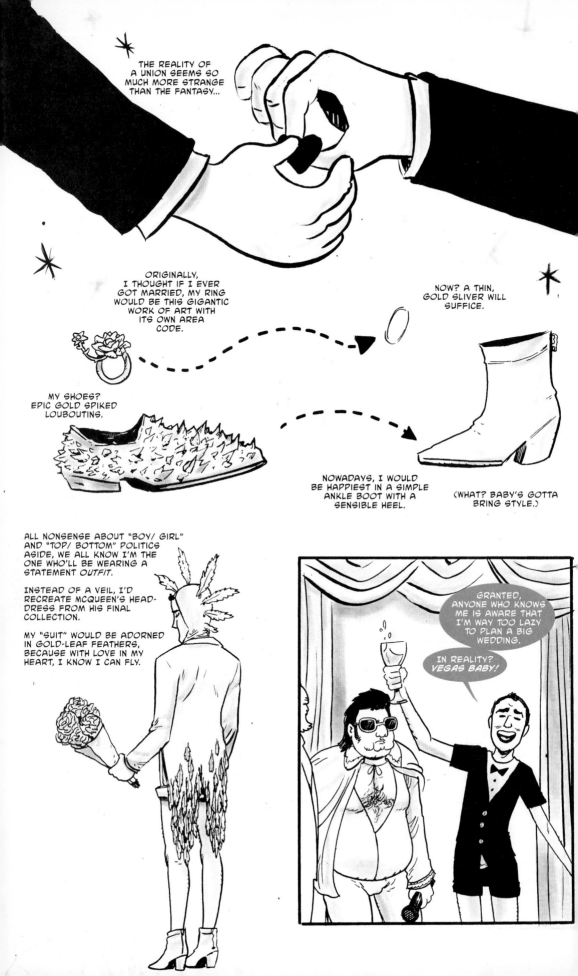

THE REALITY OF A UNION SEEMS SO MUCH MORE STRANGE THAN THE FANTASY...

ORIGINALLY, I THOUGHT IF I EVER GOT MARRIED, MY RING WOULD BE THIS GIGANTIC WORK OF ART WITH ITS OWN AREA CODE.

NOW? A THIN, GOLD SLIVER WILL SUFFICE.

MY SHOES? EPIC GOLD SPIKED LOUBOUTINS.

NOWADAYS, I WOULD BE HAPPIEST IN A SIMPLE ANKLE BOOT WITH A SENSIBLE HEEL.

(WHAT? BABY'S GOTTA BRING STYLE.)

ALL NONSENSE ABOUT "BOY/ GIRL" AND "TOP/ BOTTOM" POLITICS ASIDE, WE ALL KNOW I'M THE ONE WHO'LL BE WEARING A STATEMENT *OUTFIT*.

INSTEAD OF A VEIL, I'D RECREATE MCQUEEN'S HEAD-DRESS FROM HIS FINAL COLLECTION.

MY "SUIT" WOULD BE ADORNED IN GOLD-LEAF FEATHERS, BECAUSE WITH LOVE IN MY HEART, I KNOW I CAN FLY.

GRANTED, ANYONE WHO KNOWS ME IS AWARE THAT I'M WAY TOO LAZY TO PLAN A BIG WEDDING.

IN REALITY? *VEGAS BABY!*

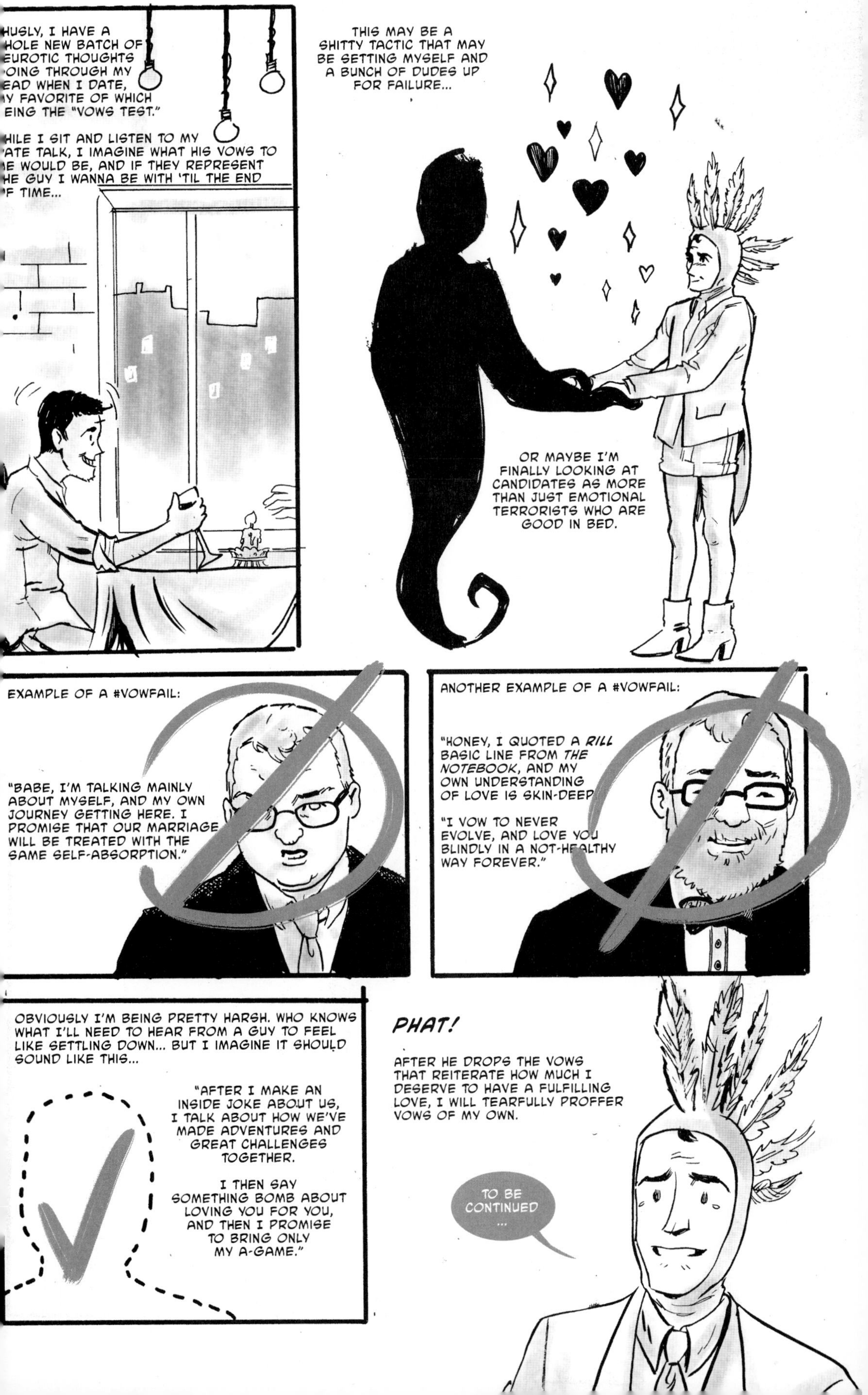
HUSLY, I HAVE A
HOLE NEW BATCH OF
EUROTIC THOUGHTS
OING THROUGH MY
EAD WHEN I DATE,
Y FAVORITE OF WHICH
EING THE "VOWS TEST."
HILE I SIT AND LISTEN TO MY
ATE TALK, I IMAGINE WHAT HIS VOWS TO
E WOULD BE, AND IF THEY REPRESENT
HE GUY I WANNA BE WITH 'TIL THE END
F TIME...
THIS MAY BE A SHITTY TACTIC THAT MAY BE SETTING MYSELF AND A BUNCH OF DUDES UP FOR FAILURE...
OR MAYBE I'M FINALLY LOOKING AT CANDIDATES AS MORE THAN JUST EMOTIONAL TERRORISTS WHO ARE GOOD IN BED.
EXAMPLE OF A #VOWFAIL:
"BABE, I'M TALKING MAINLY ABOUT MYSELF, AND MY OWN JOURNEY GETTING HERE. I PROMISE THAT OUR MARRIAGE WILL BE TREATED WITH THE SAME SELF-ABSORPTION."
ANOTHER EXAMPLE OF A #VOWFAIL:
"HONEY, I QUOTED A RILL BASIC LINE FROM THE NOTEBOOK, AND MY OWN UNDERSTANDING OF LOVE IS SKIN-DEEP.
"I VOW TO NEVER EVOLVE, AND LOVE YOU BLINDLY IN A NOT-HEALTHY WAY FOREVER."
OBVIOUSLY I'M BEING PRETTY HARSH. WHO KNOWS WHAT I'LL NEED TO HEAR FROM A GUY TO FEEL LIKE SETTLING DOWN... BUT I IMAGINE IT SHOULD SOUND LIKE THIS...
"AFTER I MAKE AN INSIDE JOKE ABOUT US, I TALK ABOUT HOW WE'VE MADE ADVENTURES AND GREAT CHALLENGES TOGETHER.
I THEN SAY SOMETHING BOMB ABOUT LOVING YOU FOR YOU, AND THEN I PROMISE TO BRING ONLY MY A-GAME."
PHAT!
AFTER HE DROPS THE VOWS THAT REITERATE HOW MUCH I DESERVE TO HAVE A FULFILLING LOVE, I WILL TEARFULLY PROFFER VOWS OF MY OWN.
TO BE CONTINUED ...

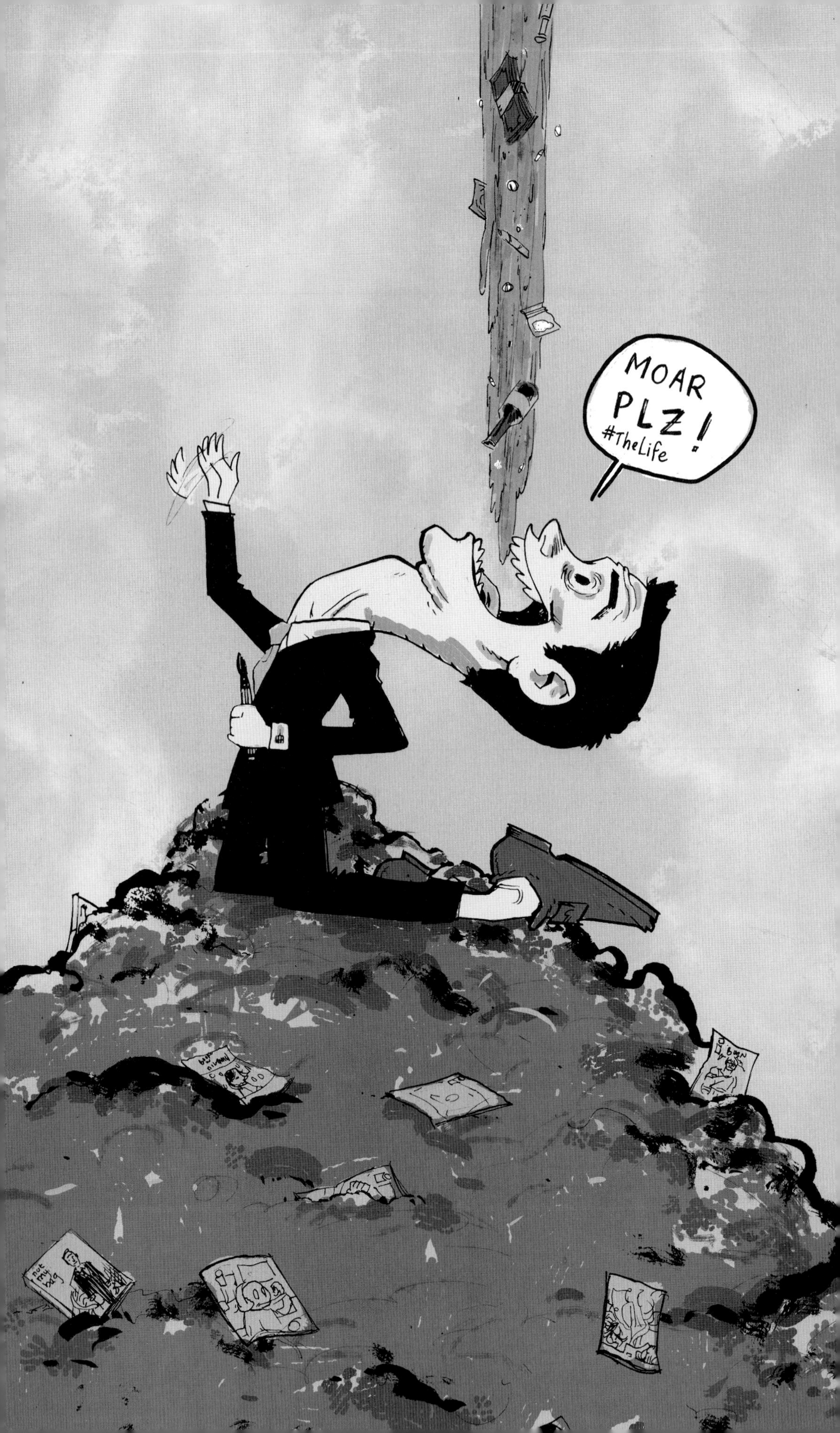
MOAR PLZ!
#TheLife

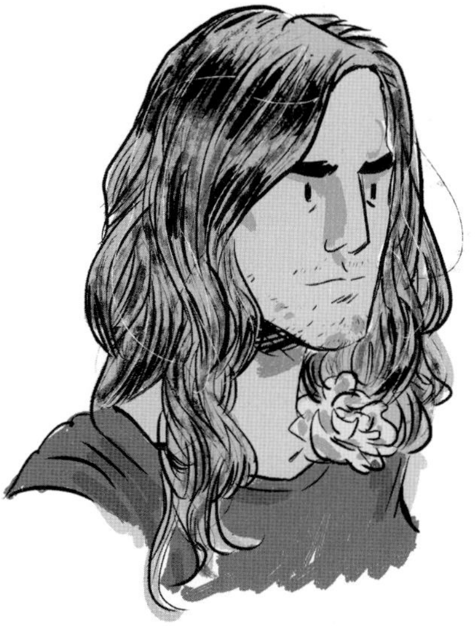

I AM NOT CARRIE BRADSHAW

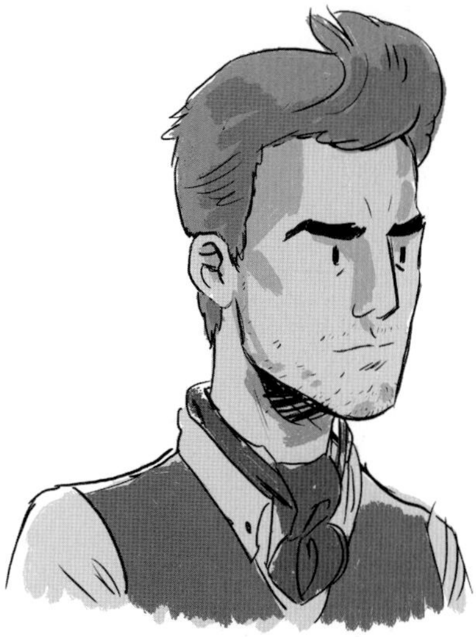

I AM NOT KURT HUMMEL

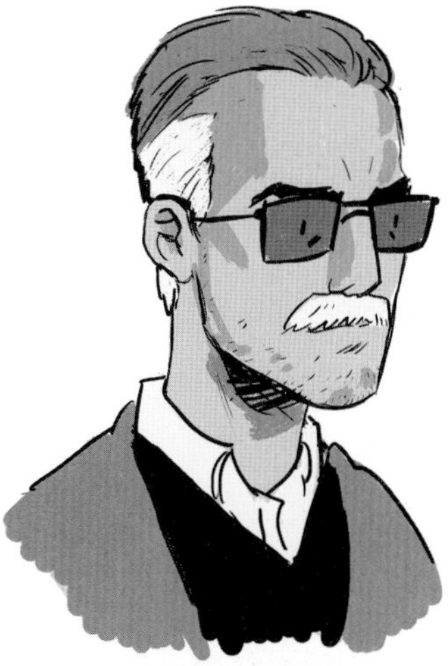

I AM NOT STAN LEE

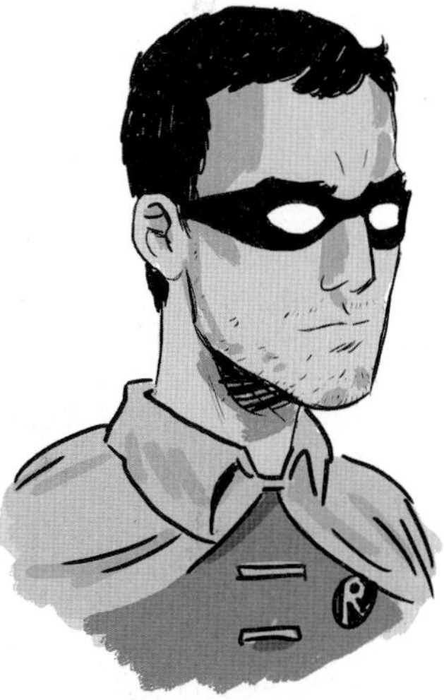
R

I AM NOT A BOY WONDER

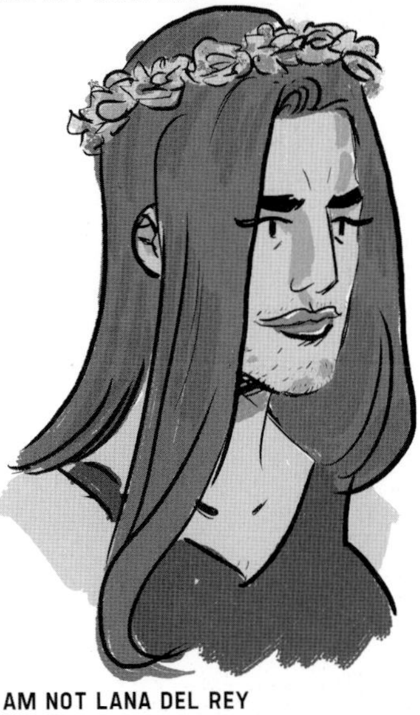

I AM NOT LANA DEL REY

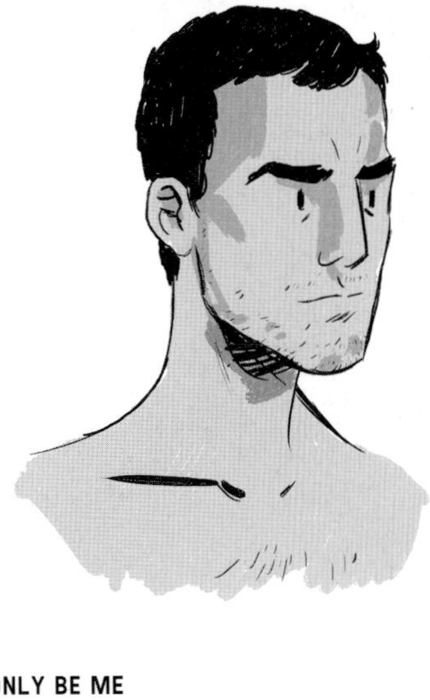

I CAN ONLY BE ME

"what it is and where it stops
Nobody knows,
You gave me a life I never chose,
I wanna leave but the world won't
let me go."

—Metric
"Blindness"

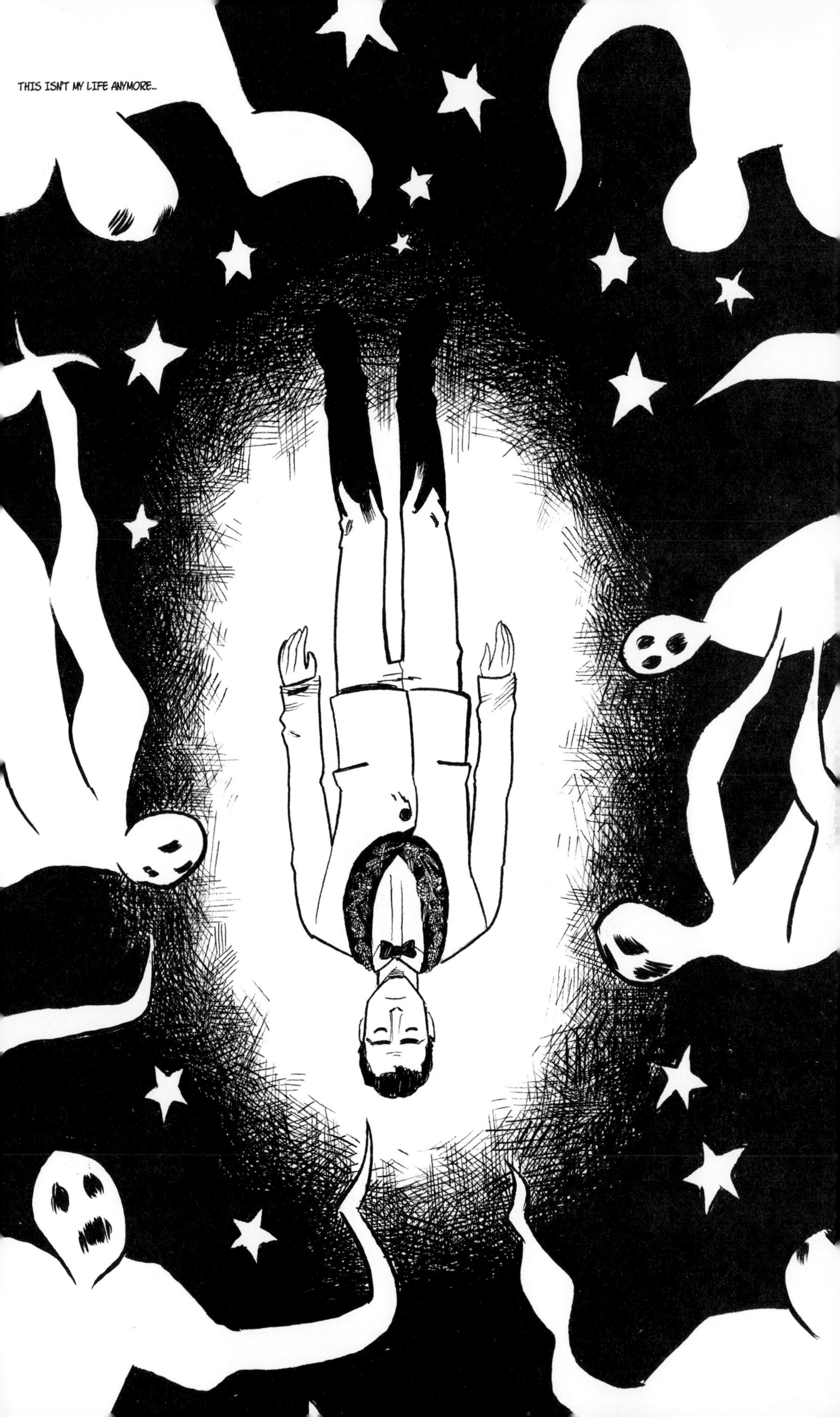
THIS ISN'T MY LIFE ANYMORE...

Progressions

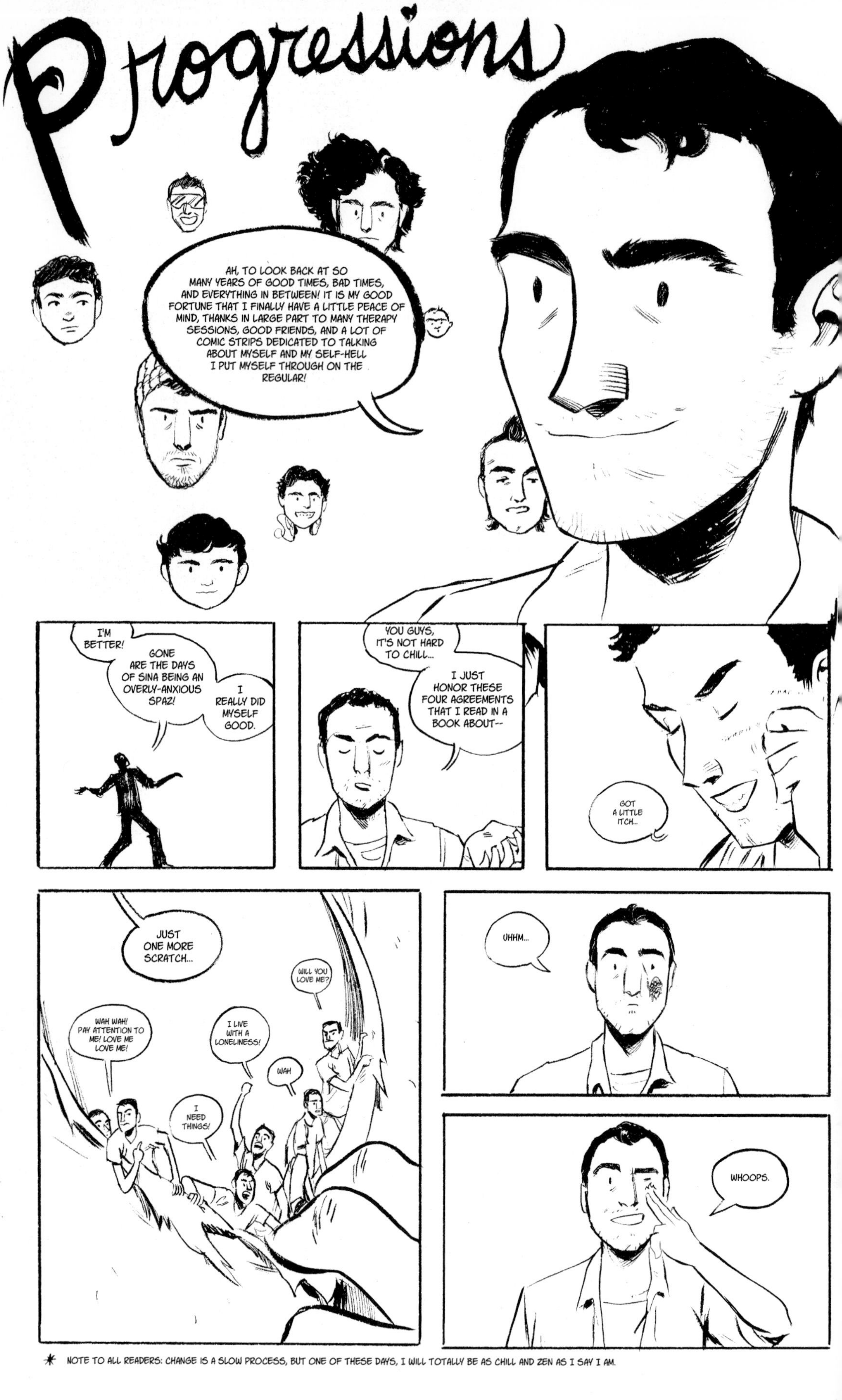
Progressions
AH, TO LOOK BACK AT SO MANY YEARS OF GOOD TIMES, BAD TIMES, AND EVERYTHING IN BETWEEN! IT IS MY GOOD FORTUNE THAT I FINALLY HAVE A LITTLE PEACE OF MIND, THANKS IN LARGE PART TO MANY THERAPY SESSIONS, GOOD FRIENDS, AND A LOT OF COMIC STRIPS DEDICATED TO TALKING ABOUT MYSELF AND MY SELF-HELL I PUT MYSELF THROUGH ON THE REGULAR!
I'M BETTER!
GONE ARE THE DAYS OF SINA BEING AN OVERLY-ANXIOUS SPAZ!
I REALLY DID MYSELF GOOD.
YOU GUYS, IT'S NOT HARD TO CHILL...
I JUST HONOR THESE FOUR AGREEMENTS THAT I READ IN A BOOK ABOUT--
GOT A LITTLE ITCH...
JUST ONE MORE SCRATCH...
WILL YOU LOVE ME?
WAH WAH! PAY ATTENTION TO ME! LOVE ME LOVE ME!
I LIVE WITH A LONELINESS!
WAH
I NEED THINGS!
UHHM...
WHOOPS.

✱ NOTE TO ALL READERS: CHANGE IS A SLOW PROCESS, BUT ONE OF THESE DAYS, I WILL TOTALLY BE AS CHILL AND ZEN AS I SAY I AM.

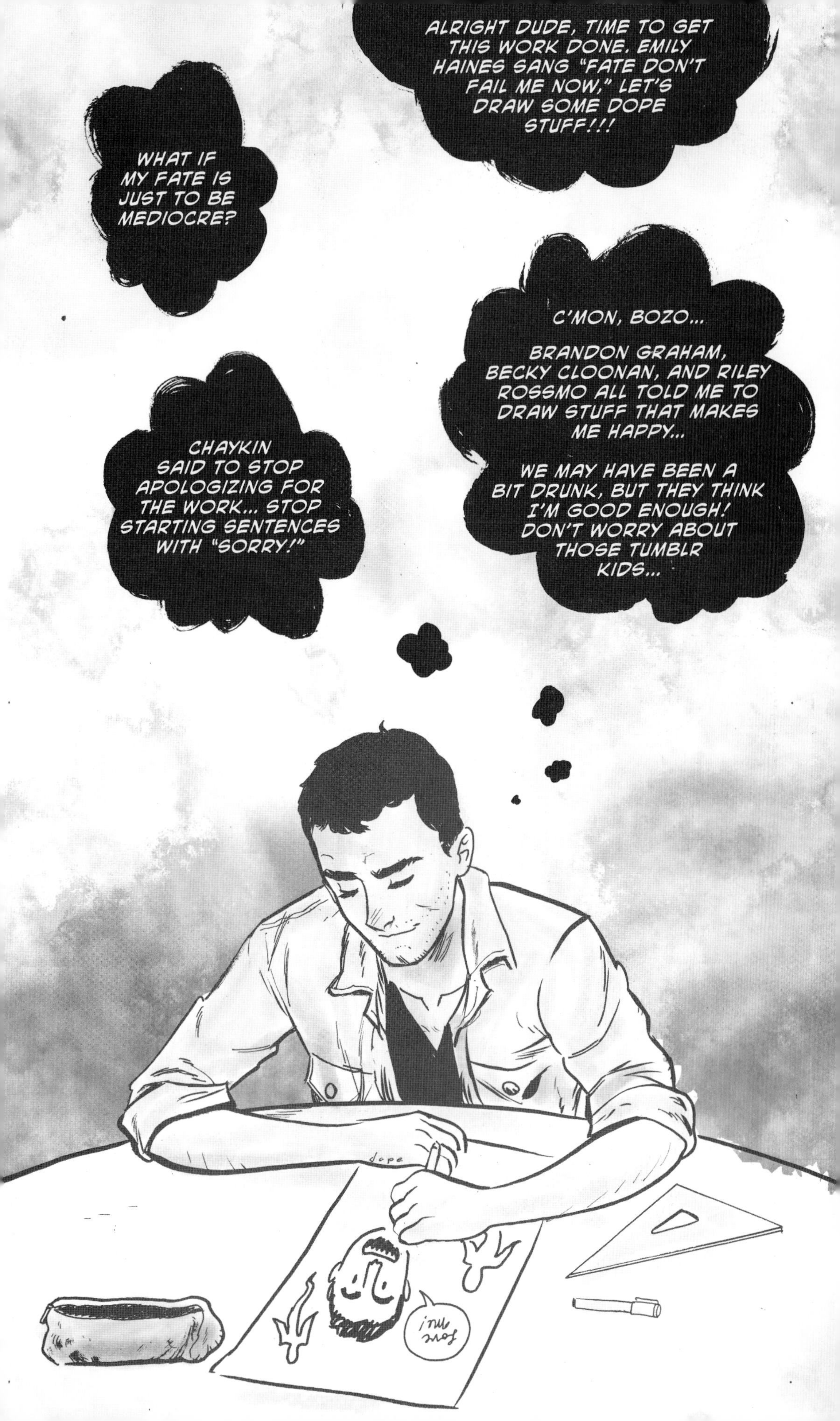
ALRIGHT DUDE, TIME TO GET THIS WORK DONE. EMILY HAINES SANG "FATE DON'T FAIL ME NOW," LET'S DRAW SOME DOPE STUFF!!!
WHAT IF MY FATE IS JUST TO BE MEDIOCRE?
C'MON, BOZO...
BRANDON GRAHAM, BECKY CLOONAN, AND RILEY ROSSMO ALL TOLD ME TO DRAW STUFF THAT MAKES ME HAPPY...
WE MAY HAVE BEEN A BIT DRUNK, BUT THEY THINK I'M GOOD ENOUGH! DON'T WORRY ABOUT THOSE TUMBLR KIDS...
CHAYKIN SAID TO STOP APOLOGIZING FOR THE WORK... STOP STARTING SENTENCES WITH "SORRY!"
dope

I WANT TO GROW UP, I THINK

I made this book because I didn't know what else to do. My grandmother died, the comics I was working on were struggling to sustain sales, and as a result of a difficult – albeit prolific – year, I had no love to give in my relationship. Tapped out, lost, and hollow, I left Los Angeles to figure out what I needed to become whole again.

There's a sickening feeling when you can no longer trust your own decisions – when you can't rely on your brain chemistry to guide you towards self-protection. My boyfriend at the time urged me to take anti-depressants. I told him I was scared to, that I couldn't be a stranger in my body. The truth that hindsight presents is such: I had compartmentalized to the point where everything I was doing was to make others happy. My emotions were packed up in tiny boxes to be dealt with later. There were dozens of necessary arguments I should have had that I swept under the rug to keep the peace. All of my work commitments were serving the needs of writers I loved and respected, but ultimately I was fueling their agendas, and not my own. Had I opted for medication during this particularly cruel winter, that would have sealed the deal for me. The numbness, the overwhelming nothingness . . . I felt that I would remain ill-equipped to understand how to communicate with the soul hiding under my pain. There is no solace in the prospect of living even-keel.

The nights spent on air mattresses, couches, and floors were the ones where I felt the most privileged. In a strange turn, I didn't have the financial or emotional freedom to explore my own feelings until I'd relinquished the nice apartment, the high-paying freelance jobs, and responsibilities that come with pursuing romance. When I was left with nothing, I had the bandwidth to look at myself again. It was during those months that I could actually hear the advice being given to me through the years. I spent my time reading material that had nothing to do with comics. My notebook slowly began to fill up with drawings and sentences remarking on my experiences with the texts.

During my last exchange with Robert Kirkman, the first thing he asked was why I wasn't doing more autobio comics. I laughed and said they take time (a lie). When my publisher Eric Stephenson told me I couldn't produce more of the comic *Burn the Orphanage* with sales as they were, I mentioned an idea about a past relationship, and he said, "That sounds like a good book, especially if it's something you've been thinking about and really want to do." Two men, both successful and at the forefront of Image Comics' renaissance, advising me, in essence, to do me. This message, after years of being bullied into hiding my eccentricities and being encouraged to subdue my agenda, was so tough to take in.

When I began creating strips for this edition of *Self-Obsessed*, I kept asking myself, "What's the point? What is the message I'm delivering to the reader?" At the same time, Fox's TV series *Glee* was on its way out the door. *Rolling Stone* had a succinct summation of the show: "Ryan Murphy's weekly musical revue was a story about the great lengths people go in order to be anybody's somebody, be it a spouse or a star." Finally, an explanation for why I would go so far as to exploit and commodify my memories and personality! It's about the stuff I did in order to find value in myself through others. This thesis circled around my brain as I started connecting the tissue between strips from a decade ago and new material reflecting my current outlook. I could see the cartoon me flailing, trying to win the approval of others, to the point where he forgot to win the approval of the most important person: himself.

For that reason alone I had to dedicate this book to the kid I used to be. He was courteous, sympathetic to others, and most importantly, his inflated confidence allowed him to do whatever he wanted. I know now that I made this book because I needed to. I needed to make something I could stand by with 100% honesty and love. If I'm going to commit the rest of my life to being put in boxes, or being labeled, I have to do it as myself and not the version of myself I assumed others wanted. No more compartments. No more secrets. I can only be me.

I wish there was more time to work on *Self-Obsessed*, as I'm now inspired to do some weird ouroboros drawing of me eating my own tail. Fatalistic in a cool way, right?

SINA GRACE
A Coffee Shop in Los Angeles, CA

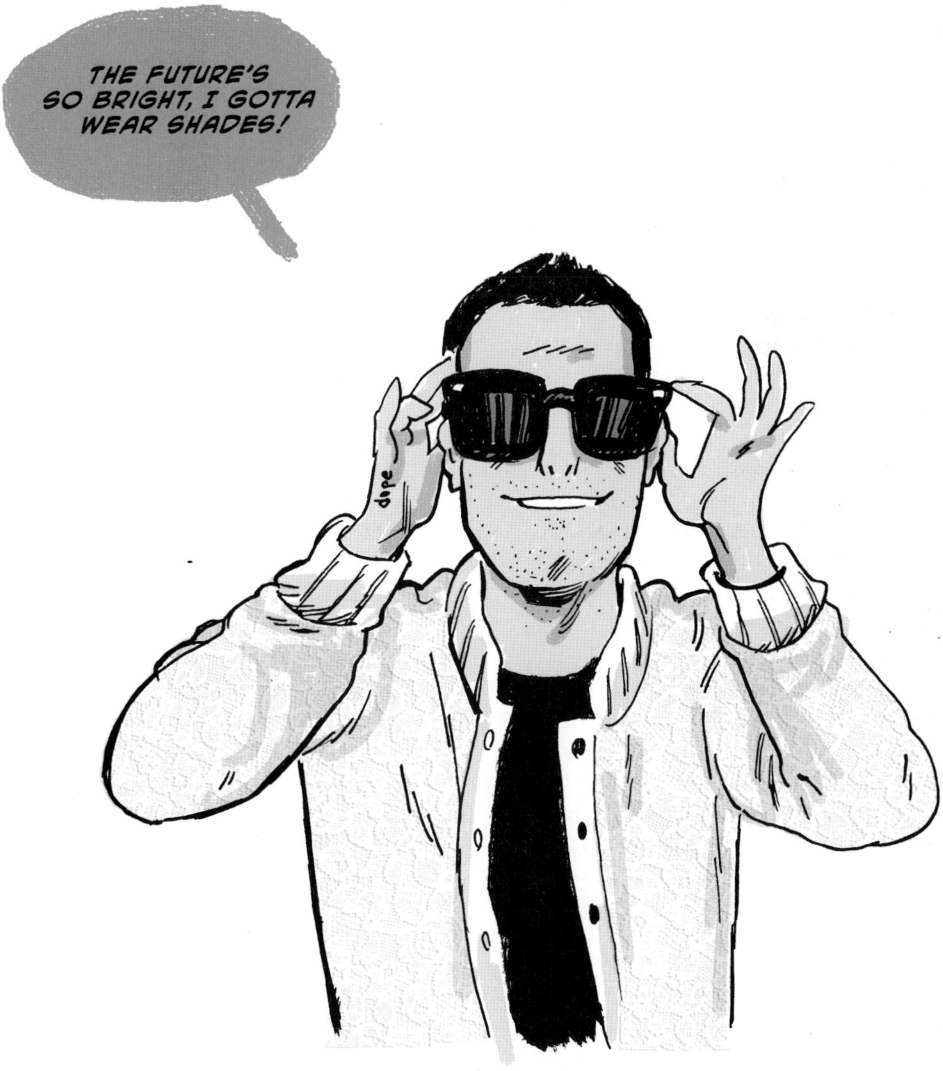
THE FUTURE'S SO BRIGHT, I GOTTA WEAR SHADES!
dope

THE
END

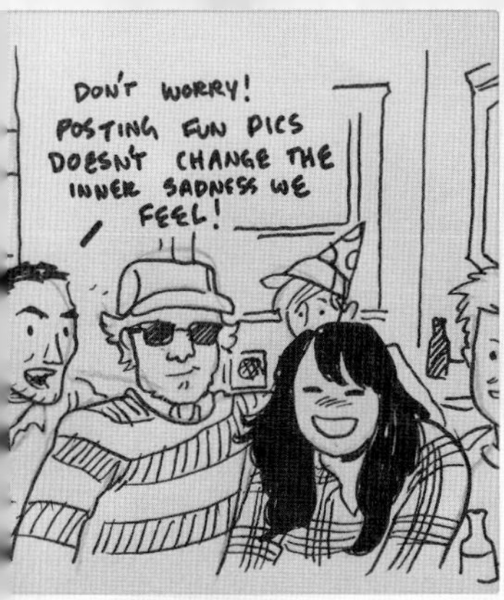
DON'T WORRY! POSTING FUN PICS DOESN'T CHANGE THE INNER SADNESS WE FEEL!

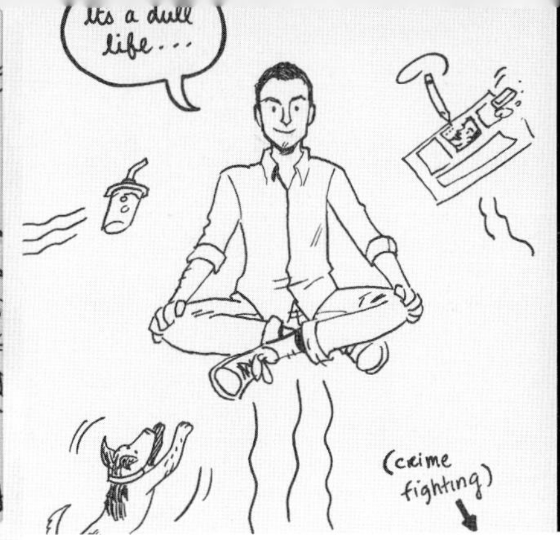
Its a dull life...
(crime fighting)

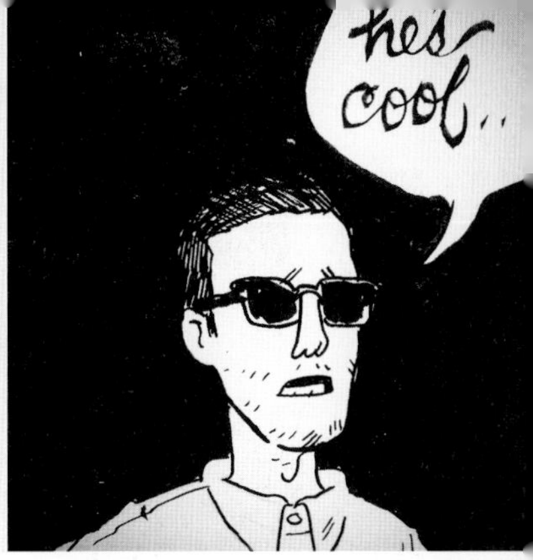
hes cool..

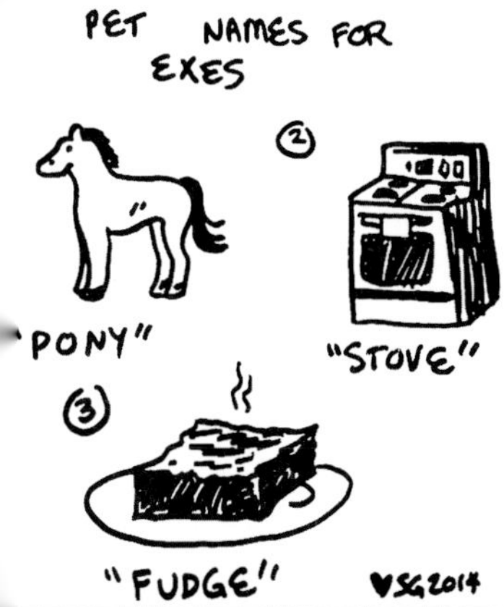
PET NAMES FOR EXES
"PONY"
②
"STOVE"
③
"FUDGE"
♥SG2014

EXTRAS

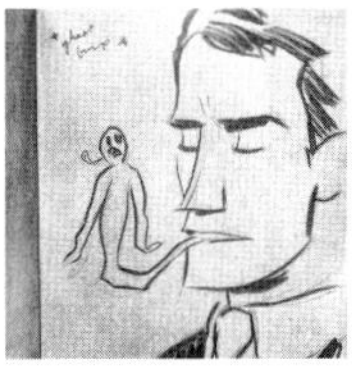

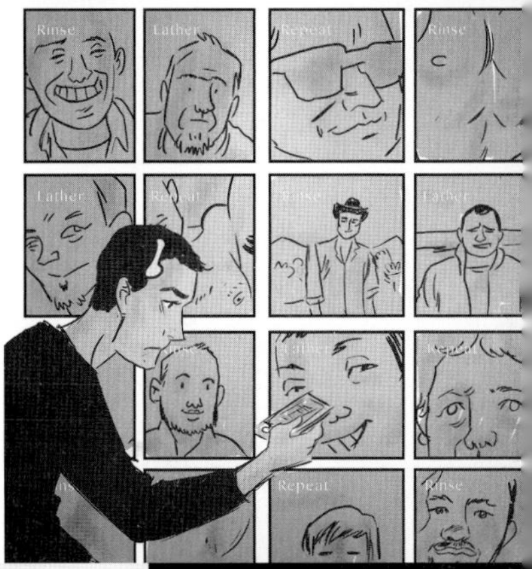
Rinse
Lather
Repeat
Rinse

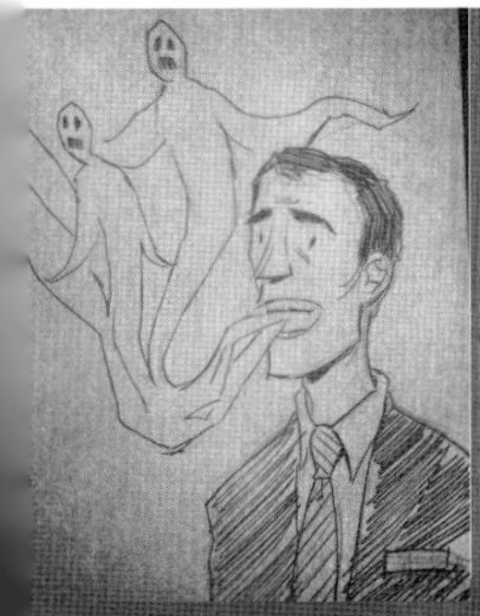

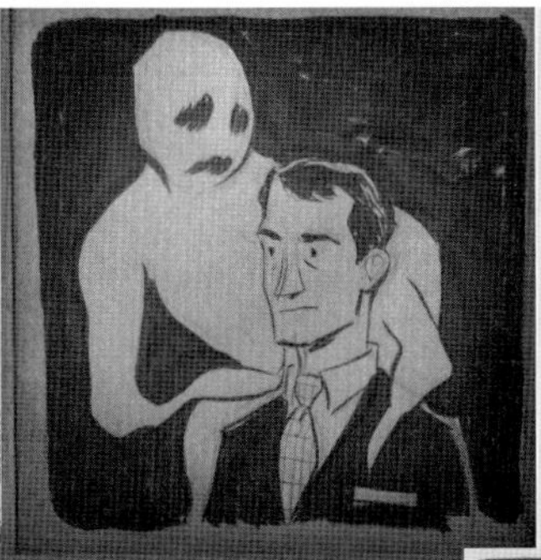

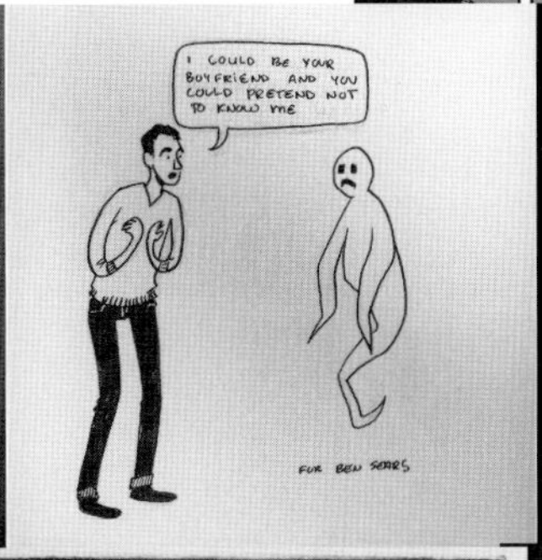
I COULD BE YOUR BOYFRIEND AND YOU COULD PRETEND NOT TO KNOW ME
FOR BEN SEARS

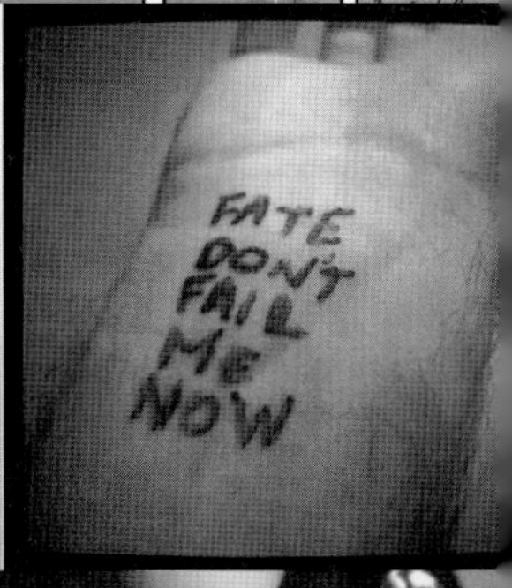
FATE DON'T FAIL ME NOW

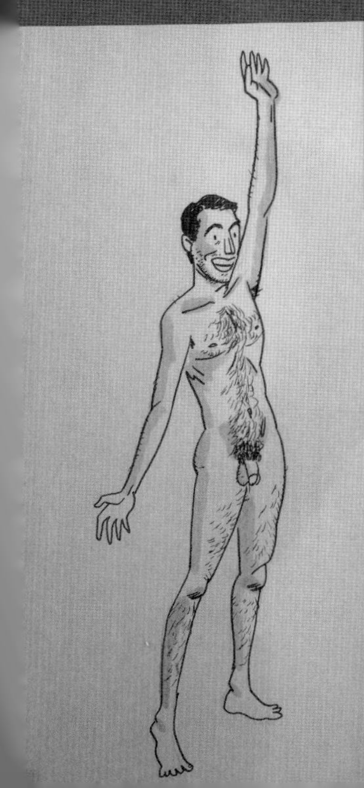

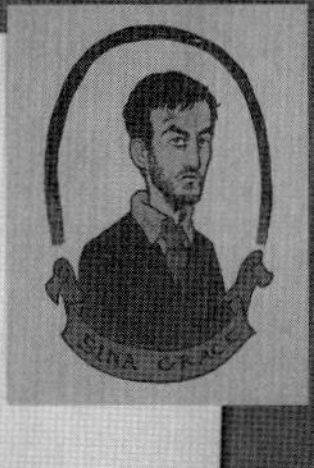

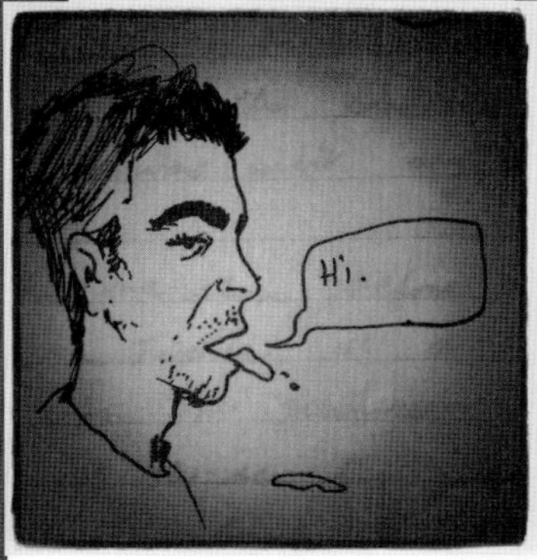
Hi.

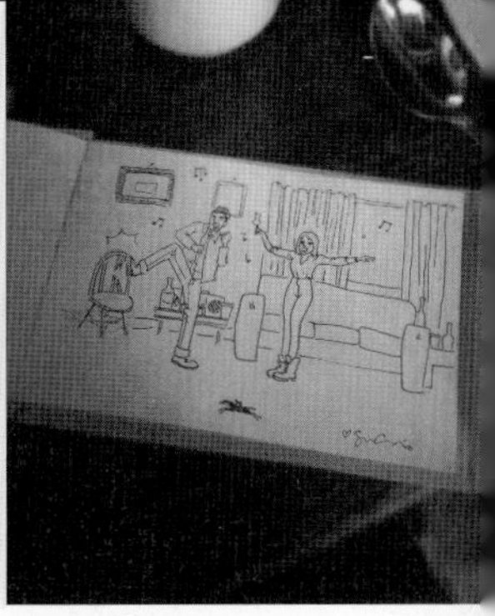

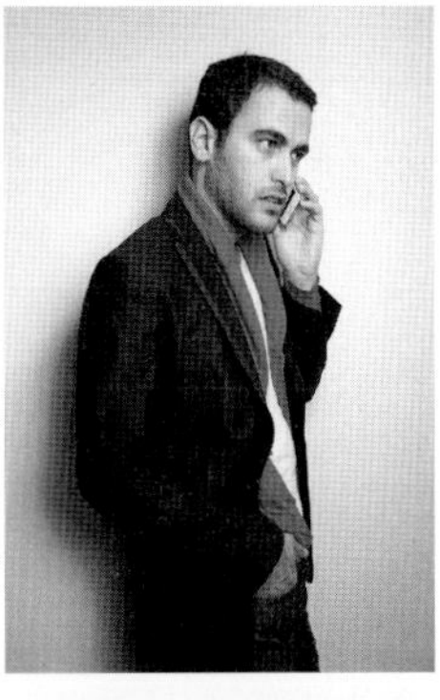

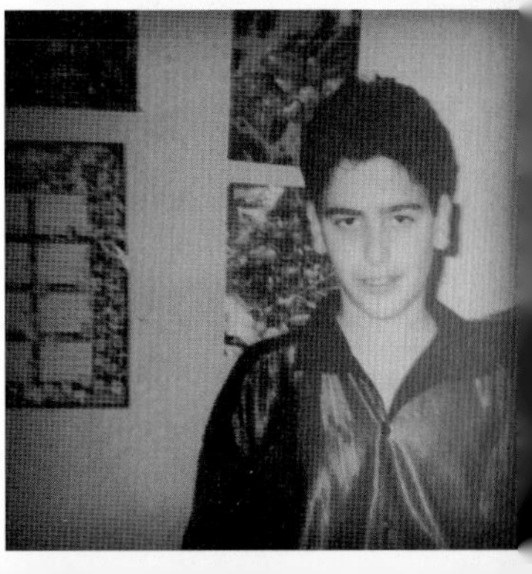

DEFINING MOMENT #37

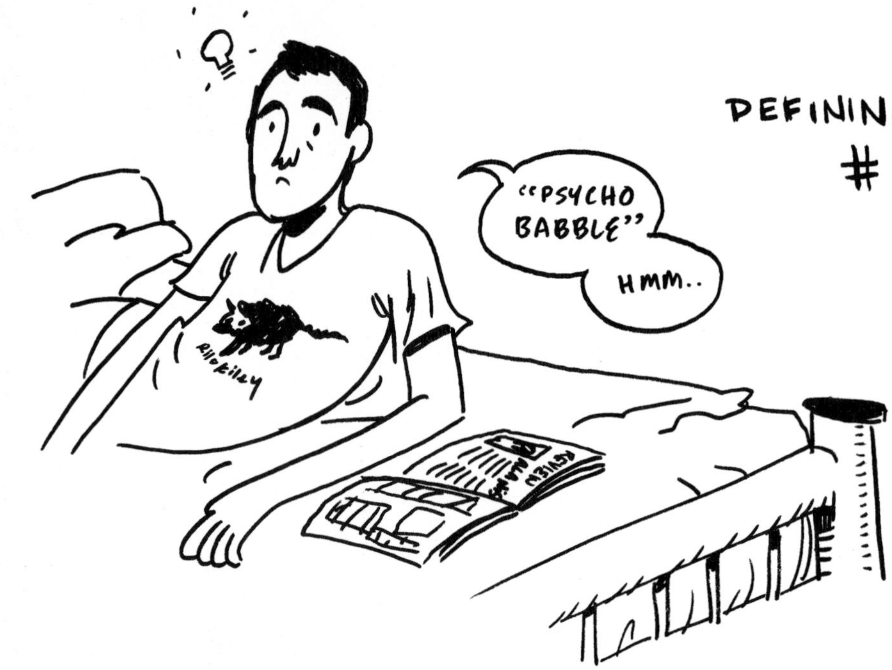
"PSYCHO BABBLE"
HMM..

Self-Portraits

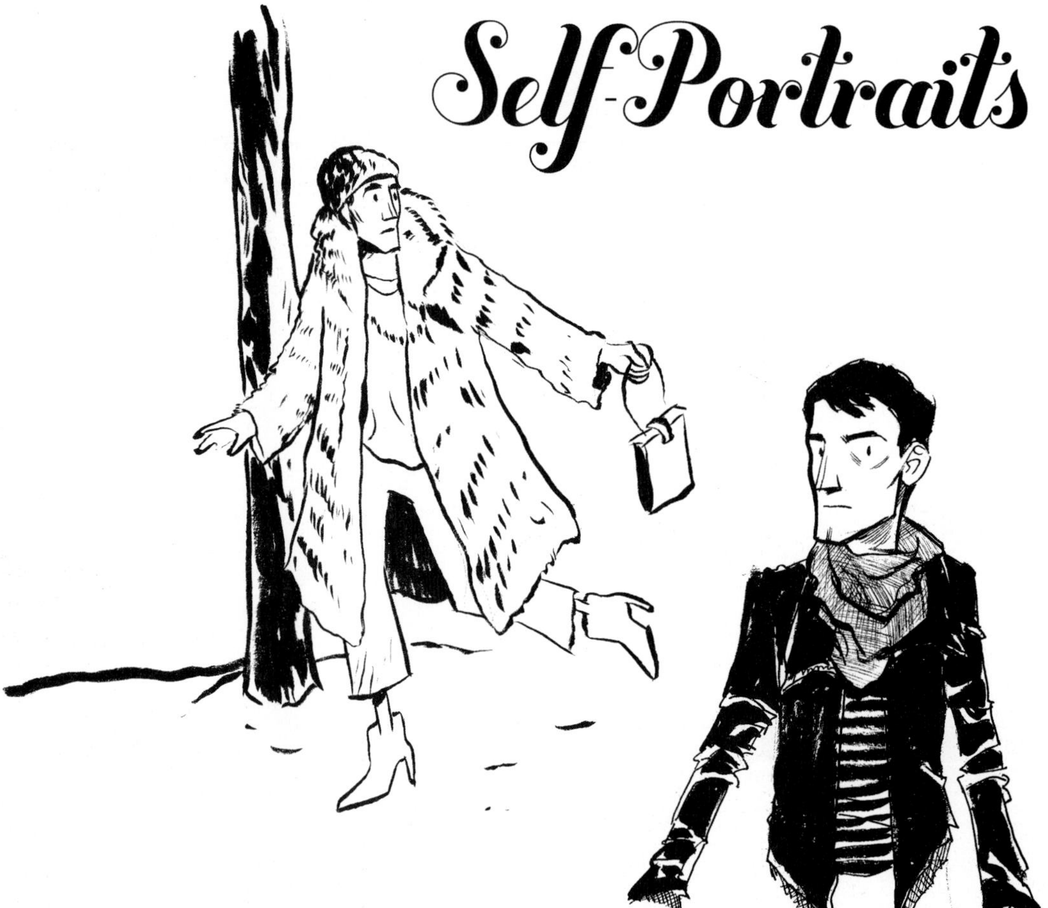

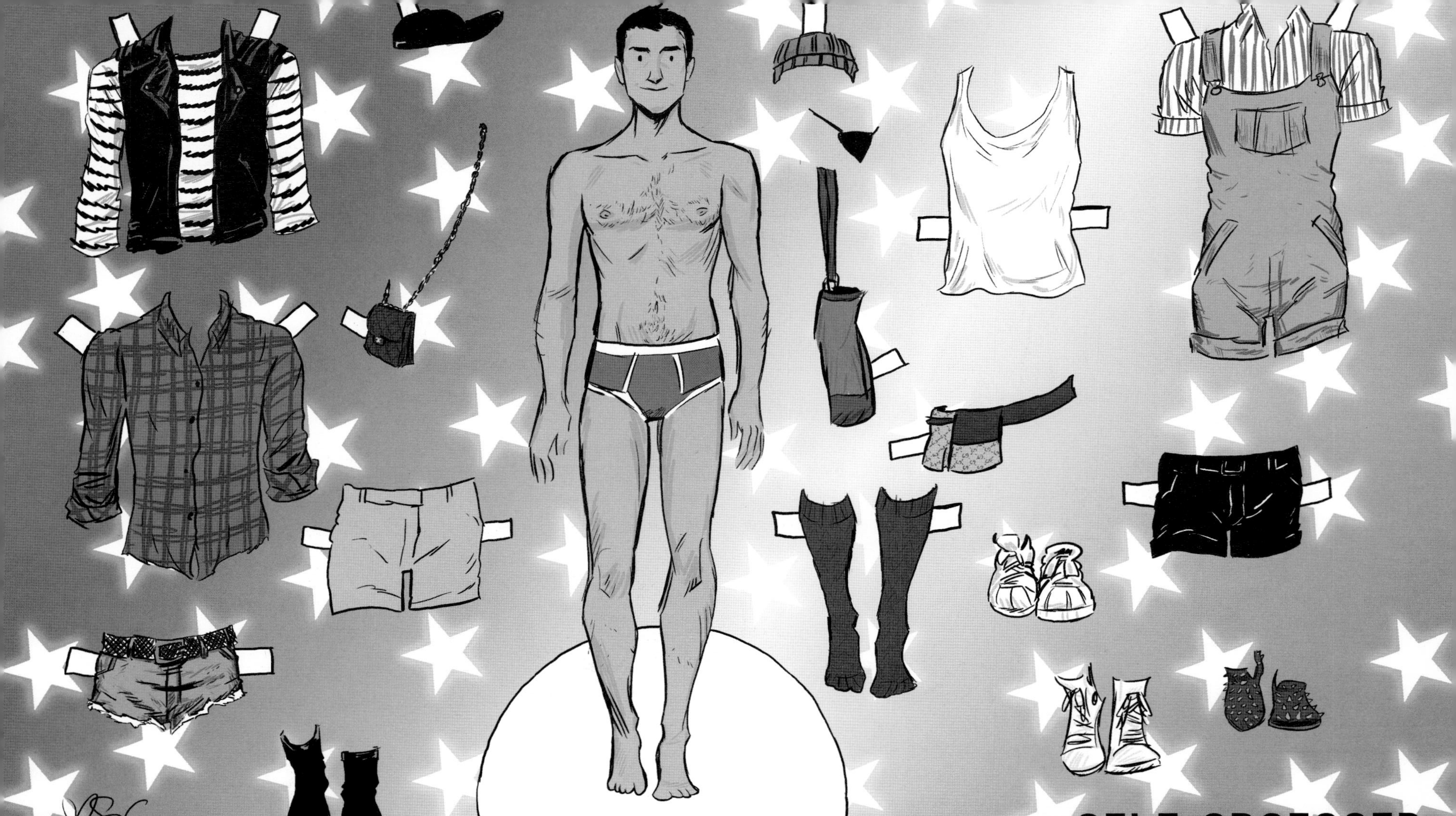

SINA GRACE SELF-OBSESSED

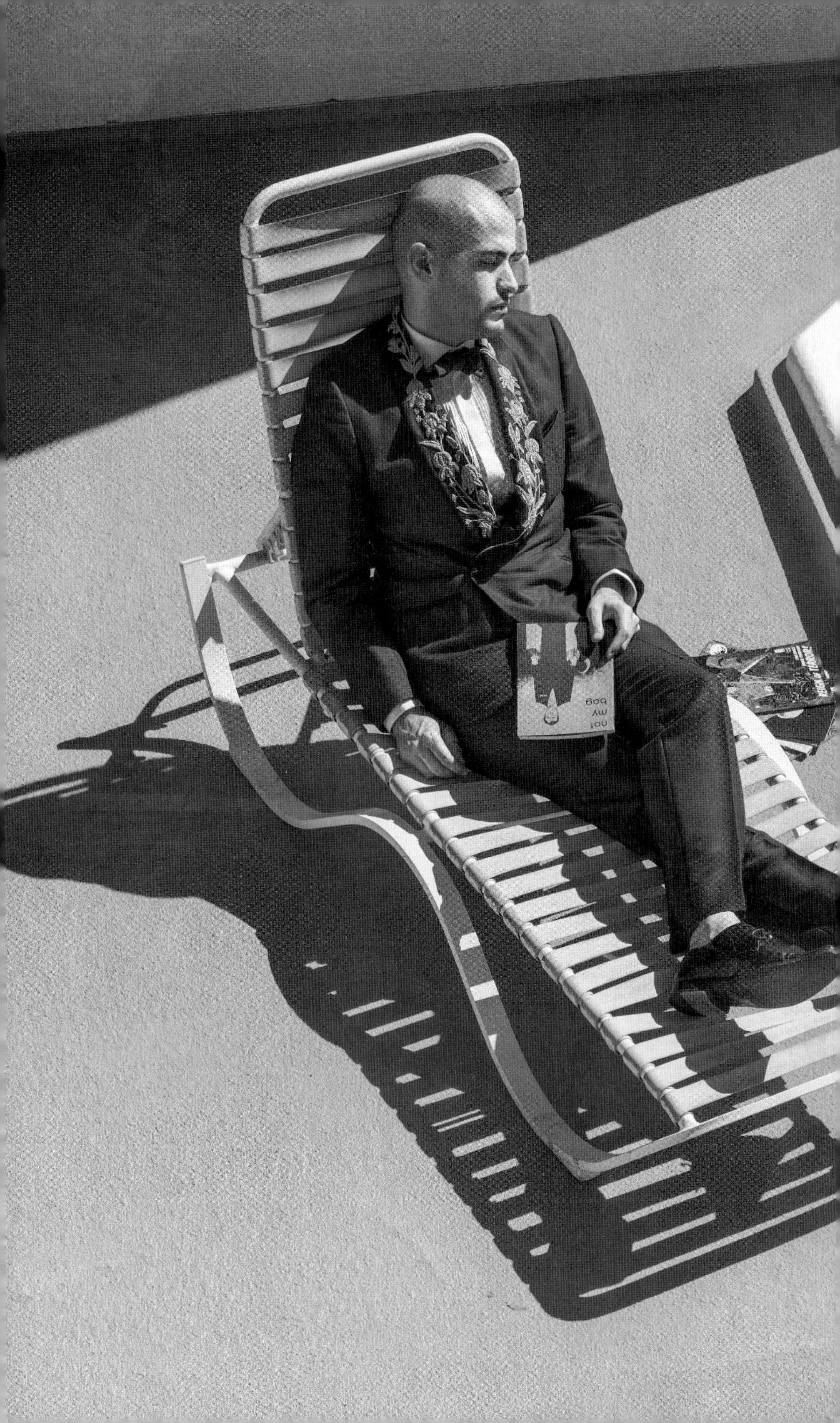
not my bag
REIGN OF TERROR

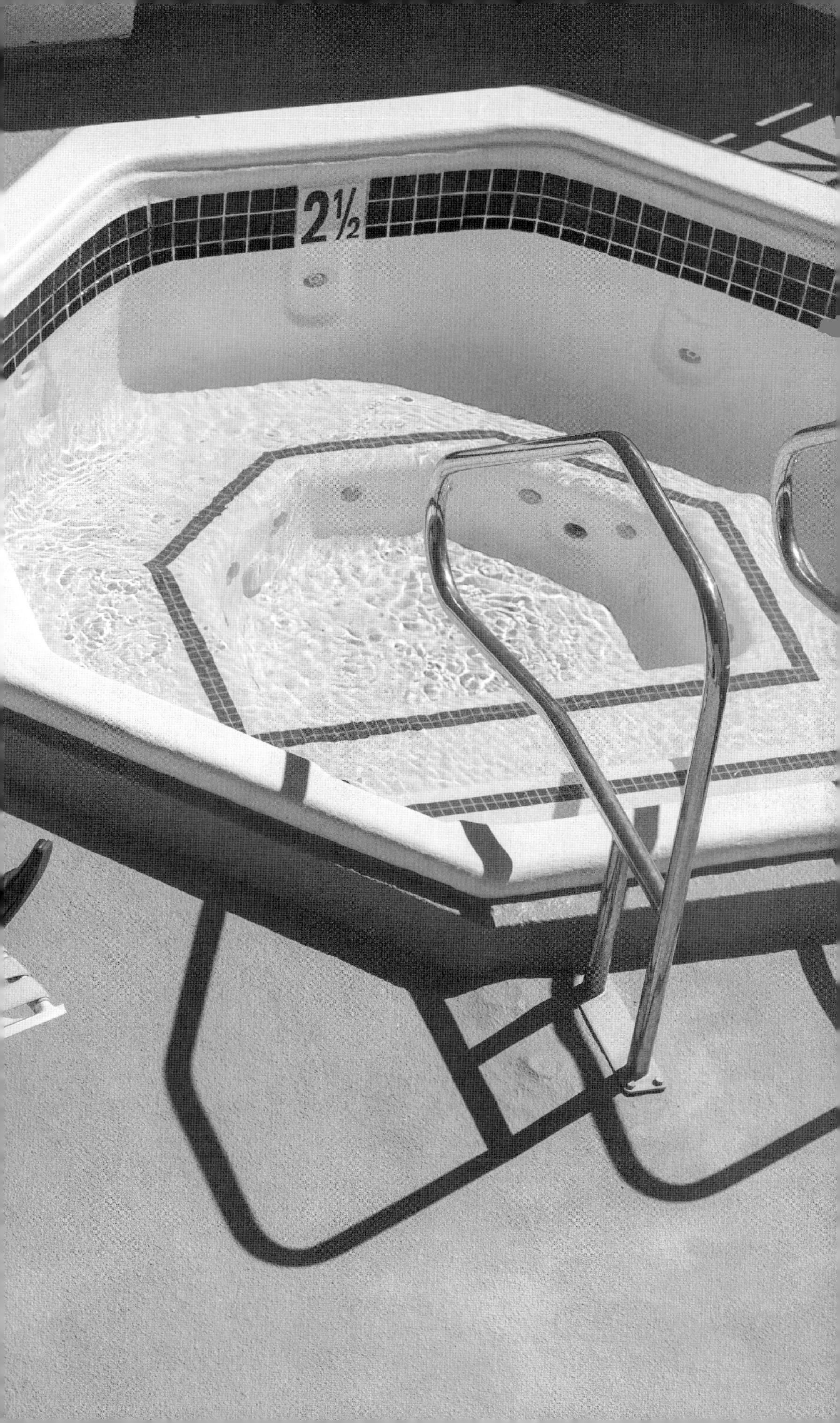
2½

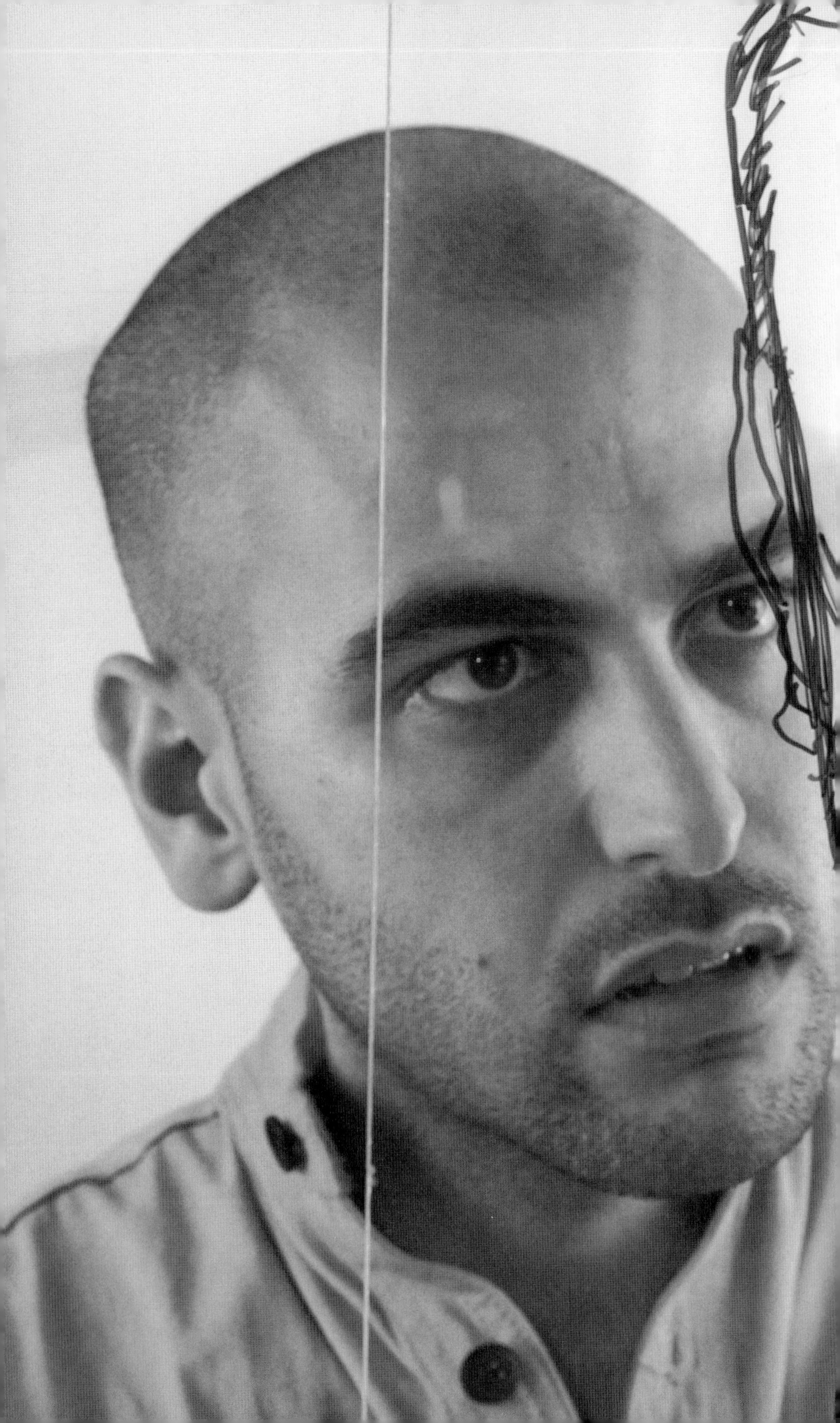

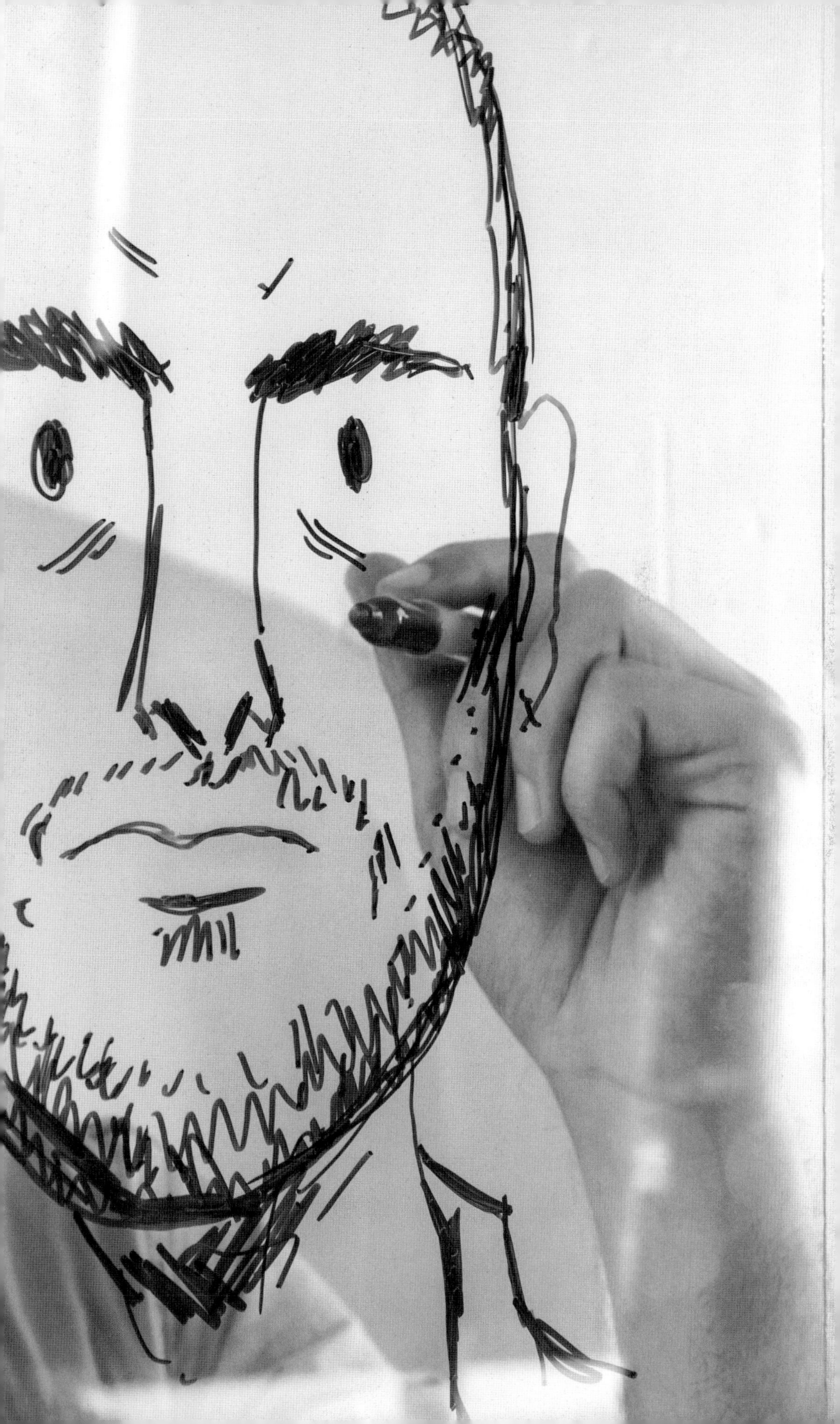

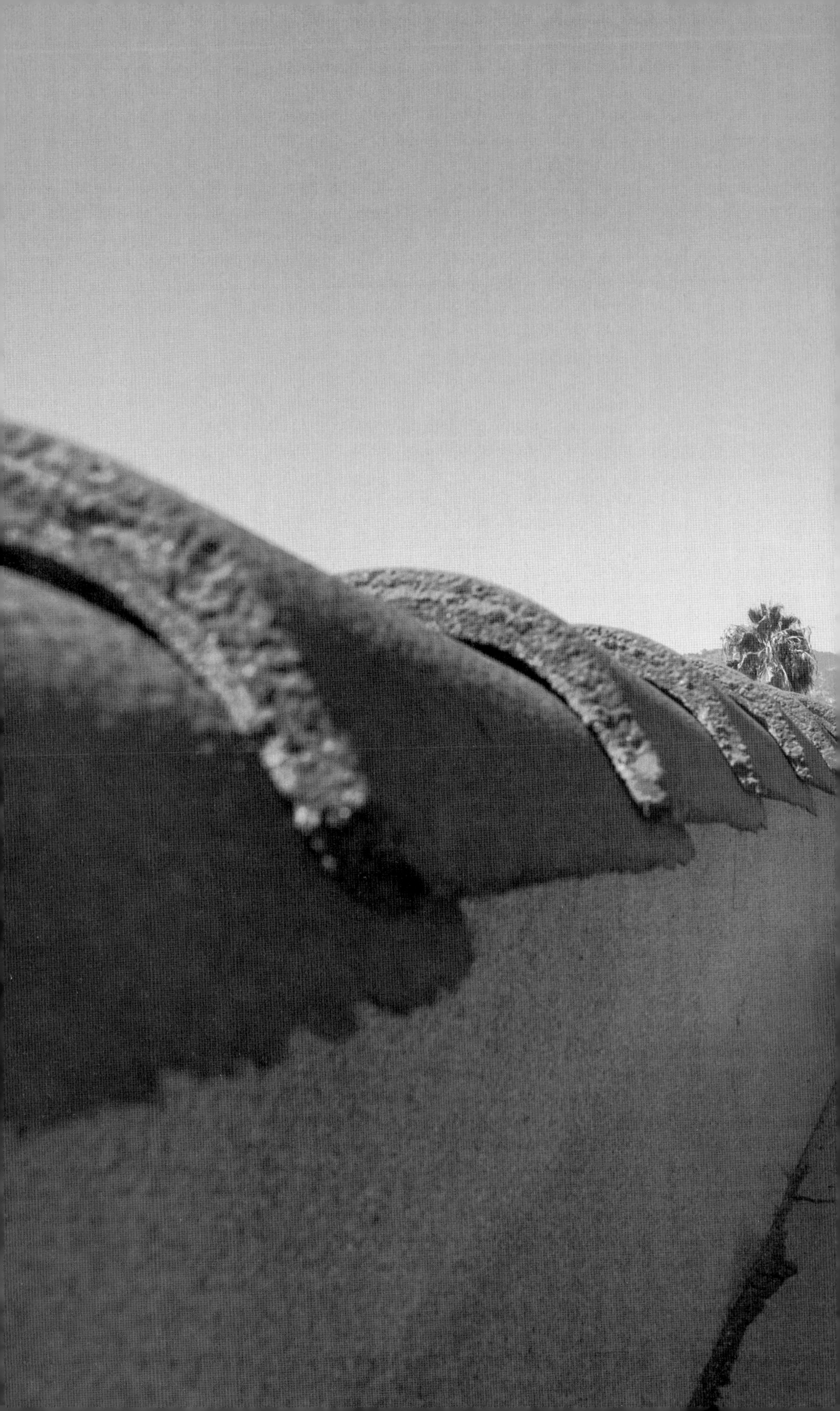

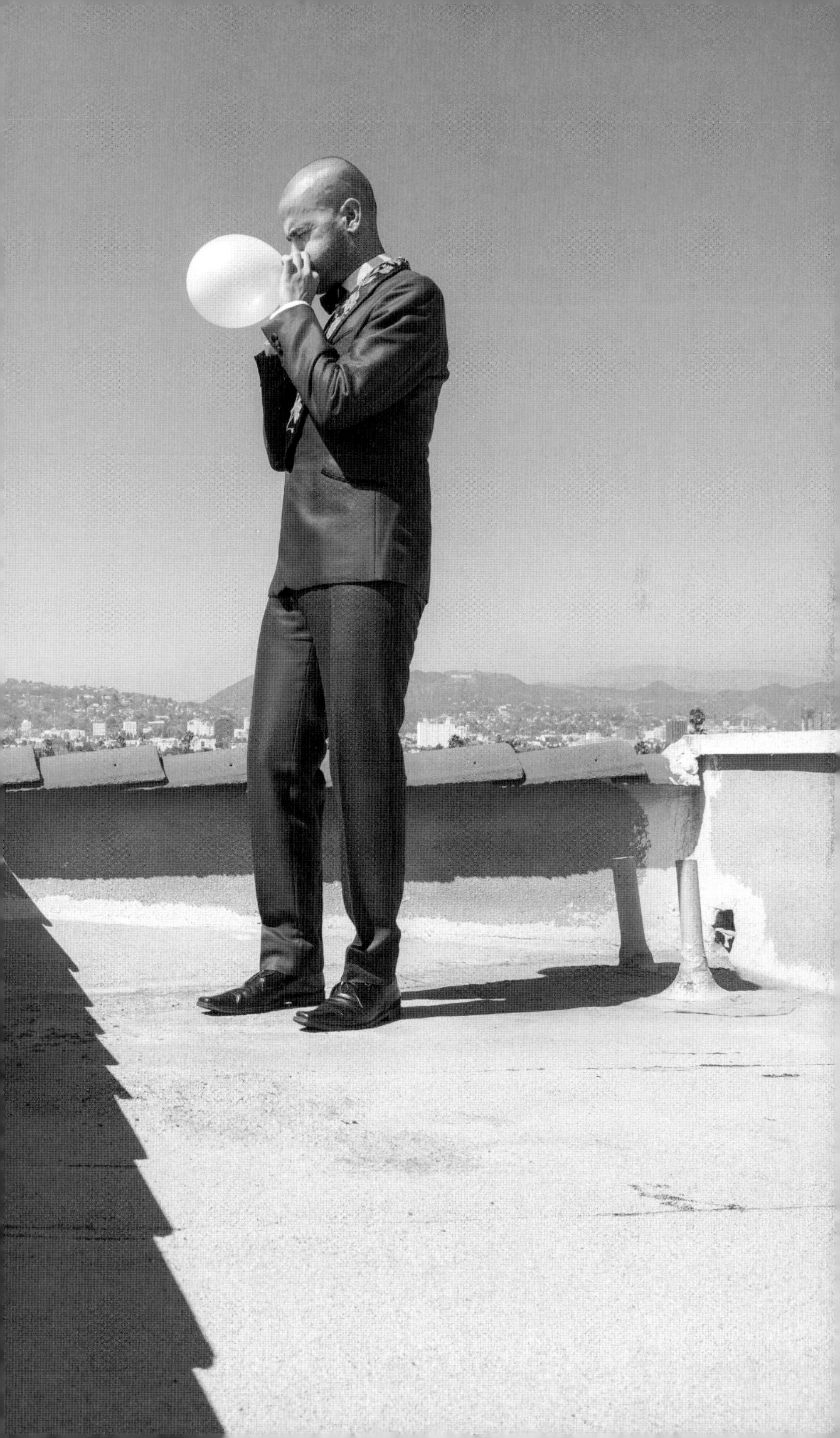

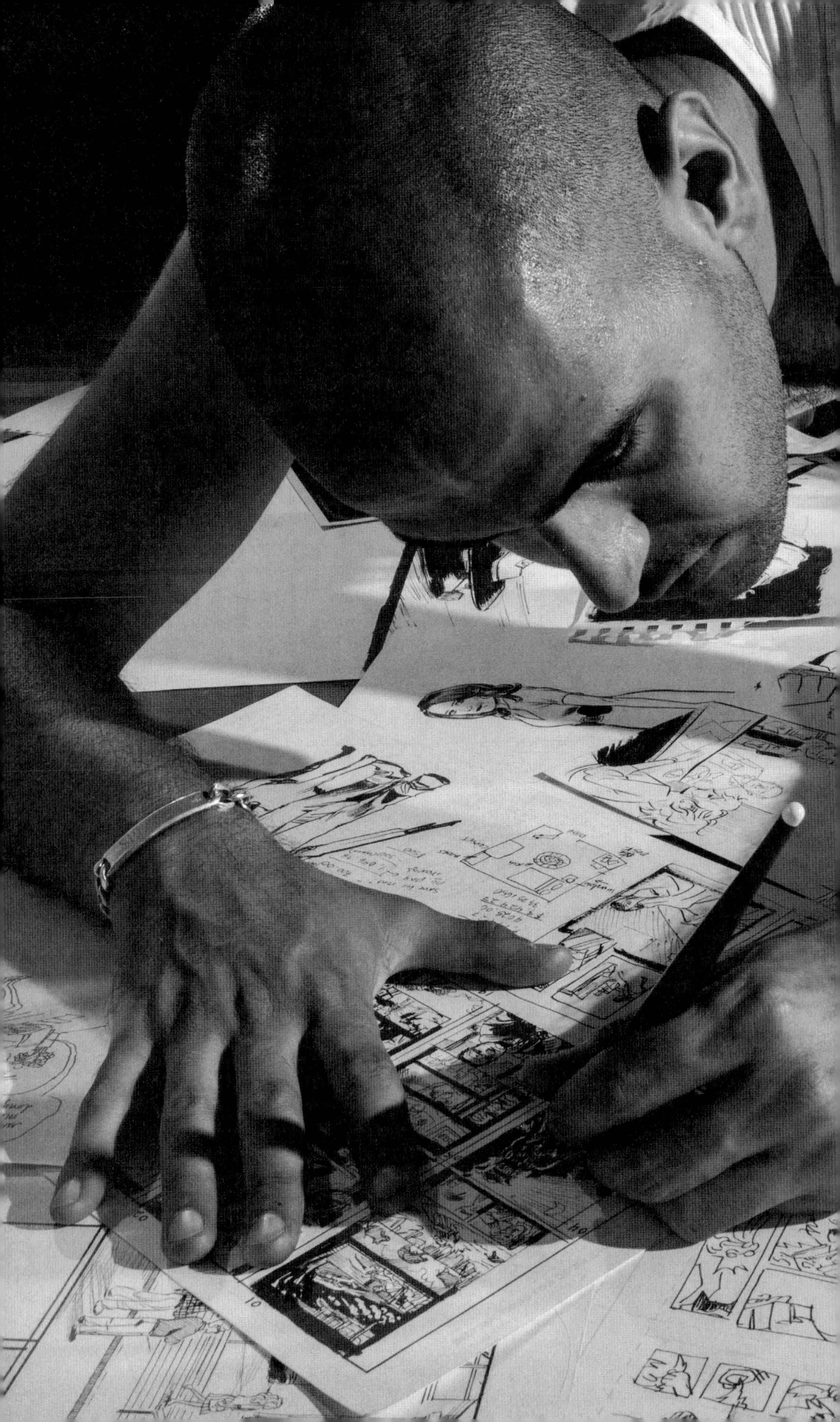

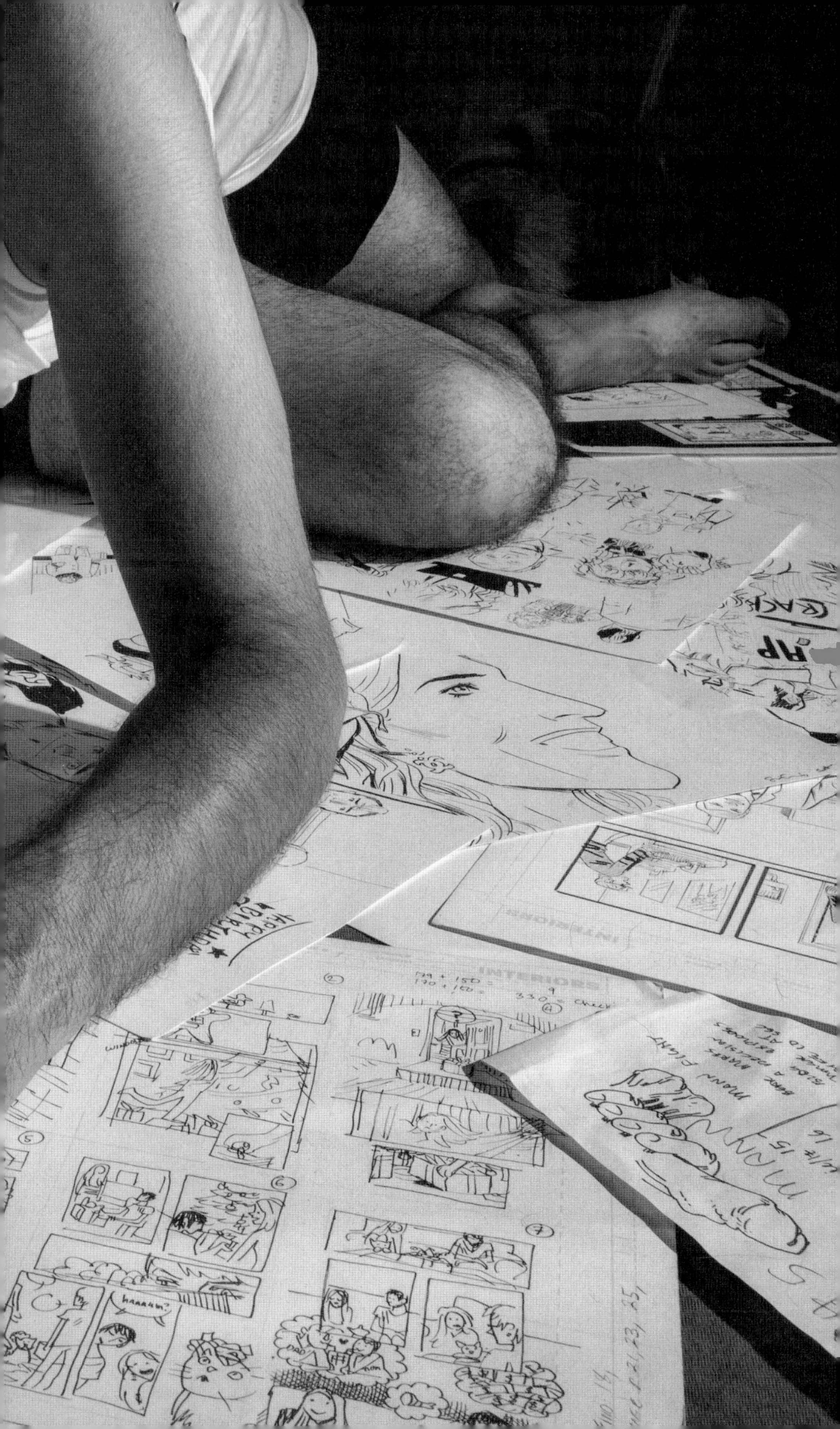
INTERIORS

COMIC-CON
OUTFIT

ACKNOWLEDGEMENTS

THIS BOOK EXISTS BECAUSE OF THE ENCOURAGEMENT, SUPPORT, AND CONTRIBUTIONS FROM THE FOLKS LISTED BELOW. THEY DESERVE FAR MORE THAN WORDS ON A PAGE, AND I WILL BE SPENDING THE REST OF MY LIVING DAYS TRYING TO SHOW THEM MY UNENDING GRATITUDE.

WITHOUT FURTHER ADO, THANK YOU:

TIM DANIEL, JEFF LEMIRE, RYAN O'CONNELL, EMI LENOX, COLLEEN GREEN, RILEY ROSSMO, SINA SPARROW, JASON FISCHER, AMBER BENSON, SPENCER ALCORN, SHAUN STEVEN STRUBLE, ENAE GEERLINGS, HARRIS MILLER, BECKY CLOONAN, BRANDON GRAHAM, KEVIN SONNICHSEN, ERIC STEPHENSON, DANIEL FREEDMAN, MEGAN MACK, NICHOLAS FREEMAN, DALE MEGAN HEALEY, CASEY GILLY, LINDSEY BYRNES, NATE JORDAN, BECKY PEDERSON, MARINAOMI, JENNY LEWIS, SYDNEY NICHOLS, AND BRYAN CARPENDER.

THERE ARE TWO FAMILIES WHOSE PATIENCE I HAVE WORN THIN THROUGH THE PROCESS OF MAKING SELF-OBSESSED... I OWE THEM A MOUNTAIN OF CHOCOLATES:

MY NUCLEAR FAMILY (MOM, DAD, SIS, BRO-IN-LAW, ETC), AND MY IMAGE COMICS FAMILY (KAT, COREY, SASHA, JONATHAN, EMILY, DREW, BRANWYN, ETC).

THIS MAY SOUND TRITE, BUT I FRICKIN' MEAN IT WHEN I SAY THAT I COULDN'T KEEP GOING IF I DIDN'T HAVE THE SUPPORT FROM THE AMAZING RETAILERS AND READERS WHO FED ME WORDS OF LOVE AND ENCOURAGEMENT THESE PAST FIVE YEARS.

THANK YOU FOR BELIEVING IN ME.

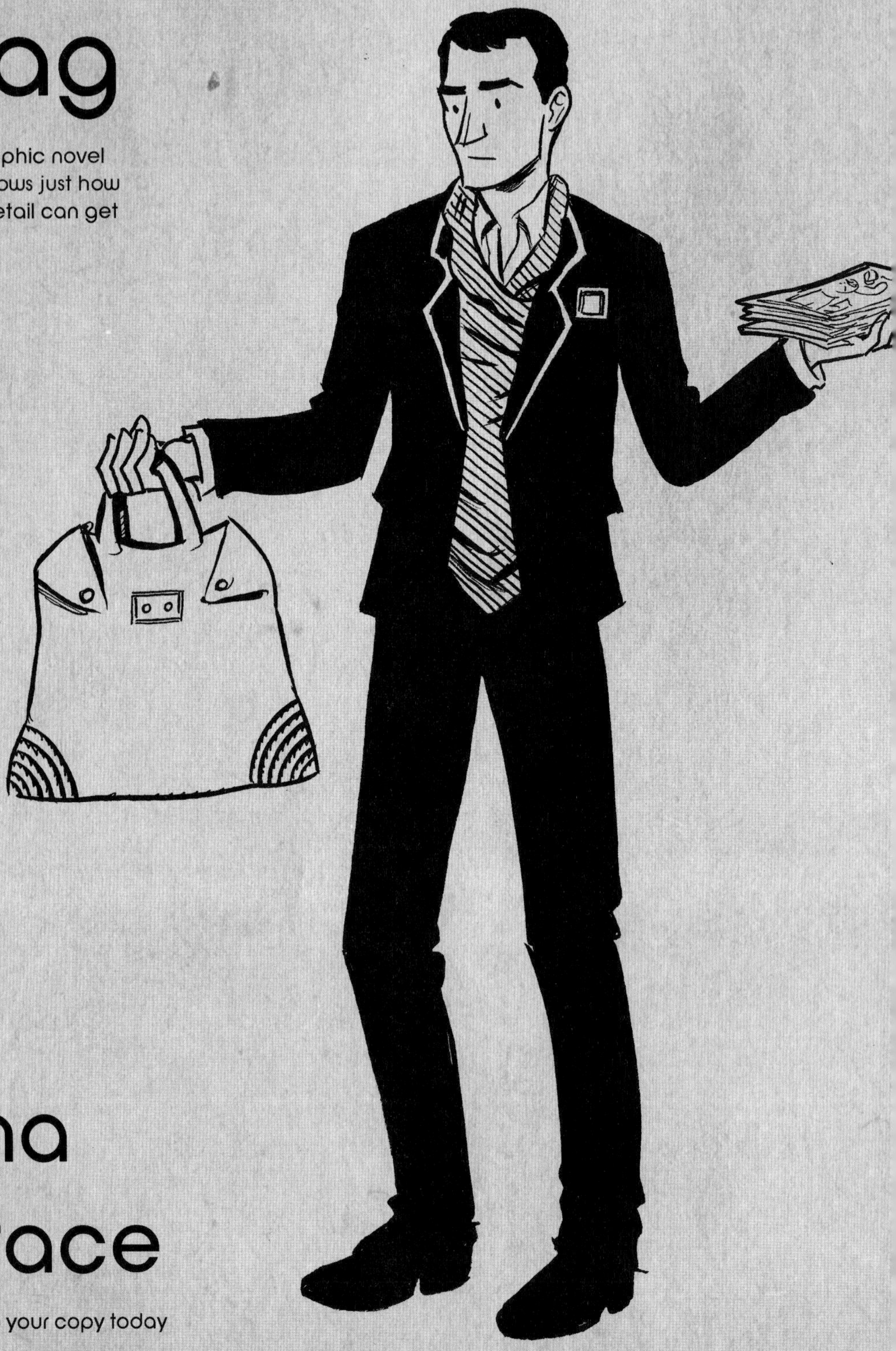

ABOUT THE AUTHOR

PHOTO BY LINDSEY BYRNES

SINA GRACE IS THE AUTHOR AND ILLUSTRATOR OF THE AUTOBIOGRAPHICAL *SELF-OBSESSED*, AND *NOT MY BAG*, WHICH RECOUNTS A STORY OF RETAIL HELL. HE ACTS AS THE ARTIST FOR SHAUN STEVEN STRUBLE'S CULT SERIES, *THE LI'L DEPRESSED BOY*, AND HANDLES ART CHORES ALONG WITH CO-WRITING THE IMAGE COMICS HIT SERIES, *BURN THE ORPHANAGE*. HIS ART HAS BEEN USED BY MUSICIANS OF ALL GENRES, MOST NOTABLY JENNY LEWIS, CHILDISH GAMBINO, KEPI GHOULIE, FEELS, AND MORE.

GRACE HAS ALSO DONE ILLUSTRATIONS FOR ALL-AGES READERS, INCLUDING *AMONG THE GHOSTS*, WRITTEN BY AMBER BENSON, AS WELL AS *PENNY DORA & THE WISHING BOX*, WRITTEN BY MICHAEL STOCK. HIS PREVIOUS WORKS INCLUDE THE SLICE-OF-LIFE *BOOKS WITH PICTURES*, AND THE NEO-NOIR URBAN FANTASY, *CEDRIC HOLLOWS IN DIAL M FOR MAGIC*. FOR A TIME, HE ACTED AS EDITORIAL DIRECTOR FOR ROBERT KIRKMAN'S SKYBOUND IMPRINT AT IMAGE COMICS. TO DATE, HE'S WORKED FOR MARVEL COMICS, IDW, BOOM, DYNAMITE, VALIANT AND MORE. HIS ESSAYS HAVE APPEARED ON SEVERAL WEBSITES, MOST NOTABLY THOUGHT CATALOG.

HE LIVES IN LOS ANGELES, WHERE HE CAN BE FOUND IN COFFEE SHOPS WORKING ON WHATEVER THE NEXT THING MAY BE.

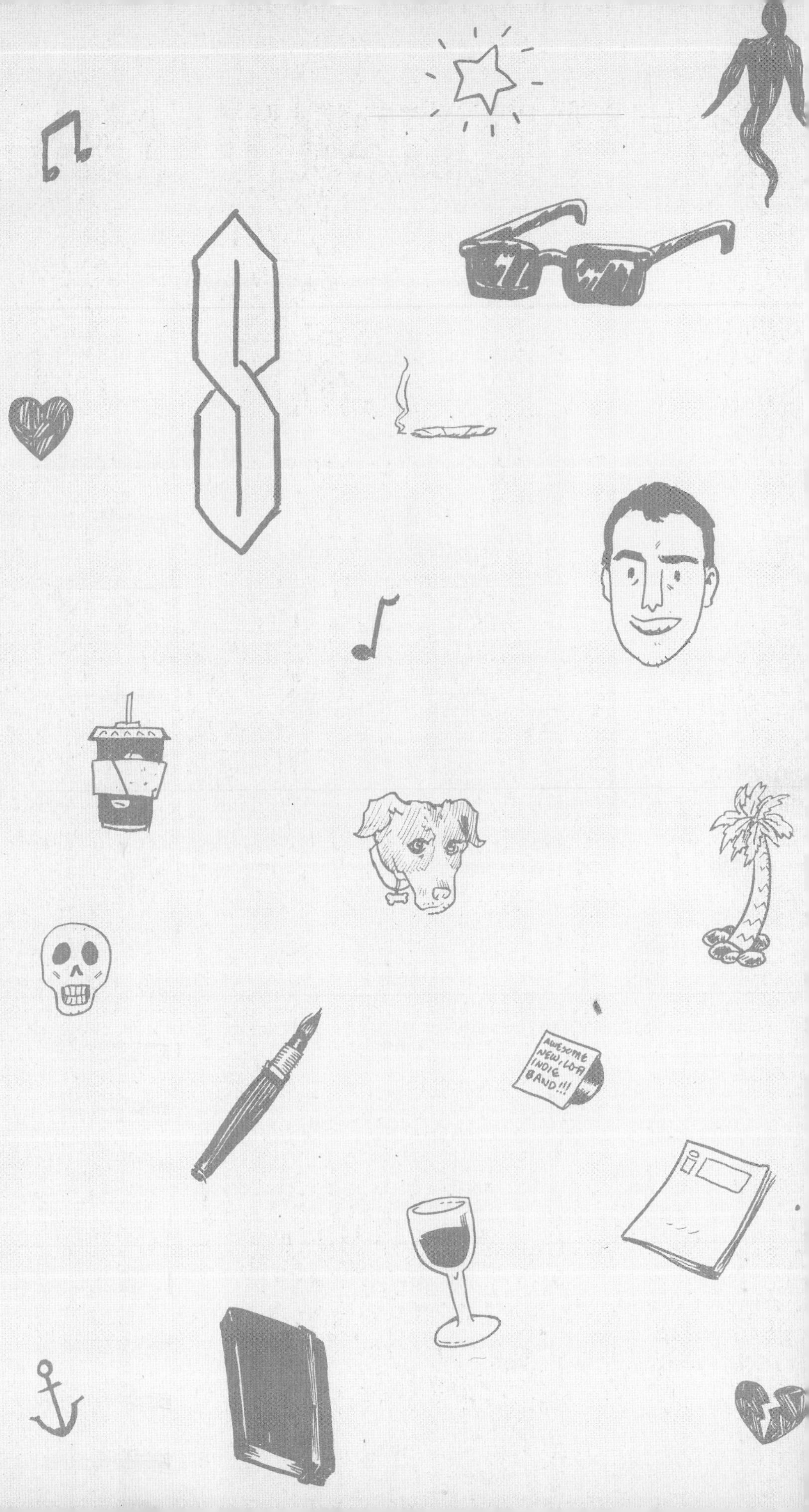
AWESOME
NEW, LO-FI
INDIE
BAND!!!